Imagination and Play in the Electronic Age

Imagination and Play in the Electronic Age

Dorothy G. Singer and Jerome L. Singer

Harvard University Press
Cambridge, Massachusetts
London, England

First Harvard University Press paperback edition, 2007

Library of Congress Cataloging-in-Publication Data

Singer, Dorothy G.
  Imagination and play in the electronic age / Dorothy G. Singer and Jerome L. Singer.
  p. cm.
  Includes bibliographical references and index.
  ISBN-13: 978-0-674-01745-0 (cloth: alk. paper)
  ISBN-10: 0-674-01745-5 (cloth: alk. paper)
  ISBN-13: 978-0-674-02418-2 (pbk.)
  ISBN-10: 0-674-02418-4 (pbk.)
  1. Play. 2. Imagination in children. 3. Television and children. 4. Computers and
children. I. Singer, Jerome L. II. Title

  BF717.S5145 2005
  306.4'81—dc22   2004053915

We dedicate this book to the memory of our parents,
and to a dear friend, Fred Rogers.
They valued play and the power of imagination.

Acknowledgments

We wish to thank Lauren Ng, Lisa Pagliaro, and Sharon Plaskon for their help with the preparation of the manuscript. We also want to express our appreciation to Elizabeth Knoll for her guidance and patience throughout the editorial process. In the course of preparing this book, we interviewed and observed numerous children's interactions in their spontaneous play, their involvement with television, video games, and computers for both educational and recreational purposes. We want to thank them and their parents for giving us the opportunity to share in their experiences. To maintain anonymity, we have made modifications in their names and have used other devices to conceal their identities.

Contents

Imagination and Play in the Electronic Age

Prologue

I dwell in possibility
A fairer house than prose
More numerous of windows
Superior of doors

—EMILY DICKINSON

The Emergence of the Electronic Age

We "dwell in possibility" when we launch our thoughts back in time to consider alternatives to decisions we made or paths we chose to follow. Even more exciting is our ability to project our thoughts into an array of possible futures. Through what Sigmund Freud called "trial action," we can explore a range of relatively realistic or more remote ways we might approach everything from potential vocations, intimate relationships, service to others, to even more fanciful considerations of space flight or even the afterlife. Who has not enjoyed and perhaps identified with the humble milkman, Tevye, in the musical comedy, *Fiddler on the Roof*, when he sings "If I Were a Rich Man"? Our capacity to venture into "mights," "woulds," "coulds," and to reshape the seeming inevitability of our futures into images of new action or even into the creative directions of the arts or sciences is one of the special miracles with which we are endowed through human evolution.

The historical origin of the human imagination is largely unknown, despite clues dating back 30,000 years to the vivid cave paintings of animals in motion found in Spain, France, and Germany. We do have increasing evidence, however, that within the lives of contemporary adults, the capacity for imaginative thought begins to appear by the third year of life when children start to play games of pretending, to verbalize their stories out loud, and to use phrases like "Let's make believe." What are the factors and contingent circumstances in the child's development that

1

evoke and foster this form of thinking, which can generate what Jerome Bruner has called "possible worlds"?

We know that parental or other adult caregiver storytelling and reading to preliterate children are certainly important sources of the content of pretend play. We can be reasonably sure that some forms of storytelling to children must have begun once humans developed speech. The visual arts of architecture, sculpture, and painting, as well as music, song, dance, and ritual all contributed to freeing humans from the perceptual dominance of the here and now. An epochal advance occurred when written language first appeared some six or seven thousand years ago. It is true that until perhaps the past two centuries the vast majority of human beings could not read. Still, many millions were influenced further toward imaginative thought by the oral narrations of the small literate minority, the priests, the aristocracy, the developing merchant class, and by occasional exposure to forms of theater both religious and secular. By the mid-1400s, the invention of moveable print opened the way for more widespread reading. The availability of books and other reading material further stimulated adult imagination and fostered children's pretend capacities and eagerness for literacy.

In contrast to the many years of slow growth of the arts and of print literacy, consider the impact of the popular electronic media that have emerged just in the last century. Silent films dominated the attention of vast multitudes of adults and children in the first quarter of the twentieth century. Many millions of nonreaders all over the world could laugh at the antics of Charlie Chaplin even when they could not decipher the occasional printed dialogue on the screen. Once "talkies" were perfected in the early 1930s, the storytelling of film became the dominant popular medium in the world. It continues to be the most widespread medium to this day on big screens in theaters and in video form on the television sets that now are found in so many homes on this planet.

Radio broadcasting became a widely popular medium at the same time as the talking films. Because of its availability in the home, radio enjoyed about a quarter of a century as the major storyteller via soap operas, dramatic shows, and live news broadcasts before television was perfected and took over in the home. Many of the generation born in the first forty years of the last century still attribute much of our childhood fantasies and pretending to the impact of listening nightly to stories like *Little Orphan Annie*, *Jack Armstrong, the All-American Boy*, and *The Lone Ranger*.

Even more challenging were dramatic series such as the fairy tale re-enactments of *Let's Pretend,* the space adventures of *Buck Rogers in the 25th Century,* or the gripping reconstructions of classic literature on weekly broadcasts like Orson Welles's *Mercury Theater.* Many members of the radio generation are likely to insist that their imaginations were powerfully stimulated by having to listen to and then reconstruct picto-rially the visual scenes. In this regard, listening to radio is more akin to reading where one has to fill in through personal effort a range of sensory experiences—auditory, visual, even tactile and olfactory.

While television, and now video games and computer imagery, "do it all" for you, are they preempting our capacity to practice the imaginative skills we need to make effective use of "possible world" abilities in our personal lives? There are some of us, researchers, critics, or literary scholars, who claim that the almost overwhelming proliferation of the electronic media—film, cable television with its hundreds of channels, video games in arcades, in-home play stations and computers, and the unlimited uses of the internet—may be interfering with reading skills and with the more effortful penetrations into art, literature, and science that require more advanced literacy. Might such easy viewing and minimal interactivity be changing our private mental exploratory abilities? These are questions we hope to address in this volume as we also consider some of the potentially constructive influences of the electronic media on our thought processes.

Has Exposure to Television and Computers Altered Our Thinking?

In the March 1984 issue of *Harper's Magazine,* America's oldest and ar-guably most prestigious monthly, editor Lewis Lapham introduced a new format of shorter articles and artwork designed to be easier to read. As Lapham wrote, "The new version of *Harper's* addresses the sensibility of an age in which people have become accustomed to the techniques of film, to shorter literary forms and the juxtaposition both of ideas and of images" (Lapham 1984, p. 3). This shift toward shorter, less complex content, simpler writing styles, and more pictorial content was already underway in the last half of the twentieth century. It was typified by the emergence of newspapers like *USA Today* whose terse and simplified ar-ticles and graphic emphasis contrasted with the more detailed reportage of dailies such as *The New York Times, The Washington Post,* or the *Los*

Angeles Times. News magazines like *Time* and *Newsweek,* already designed earlier in the century for briefer and tighter styles, responded to the impact of the fast pace, pictorial vividness, and commercialism of television by further abbreviating their texts, introducing more graphics and colors, and to some degree blurring the visual distinction between articles and commercial advertising. In the political sphere, public addresses by elected officials or candidates became shorter, moving ultimately toward the 30-second sound bytes that now have replaced the once-elaborate arguments and reasoning that characterized the speeches of presidents like Abraham Lincoln, Woodrow Wilson, and Theodore and Franklin Roosevelt.

Consider a more recent example of how the electronic media may be reshaping even the basic textbook reading material available to children. In an aptly named technical monograph, James LaSpina's *The Visual Turn and the Transformation of the Textbook,* we find an elaborate case study of how a major publisher planned and produced a series of social studies textbooks that were adopted by the state of California in the early 1990s (LaSpina 1998). The author concentrates not on the rather controversial *content* of the series, but rather on the *style* and *presentation* of the material. The format of the texts at each grade level involved a great emphasis on pictorial material and on a structure that seems to mirror the web sites and menus of computers. Short paragraphs interspersed with charts, pictures, and texts in different fonts creates a kind of multisensory experience for the user.

The elaborate theorizing and systematic reviews and testing that went into the production of this social studies textbook series are described in detail by LaSpina. The meticulous care in production belies any hasty criticism that our multitasking, fast-paced visual age has cheapened the quality of textbooks or undermined reading. LaSpina calls attention to the reality that natural human experience often takes place in a daily world of complex stimulation. As we go about our business we are taking in new sounds, sights, and smells, waving to friends, watching out for traffic as we cross streets, observing peculiar passersby, and along with such activity, learning about our neighborhood and how to navigate its boundaries. This imagery calls to mind Virginia Woolf's acute sensitivity to such reality of human experience in the opening of her novel, *Mrs. Dalloway.* As one of the developers of the California textbooks pointed out to LaSpina, many young readers eventually tired of the "multisensory, multicomponent" format. The production staff recognized that what they could best offer was more of a guide book than a "read about it" book (LaSpina 1998, p. 209).

It seems likely that we will still need to offer students some opportunity not just for varied experience as the cognitive scientist Donald Norman (1993) has proposed, but also for reflecting and interiorizing the deeper meanings of events. We believe that this use of one's private thoughts for conscious examination of external experiences and their implications has been trained inadvertently by the pretend play of the young child and later by combinations of storytelling, reading, and mental reenactment of what we have seen or read.

Have the new electronic media introduced changes in the attention capacities of children and adults and in the style and structure of their consciousness and imagination? We know with reasonable certainty that children and adolescents who are heavy viewers of action television shows and frequent players of violent video or computer games are more likely to show higher levels of aggression and disruptive noncooperative behaviors (see Chapter 4). From some early studies, we have found that preschoolers who were heavy viewers of television were less imaginative than lighter viewers (J. L. Singer and Singer 1981). Television viewing may also affect fearfulness, cognitive skills, and social or racial stereotypes (D. G. Singer and Singer 2001). What is more difficult to assess is whether television viewing, computer use, or videogame playing are altering the very structure of how children think and imagine, and how various electronic exposures influence their potential for creative thought.

To whet the reader's curiosity, let us first look at some vignettes of children as we observe them today in relation to their sources of influence from the media surrounding them at home and in school.

Billy, a Child of the Twenty-First Century

Very recently we were in a local magnet school producing a videotape for inner-city parents and daycare providers. The tape and accompanying written material were designed to demonstrate to adults how playing an imaginative game with a child could contribute to preschool children's readiness for effective school entry and cognitive, social, and literacy preparedness. Our producer, Harvey Bellin, and his camera crew had set up a large room where the various scenes were to be filmed. The child participants (four-year-olds of diverse ethnic backgrounds) and their parents had assembled early on this snowy day in the school library, a room not only replete with attractive children's books but also with a television set, a VCR, and four computers. Billy bounded in and before even taking off his coat he had seized two prominently displayed books on animals and machines and was examining them on one of the library tables. He even pointed to and sounded out a few letters on their pages and pretended to be reading, actually narrating accurately the contents from the pictures even though he could not yet read.

An hour or so later, after his first "acting" stint, Billy returned somewhat wearily to the room where parents and some siblings were assembled. He munched on a bagel and watched a talk show on the TV with some of the parents. Soon, however, he found his way to one of the computers where he switched on a game of a very simple educational nature. Billy seemed energized by the game. It called for using the computer mouse to point and click on the different objects in the setting of a countryside walk. A voice pronounced the name of the object or animal, the spelling of the name was printed out, and sometimes sound effects or music were added. Billy eventually returned to the filming room. Later, as the long day of "takes" and "retakes" wore on, and as Billy once again lost interest, he returned to the library and found a more humorous, slapstick video game that he played with some occasional laughter and verbalization as he pointed and clicked.

Will the ease of television or of the simple point-and-click computer and video games lure children away from less exciting but necessary activities, and the more demanding but "internalizing" task and *promise* of reading, perhaps altering the depth and complexity of their private imaginations?

Our next example drawn from interviews with an older child suggests some further questions we hope to examine in this volume.

Jesse, the Builder

We were introduced to nine-year-old Jesse long distance via his grandmother, who had told us about his love of construction toys and his progress through the LEGO™ series starting at age four. She arranged a taped interview with him about his play. Jesse loved to put together as many buildings or vehicles as possible with each successive LEGO series, sometimes following the instructions once he could read and sometimes reshaping the plastic blocks into structures he conjured up himself. Jesse had recently acquired one of the most advanced sets in which the physical construction was also represented on a computer screen (see Chapter 5). Players could manipulate the toy using the keyboard so that it appeared in cyberspace on the computer monitor or they could maneuver it by hand on the floor. Jesse said he had chosen this particular set because "This one had more to build. Also, it was 50 percent off! This one looked really cool. It could do a lot of things."

Jesse reported that he enjoyed building the toys about as much as playing with them. He reported that he followed the instructions carefully and liked to move back and forth between the computer image and the floor toy when playing. He enjoyed playing alone, but also welcomed opportunities to share his construction games with a friend. When asked by his grandmother if he made up stories about adventures, he replied, "I don't make up stories. I just like to make the toy flip and roll over and shoot missiles. The best part is building it."

This young engineer poses a problem. Is Jesse unwittingly sacrificing the opportunity to develop his imaginative skills and narrative thought to the processes of construction and computer manipulation? Although he may not verbalize elaborate adventures, he is creating miniature, even somewhat violent scenarios with this toy. More than anything else, Jesse loves the construction, an act in which he is personally involved through his senses and muscles as well as his mental powers. He also gains a sense of control through using the computer to produce the toy's virtual counterpart.

We have observed large numbers of children at play in the LEGO theme parks in Billund, Denmark, and in Windsor, England. We can attest to the varied ways that youngsters become involved, some like Jesse, more caught up in the construction itself, others moving into more elaborate interactive play with relatively complex narrative structures. The play of the former group was similar to the style of children who are called *patterners* who enjoy playing with blocks, clay, and markers, whereas the latter group may be compared to the *dramatists* who prefer dressing up and playing with less structured toys (Wolf and Grollman 1982). Some combination of these two styles may ultimately lead to more optimal and adaptive thought.

For almost half a century as researchers in the psychology of ongoing consciousness, daydreaming, and speculative thought in adults and children, we have had to confront the impact of television viewing, and more recently video games, and the increasingly elaborate computer domain and their impact on our conscious thought and imaginative skills. Our objective in this volume is to focus on what research tells us about the origins of the human imagination in the family life and play of children.

In our first chapter we seek to establish the role of conscious thought and its components for adult adaptation and then, in subsequent chapters, to guide the reader toward an examination of how such adult processes may have their origins in the play and exploratory behavior of children. We show how we can study the phenomenon of ongoing thought for scientific purposes and call attention to how consciousness, as Emily Dickinson's poem suggests, can open doors to the countless possibilities and alternatives that free us from the strictures of "here and now."

Our second chapter points to the possible links between the beginning of play in children and the flowering, through pretending and symbolic games, of an increasingly elaborate interior, private world. We stress that such play is fun for children, a worthy contribution to the happy childhood all children deserve, but that it may also serve as a precursor for school readiness and for literacy. Reading and a more complex imaginative life are often closely linked, but as we suggest in Chapter 3, a new source of input competes for "channel space" in the cognitive processes and internalization of imaginative thought in children. This is television whose omnipresence in the home may be even more influential and at earlier ages than was the movie theatre of the first half of the twentieth century. How has TV influenced imaginative thought in structure and content? What positive and possibly hazardous impact can it have on our children's emerging consciousness?

In Chapter 4, we carry the theme of the potential hazard of the electronic media further because of a particular feature of television and, even more recently, video games in arcades or on computers. We refer here to the extremely high frequency of violent content that pervades these electronic media. Certainly stories in books and movies have always involved aggressive themes, but young children had relatively less access to this material. Nowadays our society appears to authorize the acceptance of violence by providing easy opportunities in one's home for children to model aggressive acts by watching television or to practice them by playing video games. For many children, especially those less gifted or practiced in reading, watching television or choosing to play the more violent video games may be less demanding than even reading comic books or adventure stories. We also consider the constructive uses of nonviolent video games.

In Chapter 5, we turn to some more complex features that have emerged as a result of the child's interaction with the vast and expanding reaches of cyberspace, the computer's domain. We consider the possibilities for new learning opportunities and perhaps for developing a richer consciousness. There are also serious risks for confusions of identity, for blurrings of reality and fantasy, and for actual exploitation of children as they explore the Internet.

We conclude our study of play and imagination in Chapter 6 by pursuing the possibilities of imaginative enrichment and constructive learning through play and pretend games. We confront a serious issue that educators and parents have been faced with in the early years of the twenty-first century—is play a distraction, even a detriment, to literacy and effective education? The current federal administration with the so-called "No Child Left Behind" policy is emphasizing a national push toward early literacy in preschoolers. For many parents, early childhood teachers, and child caregivers, this proposal has signalized an effort to use drill, phonemic exercises, and national testing of children as young as three.

Play has actually been abolished in many Head Start centers presumably as irrelevant to this national literacy and school readiness effort (Zigler et al. 2004). Does this omission of play subvert the ostensible goal of fostering school readiness and effective social development? In this last chapter, we also address the constructive possibilities of imaginative play for cognitive growth, social and emotional development, and school readiness. Examples are presented of print and electronic media programs and of the research bearing on how parents and teachers can use guided play to enhance ready-to-learn abilities in children.

As summarized in the Epilogue, children's play and the growth of imagination may be seen as critical opportunities to enhance school readiness. Beyond this more focused goal, there is the further benefit that the early play and imagination of children can enrich personal growth and the capacity for enjoyment and creativity throughout life. What is new in human history is that such growth must now occur in an environment in which the electronic media surround the child and afford temptations and risks as well as opportunities. How will that great miracle of human consciousness fare when the child develops in this new atmosphere?

— 1 —

Our Conscious Imagination

From deep analogies by thought supplied
Or consciousness not to be subdued,
To every natural form, rock, fruit and flower,
Even the loose stones that cover the highway,
He gave a moral life; he saw them feel,
Or linked them to some feeling. In all shapes
He found a secret and mysterious soul,
A fragrance and a Spirit of strange meaning,
Though poor in outward shew, he was most rich;
He had a world about him—'twas his own,
He made it—for it only lived in him,
And to the God who looked into his mind.

—WILLIAM WORDSWORTH, "THE PEDLAR"

In a Duke University laboratory, a macaque monkey sits before a video screen manipulating a robot handlebar that captures shapes on the screen in a computer game. Rewarded by real food treats for each successful "capture," the monkey gets quite good at playing the game. Electronic wires have been implanted in the fronto-parietal area of his brain. As he *mentally* starts to direct his eyes and arms toward his intended movement, the electrochemical activation of his relevant brain neurons sends a signal to the computer, which leads to the attempted and successful capture on the screen. At first the monkey, not knowing of his surgically implanted signal system, goes through the motions of manipulating the keyboard lever before him. After a while, as his success continues, he stops doing so and drops his arm—his mind alone seems to be doing the work for him. Research of this type has the ultimate goal of aiding humans with various brain diseases or spinal injuries to sustain or control effective actions even when paralyzed or suffering from the spasmodic trembling characteristic of a condition like Parkinson's or other cerebellar illness (Blakeslee 2003a,b; Carmena et al. 2003).

Although harnessing the mental energy of our thoughts to play video games may still be a fantasy, the real experiments with monkeys point to the significance of our private thoughts and ongoing consciousness. It may be that our fleeting private images, our plans for future engagements, even our long-term hopes are building habit-strengths that can result in rapid actions under particular circumstances. Human consciousness is not merely a superficial phenomenon, but a critical capacity we have developed through evolution for important adaptive purposes. We are proposing that our human stream of consciousness emerges gradually in childhood from children's play and from their pretend games. Certainly the pioneers of psychology as a science, such as Wilhelm Wundt in Germany and William James in the United States, placed consciousness at the heart of the field. But finding scientific methods to get at the *privacy* of our thoughts, as our poetic quote from Wordsworth suggests, stymied research for many years. Only in the past half century or so have behavioral scientists been able to move beyond the rich clinical anecdotes of psychoanalytic treatment to more rigorous methods for capturing and evaluating the functions of consciousness.

Studying Consciousness

Suppose that you are asked to perform a simple task like wearing earphones and listening to single tones or "beeps" coming about one per second, and then reporting by pressing a button whenever you hear a beep that is louder, higher, or lower than the one that came just before it. We'd have to pay you to maintain accuracy, especially if we require you to perform this task in a lightproof, soundproof booth for an hour. It's natural that your mind will wander, so you have to try really hard to focus on those beeps. You're being reimbursed each time you push the button when the tone is different from the one that came before it. But even if you're keeping to a level of 90 percent accuracy, over an hour's time we find in such experiments that your thoughts drift considerably into memories, interior monologues, or speculations about events that are fairly remote from your current chore of signaling differences in the beeps. Sometimes we interrupt you every fifteen seconds during the hour and have you move a switch to tell us whether you have had any task-unrelated intrusive thoughts or what we call TUITs (Antrobus 1999; J. L. Singer 1999).

Laboratory experiments like these have been extended by more "natural" ones like those devised by Eric Klinger, Mihaly Csikszentmihalyi, and Russell Hurlburt, in which people carry message pagers and are interrupted randomly throughout the day. They have to report on forms what they were doing, thinking, or feeling. We find ample evidence that part of being human is to experience a good deal of shifting thought and conscious imagination as we go about our daily business (Antrobus 1999; Csikszentmihalyi 1990; Hurlburt 1990, 1993; Klinger 1999; Pope 1978; J. L. Singer 1995). Samples of the thoughts of "ordinary" adolescents or adults obtained in the kinds of research we have just described may not have the richness of vocabulary or the poetic and literary allusions of a character in a James Joyce or Saul Bellow stream-of-consciousness novel. Still, they are often more complex, varied, and potentially creative than you'd expect from an ordinary conversation with the individual.

When psychology emerged as a scientific discipline in the last quarter of the nineteenth century, human consciousness was a central topic of study, as evident from the placement of the chapters on the "mind" and "the stream of thought" toward the beginning of William James's great 1890 textbook, *Principles of Psychology* (1890/1950). Because of difficulties in developing scientifically reliable methods for studying consciousness, psychologists largely shifted their approach to behaviorism and the study of learning in small animals beginning in 1910. It was left to great writers of fiction, such as Virginia Woolf, James Joyce, and later in the twentieth century, William Faulkner, Thomas Wolfe, and Saul Bellow, to explore in vivid and creative literary prose the workings of our human stream of consciousness. After a hiatus of fifty years between 1910 and 1960, psychologists and philosophers of science broadened their theory and methods and began to explore human information processing, cognition, and its relation to emotion, and thus, inevitably, the field has returned to more serious study of our conscious, ongoing thought (Ciba Foundation 1993; J. L. Singer 1995).

Let us consider some examples of the way the stream of conscious thought meanders between the shoals of immediately perceived objects and the central current of recollections or fantasies drawn from our long-term memory. In Virginia Woolf's novel *Mrs. Dalloway*, referred to in our Prologue, we find the young matron Clarissa walking through the London streets, buying flowers, reacting to the weather, watching the curb as she crosses a street, noticing the splendor of the architecture of Westminster—all acts of direct conscious response to her physical surroundings. After conversing with a friend she meets in the street, she then engages in memories of events twenty years earlier. She recalls conversations with a distant friend, who may be visiting soon, and eventually she drifts to self-conscious reflections about how energetic and alive she felt earlier in her life (Humphrey 1954, pp. 51–52).

Perhaps the most extended and masterful examples of a writer capturing the flow of our consciousness are found in James Joyce's *Ulysses,* widely voted at the turn of the millennium as the most important or influential novel of the twentieth century. It begins with Stephen, young teacher and would-be artist, gazing out at the ocean from his tiny seaside apartment window and first noticing the crash of the waves. Soon his thoughts shift more and more deeply into memories of the recent death of his mother, recalling how, as a lapsed Catholic, he resisted praying for her. Guilty emotions are roused in him and he remembers a dream in which she appeared to him out of her grave as if summoning him to return to religion or to the family ways. In his mind he seems to scream out his determination to be an independent person and an artist: "No mother. Let me be and let me live" (Joyce 1934, p. 11).

Joyce's long novel eventually ends by giving the "last word" to a woman, Molly Bloom, as she lies in bed with her husband, Leopold, trying to go back to sleep after he awakened her by returning from a late-evening carouse with Stephen. Her stream of consciousness is represented by a single sentence of forty-five pages in length that displays with amazing vividness and in an almost poetic form how our thought swerves between processing external sights and sounds to extended memories and speculations. Some of Molly's associations are to dramatic events from that very day and others from years before, culminating, as she falls asleep, in a loving memory of the beginning of her relationship with Leopold, the Ulysses of this novel: "how he kissed me under the Moorish wall . . . and his heart was going like mad and yes I said yes I will Yes" (Joyce 1934, p. 768).

A lucid analysis of this vast mixture of monologue and imagery has been provided by Humphrey (1954). He shows how Molly's thought first reacts to an external cue, the clock. She then shifts her attention to somewhat impersonal thoughts about other people's sleep patterns. She notices her wallpaper, remembers a former apartment, and after she lowers the lamp, she moves gradually from imagining future scenes to more extended memories of her courtship.

A final example is one taken from a tape of one of our research studies in which ordinary adults talked aloud for extended periods of time, but with earphones on so that (as with our thoughts) they could not actually hear their words. This participant, a young New Haven man, said at the start of a lengthy period of continuous talk:

> Ok so I'm looking at that piece of wood down there in the corner. I'm thinking that this is a really, very interesting stream of consciousness. I'm looking at my coat now. I got it from uhm Hadassah. And there's this great Jewish lady there that was uh, oh, I'm thinking about this tie that I had. Oh, now I'm thinking of a tie of my grandfather's. I'm thinking about the day that my grandfather died. I was at junior high school and [name] walked into the office. I was in the office and I was crying and I didn't really care if he, if he cared that I was crying uhm. I walked outside. I remember walking down by the football field. It was a long, curvy driveway sort of and I remember looking over through my tears at them playing football. (Pope 1978, p. 288)

We have taken some space to exemplify the stream of thought as a central feature of human consciousness because we believe, following William James, that it is a critical feature of human psychology. As we shall suggest in our next chapter, it may well be an internalized continuation of the make-believe play accompanied by "out loud" verbalizations of preschool children. Before we move on to a discussion of children's imagination, and how particular environmental experiences ranging from parents' or other adult caregivers' story telling, reading, or playful interactions influence children's thinking, we want to call further attention to the structure and adaptive features of adult consciousness.

What Do We Mean by Consciousness?

Human consciousness in its simplest form is simply the awareness of one's environment and the capacity to use one's perceptions to attempt to steer one's motor apparatus through a given physical situation. A blow to the jaw may in a second reduce a previously alert and engaged prize fighter to a slack-limbed sleeper who awakens moments later without memory of the intervening period to find he has lost the battle and perhaps, his championship. Sleeping at night or napping by day involve voluntary yieldings of consciousness, although as Hamlet suggests, "Who knows what dreams may come?" We know from the sleep laboratory research of the last half of the 1900s that some form of thinking does appear to occur through any extended sleep period, though it is usually not well remembered except after the so-called Stage 1-EEG, rapid eye movement (REM) phase of the sleep cycle. Such sleep mentation may well be a continuation, in modified form, of the stream of thought during waking consciousness that William James first described, except that, with limited *external* input, dream consciousness primarily reflects the seemingly random inputs from one's long-term memory activity (Antrobus 1993, 1999; Epstein 1999).

A second meaning of consciousness, which is perhaps unique to humans, involves assigning meaning to experience. We do this by associating new scenes or events to related earlier images. For children, once they have learned to talk, they may also give verbal labels or even form conceptual categories to experiences, shaping them into the schemas and scripts that allow efficient retrieval of memories (Johnson and Multhaup 1992; J. L. Singer and Salovey 1991). This manifestation of consciousness is what is best shown in the literary genres of fine writers like Joyce, Woolf, Faulkner, Bellow, Proust, and in some of the stories and novels of Thomas Mann. As our examples from *Ulysses* suggest, this form of conscious thought may involve a kind of quasiobjective mental commentary on external events, sights, or sounds or on material we are reading or watching on television. It can, however, merge into deeply personal recollections, reflections upon one's guilts or past successes and failures, as well as upon one's aspirations and determinations.

These more personal mental interactions may lead to a third form of consciousness, the self-guided or directed use of one's thought stream. The active control of ongoing thought has been described by Isaac Lewin's (1985–1986) cognitive model, which points out how we can either actively direct our thoughts or respond to them passively as a "bystander." Perhaps the prototype of all such self-consciousness is the four-year-old child's assertion, "Let's make believe this is a magic ship we can sail in!" As adults we can decide, sometimes playfully, to follow a stream of associations, if only to escape the boredom of a long airport delay, a lecture, or a business meeting. We can also learn to use such guided imagery sequences for purposes of extended planning, mental rehearsal of interviews, sales pitches, inventions, and artistry, or even for quasitherapeutic self-examinations. A good deal of modern psychotherapy and behavior modification does indeed involve training a patient to make effective use of self-steered imagery and narrative sequences (J. L. Singer and Pope 1978).

What Do We Mean by Imagination?

Imagination is a form of human thought characterized by the ability of the individual to reproduce images or concepts originally derived from the basic senses, but now reflected in one's consciousness as memories, fantasies, or future plans. These sensory-derived images, "pictures in the mind's eye," mental conversations, or remembered or anticipated smells, touches, tastes, or movements can be reshaped and recombined into new images or possible future dialogues. These thoughts may range from regretful ruminations ("If only I had said or done it differently"), to rehearsals or practical planning of social interactions, to the production of creative works of art, literature, or science (J. L. Singer 1999).

The imaginative process is broader than simply imaging a concrete stimulus. Imagination may involve elaborated verbal sequences conducted privately in consciousness, or it may take on story-like forms such as a reminiscence or wished-for future sequence of events. For individuals in particular vocational, scholarly, scientific, or artistic fields, imagination may involve elaborate potential activity. An automobile mechanic may mentally review the array of physical structures that are defective, recall the repair manual or certain key words from it, picture mentally the kinds of tools required, and become aware of certain safety precautions inculcated in his training. He then may actually begin a series of movements based on what he imagined. Mozart described how whole sequences of music appeared in his "mind's ear" and then were translated mentally into musical bars and note sequences. He often wrote out pages of musical notation, which could then be printed with relatively few corrections or changes and distributed to musicians for performance.

Some features of imaginative thought that must also be defined are fantasy, daydreaming, and night dreaming or sleep mentation. Much of imaginative thought takes the form of daydreaming, which usually involves shifts of attention away from an immediate task or concrete mental problem to seemingly task-unrelated images or thought sequences (J. L. Singer 1966, 1978). Such daydreams may range from memories, to wished-for future events, to playful storylike reshapings of current concerns, or to long-standing desires. Daydreams may also represent mental experiences involving guilt, shame, or other unpleasant emotional responses to others. They may also reflect fearful or anxious mental scenarios, more or less realistic, ranging from anticipation of a natural disaster to an invasion from outer space by hostile aliens. Although imagination can be utilized directly in a problem-solving mode, as when a writer envisions various scenes for a novel or movie script, daydreams are more commonly a feature of the naturally occurring stream of consciousness. Their adaptive function or practical utility may be harder to discern. They may seem fleeting, even trivial, or they may emerge as reactions to current emotions. Night dreams, the imagery of which we become aware shortly after awakening, may be continuous with daydreams except that they occur when our major task is to "stay asleep" and when we have drastically reduced the processing of external stimuli by shutting our eyes, reducing light, and curling up in a bed to limit motion (Antrobus 1993, 1999).

Fantasies can be wishful or pleasant in content and tone, but they can also involve frightening, hostile, or dependent scenarios. A fantasy of finding out that you are a long-lost relative of a billionaire may be positive and wishful. People also report fantasies about space invasions, nocturnal visits from vampires, or story lines in which they encounter teachers from childhood who humiliated them and on whom they now wish to wreak terrible vengeance. The term "fantasy" is also used by psychology when it is elicited through psychological tests, usually projective methods such as the Thematic Apperception Test (TAT). Here participants are shown ambiguous pictures and asked to make up stories about such pictures. The stories told are found by personality researchers to reflect basic recurrent fantasies about important needs. When such stories from a given respondent are accumulated across a series of pictures, one can use these fantasy scores to represent the hierarchy of needs of an individual such as desires for power, achievement, or intimacy. Extensive research has shown that such accumulated solicited fantasies produced to TAT-type pictures or to related ambiguous materials like inkblots can also predict specific overt behavior as well as reflect a vivid or rich imagination, generally with creative potential (McAdams 1990; J. L. Singer and Brown 1977).

Imagination as a Feature of Normal Thought

A division of normal thought processes along two separate functional lines can be traced to the mid-nineteenth-century British neurologist Hughlings Jackson's (1932) distinction between "propositional" (abstract or logical) and "referential" (concrete or sensation-derived) thought, with the former more vulnerable to severe brain damage, toxic conditions, or great fatigue. Sigmund Freud (1911/1948) extended this view into "primary process" and "secondary process" thought. The former involves imagery and fantasy reflecting the pressure of unconscious erotic or aggressive drives without any social constraints, whereas the latter process reflects more conscious, mature self-restraint and defensive or compensatory efforts. More recent theory and a body of research suggest that Freud's emphasis on both the immaturity and the drive-relatedness of his primary process is too narrow a view. Instead, a growing number of investigators in psychology are proposing that human thought has evolved along two semiautonomous lines, both adaptive to special circumstances of the human condition (Frank 2003; J. L. Singer and Bonanno 1990). Some examples of such theorizing as they bear on imagination are briefly summarized on the following few pages.

Jerome Bruner (1986) has proposed that human thought can be ordered along two dimensions, "paradigmatic," involving logical processes, and "narrative," constructing possible, storylike realities. The logical, sequential, paradigmatic mode is usually formulated in verbal terms in our own thoughts as well as in our communication to others. In its most advanced form, it is usually expressed mathematically. This mode seeks for truth and is, as are all scientific hypotheses, ultimately falsifiable when contradicted by new data.

In contrast, the narrative mode, although sequential only when it is communicated to others in a series of statements, may be thought of first in bursts of personal images, usually visual and auditory, but sometimes even olfactory, gustatory, tactile, or kinesthetic. It is expressed as a story and can also emerge as what cognitive psychologists call "episodic" or "event" memories, or as fantasies and daydreams. As Bruner proposed, the object of narrative is not truth, but verisimilitude or "lifelikeness." One can identify gaps in logic in a story sequence, but those very features (as in much poetry and some novels, like those of Kafka) are designed to communicate the comical, playful, even sinister irrationalities of the human condition.

Both of these modes for transforming experience into thought, formulating propositions about events into logical hierarchies, and organizing our thousands of experiences into believable or "acceptable" stories, must be mastered by growing children. As Bruner wrote, "Narrative deals with the vicissitudes of human intention" (1986, p. 16). Narrative thought reflects an effort by humans to give deeper meaning and a sense of the ineffable to the shifts and changes of our life encounters. We can propose that the various human religions reflect efforts to form narratives that make sense of the mysteries and seeming contradictions of our experiences. Whether offering miraculous and life-transcending explanations reflected in the intrigues of pagan gods or the omniscience of God in Judeo-Christian-Islamic monotheism, religions involve elaborate stories that, in contrast to paradigmatic propositions, cannot be expressed in pure abstraction or tested and falsified.

Even secular humanism and scientific thought seem to require some storylike background. Consider the importance of the accounts of Socrates's teachings and his trials in the evolution of Western philosophy. For Bruner, the narrative mode also involves a subjunctive orientation, the formulation through images and remembered dialogues of possible personal life stories of more or less realistic potential futures. The imaginative facet of human experience largely reflects Bruner's narrative process. For the production of a creative product—a fictional story, film script, scientific theory, or scholarly research study—both paradigmatic and narrative processes would have to be operative (Bruner 1986).

A more recent formulation, supported by a growing series of empirical research, has been the Cognitive-Experiential Self-Theory (CEST) proposed by Seymour Epstein. It incorporates two modes by which people adapt to their physical and social milieus, a rational and experiential system (Epstein 1999). A major extension of Epstein's approach beyond Bruner's is his linkage of the experiential system to human emotionality. The rational system is characterized by deliberateness and greater effort; it works through abstraction, verbal thought, language, and may even be a more recent evolutionary development. As Epstein's work suggests, however, the emotionality associated with the experiential mode may have important human adaptive functions that supplement our orderly, logical processes.

The experiential system involves the accumulation of concrete experiences (episodic memories) into tentative, emotionally nuanced storylike generalizations or models of one's life situation or of the world. It often proceeds rapidly and smoothly, seemingly without effort. Events are generally represented in images, but can also be expressed in metaphors, prototypes, or stereotypes, and in stories. Epstein also points out that the more mature forms of the experiential mode (a reflection presumably of imagination) function along with the rational system to become the basis for intuitive wisdom or creativity.

Both systems can work together to produce significant behavior. They can also arouse great emotion. Consider the excitement that can be produced by our ability to formulate natural events into a concise mathematical system. It is reported that the ancient Greek scientist, Archimedes, watching the displacement of water as he lowered his body into his bath, began mentally reproducing those behaviors in an experiential or imaginative mode. He then began to see a way to describe this event in the bath as a general scientific proposition. Finally, in the thrill of his discovery of a mathematical formula concerning displacement, he ran naked down the streets of ancient Syracuse shouting, "Eureka!" ("I've found it!").

Although many of the features of an ultimate creative product emerge from images, fanciful or realistic, or from language-focused thought, which can also be fanciful or realistic, the product (anything from a good business idea to a scientific or literary work) requires an active and controlled orientation (Lewin 1985–1986). One can make a distinction between imaginal processes, which may involve concrete sensory-derived and sensory-imitative experiences (a mentally simulated picture, sound effect, taste, touch, smell, or motion), and verbal processes, which specifically involve lexical processes or word sequences in roughly grammatical form. The more free-floating features of the ongoing stream of consciousness may serve as the content sources for creative products, but the final steps may call for deliberate effort and conscious integration.

One of the touchstones of an effective use of consciousness and one's verbal or imaginal repertory is the ability to summon such experiences volitionally and direct them in relation to one's objectives, whether for sheer self-entertainment or for poetic, scientific, or daily practical purposes. One must add, of course, that creative products usually emerge in a domain in which an individual has already developed specialized skills through extensive practice. Research on creativity has shown that, whereas the majority of creative products are generated by trained specialists in an area, the process of creativity—the potential for imaginative novelty—may be present in many individuals whose expertise may be tangential to a given domain (Sternberg et al. 2004).

Imagination can be regarded as a critical feature of human cognition and information processing. This human conscious information processing necessarily involves representations of the stimulus or of environmental events. Once such representations are encoded for storage, they may not only be retrieved by deliberate efforts at memory, but may recur seemingly spontaneously as daydreams, fantasies, or as night dreams when external stimulation is reduced. As William James long ago pointed out in his *Talks to Teachers*, our stream of thought and mental replay of past events, even of future possibilities, serves an important human adaptive function:

> The "secret of a good memory" is . . . the secret of forming diverse and multiple associations . . . Of two men with the same outward experiences, the one who thinks over his experiences most, and weaves them into . . . relations with each other, will be the one with the best memory. (James, 1892/1958, p. 91).

The appearance of such long-term memory material in focal consciousness, often in almost random combinatory forms, provides the content that enriches or elaborates ongoing thought, and under proper conditions, is a source for creative products or sometimes simply for self-entertainment. Under normal conditions, the average person may ignore most of these seemingly random thoughts as irrelevant to some currently undertaken task. The participants in the experiments we described at the beginning of this chapter and who reported many task-unrelated intrusive thoughts (TUITs) most likely would not have remembered most of them after their hour spent processing auditory signals. We know from laboratory studies of sleep that people report a number of dreams if awakened periodically throughout the night, but under ordinary circumstances most of us recall only the last dream, if that, in the morning.

Individuals who have defined themselves as striving for creativity in some particular domain may learn to be especially sensitive to these fleeting intrusive thoughts. They then seek in more deliberate fashion to form creative products. Autobiographical reports or direct interviews conducted with eminent writers, inventors, and scientists demonstrate that their early experiences with play in childhood or their adult uses of playful, imagery-based or narrative thought are important features of their creative process (Root-Bernstein and Root-Bernstein 1999; D. G. Singer and Singer, 1990).

Nikola Tesla, inventor of alternate current motors and generators, has written, "When I get an idea I start at once building it up in my imagination. I change the construction, make improvements and operate the device in my mind" (cited in Root-Bernstein and Root-Bernstein 1999, p. 51). Beethoven reported, "I carry my thoughts about with me for a long time, often for a very long time, before writing them down . . . I change many things, discard others and try again . . . I hear and see the image in front of me from every angle . . . and only the labor of writing it down remains." As the Root-Bernsteins note, Beethoven's capacity to draw on and reshape his mental imagery might help us to understand how someone who had become deaf could still go on to write such great music (1999, p. 58).

The Adaptive Role of Consciousness and Imagination

Our brief examples of the play and replay of imagined material point out the value of ongoing consciousness not only in improving ordinary memory, as William James suggested, but also in generating creative thought in the arts and sciences. We should not focus too much attention, however, upon the great creative achievements of a Tesla or a Beethoven. Rather we recognize that most human beings may use the same processes in conscious rehearsal, playfulness, and what Freud (1911/1962) called "trial action" to deal in a novel fashion with the hundreds of dilemmas of daily life (Runco 1994, 2004). Although phrases like "connecting the dots" or "thinking outside the box" have become modern clichés, we are proposing that our human consciousness is a kind of miraculous gift by which we can, in small ways, engage in divergent and effective problem-solving thought and adaptive action. Anecdotal accounts of animals show some usual solutions for *their* daily dilemmas: some chimpanzees stacked up boxes to reach a desired fruit, and a rare squirrel learned to hang upside-down to avoid tripping the shut-down bar on a birdfeeder. We have little evidence of such animals' conscious thought, however, or of their genuine ability for reflection (Harris 2000). What is that macaque monkey's mental awareness like when he stops reaching for the robotic lever and still produces "good captures" on the computer screen through only his own thoughts?

What we are proposing, then, is that although our stream of thought is an inherent consequence of the way the human memory operates, a major further step for human beings involves our potential for directing our thoughts into either the narrative (cognitive-experiential) direction or into the more rigorous and focused paradigmatic form. Creative individuals in science, the arts, or in business or other practical endeavors learn how to shift between the imagery and story-telling facets of thought and the more abstract and rigorous logical-sequential mode.

Studies of the creative process have shown that one can identify what psychologist Robert Sternberg calls the *legislative, executive,* and *judicial* steps in producing a work of art or a new theory (Sternberg 1999). One begins by allowing a free flow of ideas and images—little stories, so to speak—that reflect the many "proposals" of a legislative group. Many of these proposals are novel and reflect what creativity researchers call *divergent thinking.* Such novelty, however, is not sufficient to generate an effective product. The individual needs to acquire and apply technical skill within a domain, whether it be the formal musical knowledge of a Beethoven or the engineering mastery of a Tesla. Executive skills must be put into action to integrate divergent thoughts into the relevant artistic, scientific, or business forms. But as studies of creative work attest, a further step involves what Sternberg has labeled the *judicial* feature, self-criticism and evaluation of the quality of the work.

A scientist like Einstein relied heavily on his imagery and fantasy for suggesting ideas (legislative), his mathematical skills for formulating these abstractly (executive), and then his judicial abilities for proposing ways in which his ideas might be tested or might meet theoretical or empirical criticism. In 1907, Einstein tried to imagine a man falling at a varying rate of speed through space. How would this varying rate of speed impact the Newtonian concepts of gravitation? His mathematical analysis, which relied upon non-Euclidean geometry, led him to believe that light itself might bend or that space would curve. The imagery might be viewed as the fluid, speculative feature of creativity, the math as the executive or action contribution, but Einstein still, as a physicist, wanted an experimental verification of his conceptual work. He found two methods to do so. One involved using established data on discrepancies in the way the planet Mercury orbited the sun. The other called for measurements by astronomers of a total eclipse of the sun. His prediction of the extent to which the sun's gravity would bend starlights was so accurate and hitherto unexpected that Einstein's work was labeled by astronomers as one of "the most momentous . . . pronouncements of human thought" (Panek 2004, pp. 100, 101).

Although we acknowledge the tremendous reaches of the human imagination and of conscious thought, our concern in this volume is primarily with everyday potential. What we are suggesting is that we have a fine resource for adaptive life, for self-enlightenment, sometimes for escape, sometimes for practical advantage if we can pay attention to our own thought processes and even learn to direct them. Awareness and control of thought may, to some extent, be genetically determined the way forms of intelligence are, although as yet we have no research on the subject. We do know, however, that there are interesting differences in how individuals use these processes.

Extensive research on personality delineates five major dimensions, one of which, called *Openness to Experience,* is the interest in thoughtful exploration and cultural enrichment (Costa and McCrae 1995; McCrae 1993–1994). Our own research on daydreaming and imaginal processes has shown that individuals who show a constructive, positive use of their imagination are also those who score higher on questionnaire measures of openness (Zhiyan and Singer 1996). We suggested above that perhaps our adult imaginative capacities and our ability to control them may take their primordial origin in children's make-believe play. There are indications that children who, early on, engage in pretend play are also likely to be more amiable, persistent, and conscientious. Our own research has shown that children who play more pretend games are also more cooperative with teachers and they show more initiative or leadership. This constellation of the early correlates of imaginative play seems closely related to specific traits that have been shown in recent research to persist over twenty years from childhood to adulthood. This cluster of traits also predicts greater positive emotionality, less aggression or alienation, more self-control, and more avoidance of harm (Shiner et al. 2003). What guides some children earlier or more effectively into learning to play at pretend or make-believe will be the focus of our next chapter. As we shall see, direct exploration and manipulation of the young child's physical and social milieu, along with inputs in the form of explanations and storytelling by adult caregivers, are critical starting points. After examining the beginnings and manifestations of what Piaget called symbolic play, we confront the new forms of experience in childhood, those presented through the electronic media of television, video games, or the Internet (D. Singer and J. Singer 2001). How may such exposures modify the imagery, narrative, and paradigmatic thought processes of children and their ability to control and apply the stream of consciousness?

The position we will be taking in this volume is that fundamental human autonomy begins with seemingly small steps in childhood. The two-year-old who shakes her head to say "No" to a proffered spoonful of baby food may seem troublesome to her mother, but that headshake is a significant sign of early independence and perhaps even of the beginning of self-definition. Pretend play, which develops soon afterward, may have similar profound implications in asserting the autonomy of the individual and the beginnings of self-consciousness and control of one's thoughts. How does pretend play begin and what function does it serve in the cognitive and emotional life of the child?

— 2 —

Play: Its Beginnings and Stages

Definitions of Play

If we observe children as they engage in make-believe play, we hear funny voices as they take on various roles; we hear lots of giggling and witness goofy behavior. We also notice that within the context of play, with all its charm and fun, how seriously children assume their respective roles, whether playing "school," "doctor," "airplane," or "submarine." Pretend play can continue for long periods of time when children are enjoying themselves, and it may be difficult for a parent or teacher to interrupt or stop the game when it is time for a meal or a nap.

We often hear people say that play is child's work. We are more comfortable with the notion of the play researcher, Brian Vandenberg, who likens play to a clown, "culture's way of making fun of itself" (1982, p. 16). Vandenberg also proposes that play serves no biological need, appears to be divorced from immediate adaptive concerns, and is simply carried out for enjoyment (1998). Mihaly Csikszentmihalyi (1982) and Brian Sutton-Smith (1982) agree with Vandenberg that play is just plain fun.

Researchers who work in the field of play owe much to Jean Piaget, who was one of the first psychologists to present a theory of play from birth to adolescence. Piaget preferred to use his acute observational abilities rather than elaborate experimental methods to develop his theory. He also questioned children to understand how they reason, and he called this his clinical method. For most of his research, Piaget concentrated on the behavior of his own three children, Jacqueline, Lucienne, and Laurent. Both Piaget and his wife, Valentine Chatenay, a former student, kept detailed diaries of what their children wore, ate, said, and learned each day. The observations were recorded by age of the child and by a number (Piaget 1962; Singer and Revenson 1996). With the advent of more sophisticated technology, we may use a video camera, for example, to record children's behavior as they play, but regardless of the tools we use, observing children is the best way to understand how their minds work. Although today some claim that Piaget's ideas need revision and, indeed, have carried out experiments to demonstrate that babies can learn earlier than Piaget had believed (Gelman and Lucariello 2002; Philips et al. 2002; Spelke et al. 1989; von Hofsten et al. 2000), it is difficult to find a more comprehensive, carefully documented theory than that described in *Play, Dreams, and Imitation in Childhood* (Piaget 1962).

For our purposes in this book, we are concentrating on *symbolic play,* which continues, we believe, throughout a person's life, but reaches its peak from ages three to six. We like to refer to this period as the "high season" of play because a child's imagination and pretend abilities are so rich and uninhibited. Symbolic play, according to Piaget and Freud, may be a distortion of reality. Bruner and Epstein, as discussed in the previous chapter, believe that play is an alternative and a potentially adaptive way of thinking. When a child pretends that a cardboard box is a submarine and goes down into the ocean depths to find a treasure, the child is engaging in symbolic play. The fish he names as he heads below, the pebbles that he transforms into jewels in a treasure chest, the ocean that is not visible except in the child's mind are all part of the make-believe game. It is important, however, that we understand what we mean by symbolic play. The following criteria proposed by Greta Fein (1981) over twenty years ago concur with our own definitions of symbolic or pretend play:

- Familiar activities may be performed even in the absence of necessary materials or social context (e.g., a child pretends to drink from an empty cup or puts a doll to bed in a shoebox rather than in a cradle).
- Activities may not be carried out to their logical outcome (a toy soldier imprisoned in a fort escapes through the roof).
- A child may treat an inanimate object as animate (tucking a doll into bed with a hug and a kiss).
- An object or gesture may be substituted for another (a block becomes a telephone, a broom becomes a horse).

• A child may carry out an activity usually performed by another
person or especially an adult (pretending to be an astronaut,
teacher, doctor).

Lev Vygotsky, the Russian psychologist, believed that play was a result
of social interaction, a key element in his theory, and that play serves as
the primary context for cognitive development (1978). Play, as Vygotsky
envisioned, is a rich manifestation of imagination that combines elements
of reality and fantasy rather than distorting reality. "Imagination is a new
formation which is not present in the consciousness of the very young
child, is totally absent in animals and represents a specifically human form
of conscious activity. Like all functions of consciousness, it originally
arises from action" (1976, p. 537).

Scaffolding, a term introduced by Vygotsky, denotes the situation when
siblings or adults enable the child to accomplish more through their aid
and encouragement than the child would accomplish alone. Social interaction is fostered by scaffolding when the parent, teacher, or older sibling
guides the child in play by offering new ideas, words for the play script,
or even by assisting the child to build a fort or castle. The *zone of proximal
development*, another term featured by Vygotsky, refers to the fact that
when confronted with a novel object or situation, a child needs to find
a way to integrate this unfamiliar material into its realm of established
schemas and then make some sense of it. There is a lower limit, what the
child can do alone, and an upper limit, what the child is capable of with
guided instruction.

Other aspects of play, according to Vygotsky, are the *separation of
thought and action,* and the development of self-regulation. The *separation
of thought and action* implies that a child is not bound by the perceptual
qualities of an object. Vygotsky argued that when children use objects to
represent other objects in play (using a block to represent a boat), this
sets the stage for abstract thought. The child, for example, may envision
the bathtub as an ocean filled with boats, submarines, fish, or strange
animals of the deep. The ordinary bath now becomes an adventure on
the high seas. Getting clean, for the child, is secondary to the pleasure
resulting from imaginative play.

Self-regulation happens during play when a child assumes the role of
another person. In this way, children can learn to control their feelings.
In the course of a game, there may be opportunities, as Vygotsky notes,

to act out anger, sadness, or grumpiness; for example, a child pretends she is a baby, refuses to take a nap, and begins to cry. If she is told to stop crying by the "mother" during the play game, the "baby" can obey and stop. At times a child will scold her doll in play, and this may, indeed, reflect the anger a caregiver recently expressed toward the child. Play that reflects feelings is *compensatory play*.

Self-regulation is also accomplished when children talk to themselves. We often hear children say to themselves as they play, "Bad boy," or "Don't do that," or "Mommy will be angry," or in more positive ways, "You're my favorite little guy," or "Here's a kiss," or "Good job!" Vygotsky called this *private speech*, and we find numerous examples during make-believe play.

The Beginnings of Play

We can watch babies as they taste, nibble, suck, smell, and feel objects in the world around them. Although these babies are not involved in make-believe play, these sensory motor acts are a form of exploration and curiosity, the ingredients for later pretend play.

At birth we see evidence of the neonatal smile, a crooked, appealing sort of smile that triggers a joyful response in the caregiver. The baby's true smile begins at about four weeks, with cooing and babbling. Social smiles are present at about two months, and genuine laughter at twelve months. The socially elicited smiles "are unambiguously correlated to events external to the infant, in particular the perception of other people's faces engaging in play games and other social exchanges. It becomes the mark of reciprocity with other people in the environment" (Rochat 2001, p. 183). When there is no smile or vocalization from the mother, the baby becomes passive and withdraws. In severe cases, this is known as anaclitic depression, a refusal to eat, to smile, and to respond that may even lead to death. We have seen indications of this in babies left as orphans in wartime in countries in Africa, in Bosnia, and recently in Afghanistan and Iraq.

The early interactions between caregiver and child that can lead to more advanced pretend play involve the caregiver's smiling, talking to the baby, caressing and touching the baby, and responding to the baby's smile. This mutual reinforcement—mother smiles at baby and baby smiles back at mother—helps to forge the bond between the two, often called the "love dance" that leads to what Erik Erikson calls mutual trust (1968). This early social interaction, so germane to both Erikson's and Vygotsky's view of play, is another precursor for later symbolic play.

As babies begin to enjoy greater mobility, they are increasingly curious about the people and objects around them. They repeat sounds with their babbling and practice motor acts continuously until they reach their goal. We once observed a nine-month-old trying to stack rings on a pole. He kept missing, but he kept trying. This perseverance led to his eventual triumph when he successfully managed to get all five rings on the pole. Not satisfied with this, he then adorned his ankles and wrists with the rings, inventing "jewelry" for himself and a new way to play with the rings.

Watch babies in a crib or playpen and see how they reach or try to kick the dangling objects on a mobile or suck on their own toes or those of a doll. At first, their movements are tentative, characterized by trial and error, and then as the babies gain more control over muscle movements, actions are more deliberate and purposeful. When babies begin to walk, a whole new world opens up to them. Mothers may look quite apprehensive as they watch their babies appear to totter. Pablo Picasso's painting, *First Steps,* captures the frantic look of a mother as she stands behind a toddler who assumes a wild-eyed expression as she eagerly surges forward. The toddler is exerting her newly discovered autonomy or independence as she separates self from mother through this concrete act of walking.

There is evidence that children as young as 18 months engage in simple pretend play, as when a toddler feeds a teddy bear with a spoon, uses a cloth to pretend to wash his or her own face, brushes a doll's hair with a comb, or drinks from an empty toy bottle (Fein 1981; Hughes 1991). At this age, toddlers can even imitate the movements of a favorite pet by crawling on the floor, or by making "meow" sounds.

Generally, the baby plays alone in her crib or in a safe play area, but there are times when a caregiver interacts with the baby and elicits many smiles and laughter as they play together. Through mutual play, the baby can imitate a partner and play in a more complex manner (the scaffolding described by Vygotsky) than when playing alone. When the partner goes away, the baby left to its own devices may copy some of the play activities that they had engaged in together. Toddlers generally play next to each other without much interaction. This is called *parallel play*. Occasionally one toddler may reach for the other child's toy and much tugging at the toy ensues. There is little attempt to share graciously at this age. The toddler is keen about playing games with an adult such as Peekaboo, rolling a ball back and forth, or "reading" a book together, but for the most part, the child at this age is engrossed in solitary play as described above.

Symbolic Play

Symbolic play begins in a more primitive way at about age two, when the child's thinking does not reflect much awareness of cause and effect or of the functions of the human body. One of our own children, as a young three-year-old, was not satisfied when one of us was resting on a couch with eyes closed while he spoke. "Open your eyes and listen!" he demanded. Children in this period are egocentric; they believe that everything they feel or think is experienced by others around them. If a child tastes soup and it is hot to her tongue, it must be hot for the caregiver as well. We are always excited, however, to discover a young child who is able to understand another person's point of view and express sympathy or empathy despite the fact the egocentricism dominant in preschooler years. We have a vivid memory of our son Bruce, who while attending preschool, befriended a child, Rebecca, who never spoke to anyone. He often sat by her side, shared toys or books with her, and spoke to her even though she did not respond to him with words, but only with smiles or a nod of her head. The teachers were aware that Rebecca had no physical speech disability. She had been diagnosed with a psychological disturbance called mutism. Bruce had been out of school for a few days nursing a bad cold, and this child missed him very much. When Bruce returned, she shouted out his name much to the surprise of the teachers. After that, quite cautiously, Rebecca spoke to Bruce, and to him alone. Evidently Bruce's care and concern touched Rebecca in some way and her trust in him enabled her to offer him words.

Preschoolers demonstrate animism, endowing human characteristics or physiognomic properties to inanimate objects. Our son Jon, for example, bumped into a dresser in our bedroom, bent down and said, "Boo-boo" and made "nice" to it. He may have been imitating the adults around him who often kissed his "boo-boos," or according to Piaget, he was truly engaged in animism, assigning life to the dresser. Animism becomes an important element in make-believe games as when a teddy bear is a guest at a pretend tea party. Children do believe that everything that moves is alive, such as the wind "because it blows" or a candle "because it burns and is hot." The use of inanimate characters with expressive facial features such as Thomas the Tank Engine or SpongeBob on TV provide evidence of the importance of animism in the young child's imagination.

Are adults able to abandon this primitive way of thinking and make a clear distinction between living and dead or inanimate objects? Years ago, inspired by a discussion with several physician friends about the definitions of death, including brain death and the need for organ transplants, we carried out a simple experiment. It was a surprise to discover that even adults think like children when forced to make a decision concerning whether or not certain objects are alive or dead. Many of the adults questioned believed that a river was alive "because it flows" or that the sun was alive "because it has energy" (D. G. Singer et al. 1978). Our control group of medical residents, fortunately, gave correct biological answers to our list of items.

Very young children think in the experiential mode, meaning that they often encode reality in concrete images, metaphors, and narratives. Because their thoughts are more crudely integrated, more generalized, and less analytical, very young children are confused about time, space, and numbers. For the very young child, the future seems too difficult to comprehend. If you tell a preschooler on Monday that you are going to see Grandma on Sunday, on Tuesday morning, the young child thinks this is the day for the visit. Listen as they play and you will hear them travel "millions and zillions" of miles to visit a friend, but they arrive "in five minutes!"

Reasoning in preschoolers often is transductive, meaning that simultaneous events appear to involve a cause and effect relationship—the whistle of the train is responsible for its movement. Artificialism is another reflection of presumably immature thinking. This is the notion that human or humanlike divine architects are responsible for natural formations—a giant's footstep made a hole, which became a lake when it rained. As a child, one of us envisioned a god-like figure who lived in the sky and who turned on the appropriate faucet for rain, sleet, or snow. All of this experiential thinking is found in symbolic play and allows for the delightful vignettes we observe in preschool or in the home.

At about age three, when symbolic play is more frequently observed, cooperative pretend play emerges. The children can take on different roles, reverse roles, and follow a simple script or story line. There are interruptions at times when the play changes its course and a new script is introduced or when a conflict ensues, but basically, children at ages three and four can sustain cooperative pretend play for long periods and follow the rules of the play script. It is interesting to note that rules are part of the make-believe play of preschoolers. Without rules, the games deteriorate. Children set the rules when they develop their scripts for the particular play game. They hold fast to these rules and the child who does not follow the script is eliminated from the game.

Sociodramatic play, or social pretend play with many transformations of materials, more advanced language, more elaborate scripts, and numerous societal roles (doctor, teacher, even "good guys" and "bad guys") added to the repertory becomes the pattern for make-believe or symbolic play during the preschool and early school years. Social pretend play is encouraged in various communities, but varies according to the culture, as in Euro-American homes where mother-child interactions revolve around play-toy miniatures such as a toy replica kitchen or farmyard (Dunn and Dale 1984; Haight et al. 1999; Howes and Wishard 2003). Older siblings can also encourage social pretend play as observed among Spanish-speaking children in a child care center serving children from age two, along with an after-school program for children aged twelve and thirteen. Girls tended to play in mixed age groups in which the older Spanish-speaking girls organized the younger children into pretend games and, indeed, were scaffolding the play of the younger children (Howes and Wishard 2003).

As children continue in grade school, they further develop a sense of cooperation and try to abide by the rules of the game, whether board games or games of pretend. They gradually learn that rules are codified, fixed, and apply to all; rarely do we hear, "I have a new rule, so let's play this way." A sense of justice is gradually internalized through cooperation and mutual respect.

Fostering Symbolic Play

Parents and teachers can foster symbolic play if they give children *time* to play, *space* for play, and some *simple toys or props.* Many children are so over-scheduled with various lessons, sports activities, and planned trips that there is little time for make-believe play. Children need time to day-dream, sit quietly, and spin their fantasies. In terms of play space, a small corner in a room or even a place on the kitchen table is enough of an area for a child. This *sacred space* allows a child to know that when requested, a small "castle" will remain intact for a revisit the following day. The Russian writer Vladimir Nabokov recounted that his favorite play space as a child was behind a cretonne-covered divan where he could indulge in his fantasies, carrying out adventures from this "primordial cave" (Nabokov 1951, p. 23). For some lucky children, space may be a backyard with a tree house or an outcropping of rocks or a grassy hillock, features that lend themselves to becoming forts, schoolhouses, treasure islands, or strange planets.

Most of all, adults need to *sanction* pretend play and understand that the suspension of reality is part of the enjoyment of play. A parent who is uncomfortable and disapproves of a wild story or unusual characters in the play script of a child is interfering with a child's imagination and fantasy play. In effect, symbolic play enables children to have a clear sense of what is real and of what is not real or fantasy (Aronson and Golomb 1999; Golomb and Kuersten 1996). Indeed, one of the benefits of pretend play is the ability of players to switch easily between reality and pretence. If you listen to children before they engage in an imaginative game, they usually precede the game with words such as "Let's make believe" or "Let's pretend."

Recall our reference to Picasso's painting *First Steps*, which captures a mother's anxiety at her excited toddler who is thrilled at beginning to walk. Such first steps as walking or first learning to say "No!" represent great advances for the child's autonomy while arousing some fear in a protective parent. Think, then, of what a great first step it is when a child starts to say "Let's make believe." In this phrase a child comes to understand the human reality that we can live in two realms, one of the immediately given, perceptible physical milieu and one of the possible worlds we construct through our mental operations (Bruner, 1986).

As the British psychologist Alan Leslie (1987) pointed out some years ago, a child's "theory of mind"—the awareness that "I have thoughts and they are different from other people's thoughts"—may well depend on experiences garnered in pretend play. The conception of a child's distinguishing his or her own mental expectations or experiences from others' has opened an exciting and challenging area of research (Harris 2000;

Wellmann 1990). In our own laboratory, studies have shown how children engaging together in make-believe play demonstrate advances in recognizing others' thoughts or in differentiating fantasy representations from reality (Rosen et al. 1997; Schwebel et al. 1999). Parents may seem concerned at the seeming unreality of imaginary playmates or the symbolic play transformations of their children, but these activities are the harbingers of great advances in self-definition.

There are many surprises in store for the parent who may not be aware of how much fantasy exists even for the older child, and how play may change in character when another child or sibling joins in. Age is no barrier here as far as make-believe play is concerned. We have fond memories of observing and listening to one of our own school-aged children playing a game one autumn of "catch the leaves." He was on the lawn and moved gracefully trying to catch as many falling leaves as he could. His game consisted of pretending that these were strange objects from some alien planet and his mission was to catch them and find out what they were. Later, when his friends joined him, embarrassed by his fantasy game, he changed it to one of turn-taking and simple rules about where each boy could stand; now the game became "Let's see who can catch the most leaves."

Although Piaget envisioned play evolving through fixed stages, we believe that children as well as adults continue to participate in all forms of play. Pretend games and symbolic play are not always the distorting schemas or blurrings of reality and fantasy that Piaget believed. We delight in sensory-motor play when we trickle sand through our fingers at the beach or when we splash in the pool. We use practice play when we learn a new skill such as tennis, golf, or skiing. We are involved in symbolic play when we play charades, engage in mock battles with toy soldiers, join amateur theatricals, or join such groups as the Society for Creative Anachronism, where at special fairs, people can dress up as knights of old, joust, delight in singing old English songs, and eat a meal using recipes of medieval times. Finally, the adults games of chess, checkers, or games of cards are carry-overs from the six- to twelve-year-old stage when these games were of paramount importance. The video or computer games that people play well into adulthood indicate our fascination with this kind of play, which encompasses both fantasy elements and specific rules.

Benefits of Make-Believe Symbolic Play

When children play make-believe games, good things happen. In Chapter 6 we will present the research evidence for make-believe play as a naturally occurring mechanism for learning and suggest that cognitive and social gains occur when a child is engaged in this specific kind of play.

An important finding concerning the benefits of early pretend play is the predictability and stability of divergent thinking over time. Researchers Russ, Robins, and Christiano (1999) studied children who had completed a play task and a test of divergent thinking when they were second graders. When they were followed up later in the fifth and sixth grades, the quality of fantasy and imagination in early play predicted divergent thinking independent of IQ. In a series of three studies that also examined the relationship between specific forms of social and pretend play and divergent thinking, Wyver and Spence (1999) found that there is a complex reciprocal causality model in which the development of divergent thinking skills facilitates the development of play and vice versa. This suggests that children who engage in problem solving and are open to a playful approach may find that such a method will then increase later play abilities. In addition to the relationship between divergent thinking and imaginative play, further adaptive benefits emerge as children play make-believe.

During make-believe play children learn the social skills of sharing, taking turns, cooperating with each other (D. G. Singer 2002a,b,c). Vygotsky (1978) believed that pretend play served as a foundation for social awareness and social skills. We believe that of all the benefits that ensue from play, perhaps the socialization skills are the most important at this young age. If children do not accept the social norms of the game, it quickly ends, or the children who are disruptive are forced out of the game. Leadership qualities flourish among the children who initiate pretend play scripts and who designate the roles for each child. In a follow-up study of children from ages eight to twelve, twenty years later, Shiner, Masten, and Roberts (2003) found that those children who scored high in social skills, academic attainment, and work competence maintained these patterns as adults. These kinds of skills are the same as those found to emerge from imaginative play in the earlier years (D. G. Singer and Singer 1990; D. G. Singer and Singer 2001; Smilansky 1986).

A number of studies point to the fact that make-believe play in preschools or in a variety of other settings is associated with more positive emotions in children and identify an adverse relationship between imaginative play skills and the overt manifestations of anger and aggression (D. G. Singer and Singer 1990). Joy and liveliness appear during pretend games, and in general, children seem to be having fun and are enjoying the pretense. As we mentioned earlier, play offers ample opportunities to act out negative emotions for the purpose of self-regulation.

Children enhance their vocabulary when they play and learn how to use words to express themselves, as the following vignette indicates. Kayla and her grandmother were playing "restaurant." Kayla, in her role as waitress, offered her grandmother a special pie made of peaches and raspberries. When grandmother asked how much this cost, Kayla said with conviction, "Nine dollars." When the grandmother protested paying this steep price, Kayla indignantly informed her that this was a "very fine restaurant" and that "we even have weddings here." When children are in need of new words to help them to continue the story, they ask adults for help. When a child plays "restaurant," as Kayla did, words like menu, waiter, bill, and various words for food are necessary. In addition, the development of plot sequences requires the use of adjectives, future tense verbs, and extended utterances.

Children learn their colors, shapes, and numbers through play. They need four chairs for the guests at the tea party, and they can name the colors of the various objects used in the game. They recognize the shapes of squares, circles, and rectangles when they play "neighborhood" by naming the shapes of the various street signs. Children learn to be flexible when they play make-believe, substituting objects in the game for those that are not present. Children tend to persist and concentrate for relatively long blocks of time when they play make-believe. Many caregivers know how difficult it is to call children away from their play for a meal.

Through play, a child learns that there is a certain logical sequence of events in the make-believe game. Before the tea can be served at the tea party, the table must be set, the water must boil, the cookies are fashioned out of clay, the guests arrive and are seated, and then it is time to eat. It is important for children to learn to control their impulses and to tolerate delay. Preschoolers who showed delay of gratification showed better academic achievement and social competence in adolescence (Mischel et al. 1989).

When children play make-believe, indications of empathy appear when the child who is playing doctor or nurse examines a doll or puts a bandage on the arm of another child who has a boo-boo and is the victim of imaginary danger. There are physical benefits of imaginative play. Senses are sharpened during make-believe play as children use touch, sound, vision, and at times even taste and smell if food is involved. Fine motor skills improve as children build their forts or castles with blocks and make simple props using crayons or clay. Large motor skills develop as they ride their tricycles or pull their wagons, pretending these are automobiles or delivery trucks.

Colin: A Child Who Discovers Himself through Play

Let us examine how play can benefit a child's self-concept. One of the pioneers and most astute contributors to the systematic child observation literature has been Lois Barclay Murphy. In her work at the Sarah Lawrence College Nursery School in Bronxville, New York, Dr. Murphy and her collaborators made daily records over several years' time of the natural play of preschoolers. In her perennially readable and penetrating book, *Colin: A Normal Child* (1956), Murphy provides dozens of examples of the boy's make-believe play that reflect an emergent awareness of selfhood. When Colin began nursery school at four, he was at first whiny and clung to his mother. Gradually, he became immersed in the make-believe play initiated by some other children. The next day he told his mother a story growing from his play experience, but also reflecting his separation fears. The story involved a witch who visited a doctor who said she had a "heart disinfectant." Hundreds of doctors and wise men were summoned and "they cut her open and took her up to God. And God changed her into four ghosts." This seems lurid and fearful, but subsequently Colin played quite cooperatively with the other children. It was as if he had exorcised his extreme dependency on his mother and overcame his fear of his new playmates through engaging in elaborate play and storytelling.

Later in that year, Colin began to be somewhat rambunctious and aggressive in his play. He also imaged in play and story narratives that he was fighting challenging monsters, but subsequently these fantasy encounters were followed by acts of friendliness on both sides. Colin soon after began to incorporate novel stimuli from daily life that puzzled but intrigued him into his floor play. These included local sights and shops, the Meadow Brook Dairy, lumber in freight yards, and Jack Frost's house. Using the assorted geometric blocks, he piled them on a pretend train and moved them to where he could place them in neat rows. This was his lumberyard, he announced; it was located in Wyoming in the West. He called his train "The Lone Freight." Afterwards, Colin announced, "I feel so proud of myself . . . you know what, I'm not going to hit anyone in this school today." In another game he built "Jack Frost's house" and became a milk dealer.

As Murphy points out, his ability to playfully represent himself in a constructive, nonviolent, but strong manner, developed a sense of personal power. Another game followed in which he imagined himself as "a diesel motor digging," squatting on his knees and rhythmically swaying his arms while he said, "Look at the steam shovel moving on his caterpillar wheels." As Murphy notes, his fantasy games manifest the emergence of an assertive male-identified and competent sense of self (1956, pp. 48–55).

When Symbolic Play Goes Underground—The Middle Years

What happens to the wonder years of make-believe play when a child enters elementary school? Piaget wrote, "the more the child adapts himself to the natural and social world the less he indulges in symbolic distortions and transpositions, because instead of assimilating the external world to the ego he progressively subordinates the ego to reality" (1962, p. 45). Although imaginative play with the child acting out roles and speaking aloud fades by age six or seven, once children are in formal school, it doesn't disappear. Such play becomes gradually internalized into private mental activity and may also continue more openly in group play forms as when eight- or nine-year-olds climbing rock piles at the shore or in a park pretend to be explorers, pirates, or cow wranglers. We also are aware of the fact that pretense still exists for this age group despite what Piaget believed.

The late Herschel Thornburg (1979) called the early adolescent years, the upper grades of elementary school, the "bubblegum" years, a description that is pleasing to us. It connotes a time of fun, silliness, and energy, but it is also a time when the child is experiencing many conflicts and physical, social, and emotional changes. We cannot accept the Freudian notion of latency as a quiet, uneventful time for the elementary school–

aged child. The various forms of play these children engage in beautifully encapsulate the need for experimental or exploratory involvement. Manning (1998, p. 154) suggests that play for the eight- to-twelve-year-old is

- *Symbolic* of significant aspects of the child's life experiences
- *Active* in the sense that it requires participation
- *Voluntary* and *pleasurable* from some sense of satisfaction or gratification
- *Meaningful* from the child's perspective.

Children of these ages are able to play in a cooperative, socially acceptable way by taking turns, sharing, and using verbal and nonverbal means of communicating. Through the safe context of play, children learn to compromise and develop feelings of trust. If children feel that adults see play as babyish or useless, they tend to engage more in private play. The public play may be in the form of board games, mental games, and language play, whereas the fantasy games may take place when they are out of sight of adults. Children in this stage also begin to form secret clubs, invent secret codes, play rhyming games, and use more puns, riddles, and tongue twisters.

The socially acceptable make-believe play may take the form of writing poetry, acting in school plays, or participating in various forms of art or music. The Harry Potter books have inspired teachers to offer after-school programs in New York City called Wizardry 101 to tap into the imaginative powers of children. One teacher states that she turns off the lights, a sign that the children have entered a magic forest. The children lie down on the floor and imagine that they are flying out of the school window and through the clouds while their fingers and toes become feathers and claws. Children also choose magical names. Teachers take courses under a specialist, Kevin O'Keefe, who is the artistic director of Circus Minimus, an organization that teaches groups of children around the country how to create their own circuses (Mead 2001).

New forms of symbolic play may continue side by side (although for some children to a lesser degree) with involvement in physical play such as organized sports, baseball, soccer, basketball, and use of skate boards, roller skates, scooters, and even the rough and tumble play that continues to be found among boys. Interest also grows during this period in technology and playing video and computer games. Other games that are appealing to children involve constructing objects by following directions, such as making a model airplane or building with LEGO or wooden blocks. These constructions, however, can become imaginative or symbolic games when a child introduces a story context in which the objects exist. Some educators do not understand the value of play, and increasingly in our society, we see playground play being eliminated from school programs. Azar (2002) cites evidence for the importance of all kinds of play, including rough and tumble play. David Bjorkland, a cognitive and evolutionary developmental psychologist, noted "Children or other juvenile animals that do not have the opportunity to play may not develop the social skills required to interact successfully with their peers at any age" (Azar 2002, p. 51).

We are aware that play of any sort is considered a waste of time by many parents and teachers, with the increasing emphasis on the acquisition of cognitive skills such as reading, science, and math. Although these, of course, are important, we do know from the research we will discuss in Chapter 6 that children learn through guided play.

Gender Differences in Play and Sex-Typed Toys

If we are to encourage a child's imagination free of gender stereotypes, playthings must be available without the gender labels. Unfortunately, toys presented in magazines for parents or on TV are strongly differentiated by sex. It is rare that a girl will be used to promote toys such as trains or action figures. Toys that might be attractive to both sexes are shown with boys. In a content analyses of 218 advertisements aired during a week of after-school and Saturday morning children's programs, more boys than girls were featured. More boys also were shown playing outside their homes. The sex of the announcers corresponded with the sex of the characters in the ads. Overall, the ads showed stereotyped behavior for traditional sex roles (Smith 1994).

When does the preference for gender-typed toys begin? Anyone who observes babies at play will notice very little difference in the way they play and with the toys they use. Eleanor Maccoby (1980) has carried out careful studies of the social development of children. She found that during the first two years of life the play patterns of girls and boys are similar. The rattles, rubber ducks, and soft blocks are enjoyed by both boys and girls, and toys like teddy bears and other plush animals are sucked, chewed, stroked, kissed, and hugged by both boys and girls. It is only at the early toddler stage that we see differences emerging in the play styles and in the toys each sex uses. Parents and relatives may be the instigators of such differentiation. We remember an ad on TV showing a proud young father visiting his wife in the hospital. She is in bed holding their newborn son. The father is delighted with the baby's "mitts" and has brought a baseball glove as the first gift to his infant son.

The gifts of dolls and soft toys for girls and of trucks and cars for boys seem to stimulate the toy preferences that we begin to observe in the play of toddlers. Children as young as eighteen months have shown preferences for sex-stereotyped choices, and this desire continues as they get older (Caldera et al. 1989; Cherney et al. 2003; Eisenberg et al. 1984). Try as we might with our granddaughters, the trucks we offered them were politely accepted, looked at once, examined carefully, and then tucked away in the bottom of their toy boxes. Even when children respond to an opposite-sex-typed toy, they seem to return to the same-sex-typed toy and play with it for longer periods. Given the fact that very young children, even in their infant and toddler years, are watching television and video tapes (Weber and Singer 2004), it is not surprising that when these children enter preschool and are exposed to a range of toys, they will prefer toys that are advertised on TV as either girl toys or boy toys. The girls crave the dolls and doll houses, while the boys want the action figures and construction toys.

We often hear teachers in childcare centers from around the country complain about the way the boys take over the science-related toys, computers, blocks, trucks, and other big toys in the classroom, and wagons and tricycles on the playground. Wouldn't it be refreshing if the teachers allowed definite periods of the day for girls only to have access to the "boy" toys and boys only to have access to the dress-up clothes, the kitchen corner, and the dollhouse areas? Would any teacher dare to do so? Perhaps such varied play opportunities might lead to more exploratory behavior in girls and to more nurturing behavior in boys.

The literature indicates that not only do children prefer to play with toys of the same-sex type, but same-gender children prefer to play with each other beginning as early as the toddler years. Weissman (1999) found in a study with fifty-five preschoolers that boys tended to choose boys as their preferred play partner, whereas girls tended to choose either boys or girls almost equally for their preferred play partner. The children said they enjoyed the same activities or were attracted to the behaviors and/ or personality traits of the partner. Not only do children prefer to play with the same-sex partner, but play stories are different for boys and for girls. Fantasy characters in the media may also affect toy choices. Children aged four to six of both sexes played more with fantasy toys that were identified as "sex appropriate" than they did with sex-neutral comparison toys. When the toys were identified as inappropriate for their sex, the children spent more time playing with the less attractive comparison toys (Cobb et al. 1982).

Adult Influences on Gender Play

Why do children select certain play partners or playthings? It is important to examine the caregiver's use of pretend play. For example, is the adult using pretend play as a way to help a child socialize, or to learn some cognitive skills, or both? The caregiver plays an important role not only in encouraging play, but also in making decisions about the kinds of toys to offer a child and the kind of play to engage in. Interestingly, in a study where mothers used a doll to encourage play, analyses of videotaped free-play episodes between forty-two toddlers and their mothers demonstrated that mothers of the youngest children initiated and facilitated doll play. No significant differences were found in this study among the types of play exhibited by mothers of these very young girls and boys or between the types of play exhibited by boys and girls. Mothers used doll play as a means of teaching prosocial behavior rather than gender-appropriate behavior. The children used the mother as a model, and their play reflected the mother's actions with the doll (Stayna 2000). Mother-child relationships revolve around social interactions; mothers are generally more responsive and facilitative, especially if there is a secure mother-child relationship. Father-child relationships involve a more complex level of play, particularly when children are securely attached to their fathers (Kazura 2000).

When asked to offer a baby a toy, women who expressed a strong belief in sex differences were more apt to choose more masculine-typed toys for an infant boy than were women who expressed little belief in sex differences (Bell and Carver 1980). If babies were more passive, they generally were offered more feminine toys, and if more active, they were offered more masculine toys. The infant's behavior was a more important cue in eliciting responses from the women than their adult preconceptions based on stereotypes.

Parents of children aged five through seven who responded to gender role questionnaires in a traditional way were more likely to have children who chose more traditionally sex-linked toys (Repetti 1984). The labeling of sex-typed toys was significantly related to a child's tendency to stereotype occupations. Parents tend to choose toys for their children on the basis of gender, but when kindergarten and first grade children were asked which toys they would prefer from Santa, girls were more willing to add boys' toys on their lists, but boys only asked for boys' toys or neutral toys (Pennell 1999). One of our own early studies indicated similar results in a sample of preschool children observed during free play periods in their day care centers. Girls were more willing to play with boys' toys, but boys were more reluctant to play with toys considered traditionally female (J. L. Singer and Singer 1981).

Gender Differences in Group Play

Does play change when children are together in groups? This, of course, depends upon the nature of the group. In one day care center, we observed a group of boys playing in the sandbox quite diligently until another boy joined them. He was obese, ruddy-faced, boisterous, reminding us of a miniature Falstaff. As soon as he entered into the play, the noise level increased, the previously quiet group imitated his more disorganized play with the toys, screeching noises, and knocking down sand piles. When the children began to throw sand, the teacher intervened. She stopped the play and removed our young Falstaff from the sandbox. The quiet, more constructive play then resumed.

Research indicates that play in same-sex groups generally is more cooperative than in mixed-sex groups. More socially skilled children like to play with others who value these skills as they do. Obviously, our miniature Falstaff needed to acquire more adaptive social skills. When the play narratives of 652 same-sex twins were examined, girls on the whole tended to tell less aggressive and better organized stories than boys (von Klitzing et al. 2000). Those girls who did tell stories of violence appeared to have more behavior problems than boys. Probably telling such stories is so typical of boys that it does not suggest psychological problems. Children, regardless of gender, who tell incoherent, aggressive stories repeatedly appear to have more behavior problems than those who do not show this pattern. Girls tend to be more socially skilled at an early age, and as Serbin, Moller, Powlishta, and Gulko (1991) suggest, gender segregation is related to different behavioral styles, but not to specific toy and activity preferences. Our observations indicate that boys who attempt to participate in girl activities and play with girls tend to receive negative feedback from their peers (D. G. Singer and Singer 1990).

It is clear that there are differences in the way girls and boys play when they play in groups, and in the kinds of playthings they choose to play with.

Fabes et al. 2003 observed the behaviors of 203 children aged three to six during free play periods over the course of the school year. Children preferred to interact with peers of the same sex. Girls spent more time playing near adults than boys did when they played with other girls. Boys selected activities that there were more stereotyped than did girls. Boys were also more likely to engage in active forceful play than were the girls.

We find gender differences in the use of video games and in the choice of computer software, as will be discussed in later chapters. Teachers in elementary school report that during free play, the boys will gravitate more to the computers in the classroom, and generally, the girls are left to find other objects to entertain them. At a very prominent private school in California, we witnessed this gender distinction clearly during a fair at the school. While boys, mainly, were busy demonstrating to their parents computer programs that they had designed, the girls were handling the refreshments and selling articles of jewelry and other handicrafts that they had made.

Toys and Play

In addition to the gender considerations discussed above, should toys be the so-called educational ones that teach cognitive skills, or should toys be chosen for their appealing characteristics and serve no other purpose than to entertain? Since toys are the major props children use when they play, it is worth examining the kinds of toys that children play with. Many parents believe that children have more toys than they actually need. In Great Britain, for example, 74 percent of the parents surveyed recently stated that their children have many more toys than they did at the same age (PR Newswire 2003). One of the dilemmas facing many caregivers is the choice of an appropriate toy for children of different ages. The Toy Manufacturers of America, a trade organization, distributes pamphlets that describe safety features in toys and offer parents tips on which toys are suitable for their children, as well as suggestions for toys that will be useful for children who are developmentally handicapped (Toy Industry Association website 2004). Numerous parent magazines not only feature columns dedicated to play and to toys that are educational, but of course, have many ads featuring the latest toys, especially before the holiday season.

Even though a proliferation of new toys is introduced each year, the empty appliance box has been a constant source of enjoyment for young children; it becomes a house, puppet theater, vehicle of choice, fort, table, or any play object that an imaginative child chooses it to be. In one study, minimally structured toys such as drawing paper, crayons, paints, Play-Doh, blocks, pipe cleaners, rag dolls, and costumes were compared to plastic molds or cutters used for Play-Doh, a car service station, a metal dollhouse, and Barbie and GI Joe dolls with particular clothing. The minimally structured toys produced more fantasy play themes than the more structured toys. In addition, toys that were conducive to cooperative play were those that involved social interactions between children such as kitchen playthings, games where two or more children were needed as players, or miniature toys that were used in fantasy play (Pulaski 1973). These results were corroborated more than twenty years later by Bagley and Chaille (1996), who found that toys such as Transformers (a vehicle that changes into a robot) are less likely to stimulate symbolic or social play than less complicated toys such as miniature cars and figures. When social toys requiring a partner are used, more cooperative play is noticeable even among children with disabilities (Ivory and McCollum 1999).

Despite these findings, the majority of best-selling toys—about 75 percent of them—have some sort of electronics (Barnette 2001). Voted the favorite toys of the century by retailers in Great Britain are the teddy bear and LEGO, both the sort of toys that lead to open-ended or make-believe play (Young and Davies 2000). Short-list contenders were Barbie and Action Man. At the International Toy Fair in New York City, the introduction of pop-music toys was a major item for girls ages eight to eleven. Famous performers can be imitated by girls through the use of karaoke machines and video cameras (Lee 2002). Dolls still remain a favorite of girls. The American Girl dolls are quite different from the Barbie or the Bratz dolls. Each of the eight American Girl dolls has about six chapter books devoted to stories about her life. Activity books and an array of accessories are also available. Part of the attraction of the dolls is the fantasy play that occurs as the child becomes familiar with the doll's story. There is a doll that suggests the American Revolution, an Hispanic doll, and contemporary heroines from a variety of countries (Kinzer 2003).

When parents value imagination, curiosity, adventure, and creativity, their children tend to be more imaginative. Parents' own interests and personality styles, as identified on self-report measures, correlate with the degree of imaginativeness in their children (Tower 1984–1985). Perhaps these are the parents who choose toys that are more open-ended. When children are presented with an opportunity to create their own toys, they can be truly inventive. In a toy contest, prizes went to children who used ordinary materials to create their toys. Winners were a doll called Mr. Itchy Pants made out of nylon stockings, a monster spy truck with a hidden camera behind the windshield, a doll house bank that divides the money into savings and charity, and a monkey made of clay (O'Brien 1999).

From birth on, a parent can make careful choices of which toys they purchase. Dr. Richard Chase (1994, p. 8) suggests criteria for toys that he believes will enhance infant development:

1. Easily attracts a child's attention
2. Be easy for a child to handle
3. Provide consequences that reinforce a child's exploratory and play behaviors
4. Provide opportunities to practice emerging sensory, motor, social, and cognitive, and communicative skills
5. Encourage and support specific age appropriate behaviors that vary in complexity
6. "Grow with the child," by providing new opportunities for exploration and play through an 18-to-24-month span of development
7. Encourage parents and other caretakers to share in play.

Cultural Differences in Play

Do children play the same way in different cultures? It is essential when studying symbolic play to examine cultural and class differences in play stories among children and, of course, in the kinds of toys they use. On a recent visit to Thailand, we were interested to find that in many of the small villages, children played with homemade toys, usually small animals woven from straw materials or crudely carved out of wood. When outdoors, they used large banana leaves for sliding and coconut shells for boats, houses, and as storage places for their small treasures. Nevertheless, in the city of Bangkok, one could find many of the toys that middle-class children play with in Western countries.

The seminal work of Beatrice Whiting (1963) dealing with six cultures presented information on children's play that was gathered in the 1950s when the sample communities were more isolated from mass markets and the media than they are today. Those data were further analyzed by Carolyn Edwards (2000). One hundred forty children ages three to ten were observed in creative-constructive play, fantasy play, role play, and games with rules. Results comparing the six cultures indicated that children from Kenya and India scored lowest in overall play. Children from the Philippines and Mexico scored on the intermediate level, and those from the United States and Japan scored highest. Edwards proposed that the cultural norms concerning work versus play and the notion of freedom for exploration and motivation to practice adult roles through play were factors influencing the scores. When there are role models and access to materials, more creative and constructive play was found.

In a much more recent study surveying the attitudes toward play of over 3,000 parents of children in five countries—the United States, Great Britain, Germany, France, and Japan—play was considered equal to learning. Parents in all five countries agreed that more time should be given to cognitive tasks, even at the expense of free time, yet 94 percent of the parents agreed that time spent playing is time spent learning. It is clear from these data that parents seem uncertain about play and learning. The play of the children in these countries did not differ in terms of the activities they were engaged in, but it was interesting to note that 38 percent of the parents considered shopping in stores as play (LEGO Learning Institute, 2002).

Some of the findings of this five-country study are similar to one conducted earlier in the United States by *Nick Jr. Magazine* with 500 parents of children aged two to five. Although play was considered important by 62 percent of the parents in the survey, 90 percent believed that educational activities were more important (Wood 2001). Both of these studies suggest that parents are confused about the relationships between play and formal learning and do not understand or appreciate the notion that guided symbolic play can lead to the acquisition of skills, a main premise in this book.

Toys, Games, and the Media, a conference held in London in August of 2002, sheds further light on cultural differences regarding toys and play. One symposium presented studies conducted in Sweden, Austria, Italy, Australia, and Brazil. Data presented from Sweden, gathered from a nationwide randomly chosen sample of 450 child care centers, indicated a strong uniformity in the selection of toys and play materials in all centers surveyed (Almquist 2002). Surveying a total of 311 kindergarten teachers and 1,244 children in Vienna, Austria, and 353 kindergarten groups and 644 children in South Tyrol, Italy, Hartmann (2002) found that toy culture in these areas is comparable to that in Sweden. War toys, action figures, and novelty toys are prohibited in the kindergarten. As in Sweden, conventional play material, based largely on the theory of Friedrich Froebel, a pioneer researcher in education in the early nineteenth century, is complemented in Austria and South Tyrol by traditional Montessori play material. Media equipment consists of picture and reference books. Concerning electronic media, only the cassette recorder is found in the kindergarten; TV video recorders, slide projectors, computers, and electronic games are rarely part of the toy equipment. Despite the rejection by teachers of toys that are advertised in the media for kindergarten use, girls named Barbie as the toy they want most at kindergarten, and boys requested vehicles.

Similar to Sweden and to the Austria and South Tyrol study, many Australian child care centers have "war toy–free zones." Teachers hold the belief that children can and should be taught to play and that toys should always have measurable and developmental benefits (Jenvey and Jenvey 2002). These Australian researchers questioned 69 children aged four to six about their toy preferences and found that they liked the more active and outdoor toys at school and had more imaginative toys at home, as well as access to electronic playthings and computers. Brazil's child education culture favors an adult-centered philosophy, the teaching of writing and arithmetic in kindergarten as well as the use of toys that are conducive to educational purposes. The teachers demand immobility and silence in the classrooms. According to the teachers, play is best served on the playgrounds, while the classrooms are primarily for learning. Results indicated that toys and materials for symbolic building and socializing activities were the *least* represented in the classrooms. Most of the games with rules were related to the acquisition of skills in arithmetic and in the Portuguese language (Kishimoto 2002).

Again we find that the frequency and content of play is influenced by the culture. The play of younger children one and two years old in four communities—Guatemala, Turkey, India, and the United States—indicates that social play occurs in all four samples studied (Goencue et al. 2000). Although the sample size was small, the researchers are in agreement with Edwards' findings in the six-culture study described above. Other work with Indian children found that the parents studied in this sample were not vigorous play partners with their children. Interactions of 341 mothers and fathers were examined as they played with their year-old infants in their homes. Mothers were more likely to engage in object-mediated play than were the fathers. The authors state that the parent-infant rough play in nonindustrialized countries may be culture specific and not related to biological underpinnings (Roopnarine et al. 1992).

When we compare Western cultures with those in Asia, distinct differences emerge in attitudes about play, even among Asian countries. Two studies, for example, that compared Korean-American and European-American children suggested that there were similar patterns for pretend play between the two groups, but that individual factors related to pretend play transcended the culture (Farver et al. 2000; Farver and Lee-Shin 2000). In the Farver and Lee-Shin study, the acculturation of immigrant Korean mothers played a part in the encouragement and acceptance of creativity and play. As mothers became more assimilated into American culture, their children's play reflected this and became more creative. We believe too, as TV expands into Asian society, the role models presented in children's programs will affect the kind of play that ensues.

Other studies looking at two samples of children aged two to four years in South Korea, and at two samples in North Carolina, of both middle-class and working-class parents indicated that children of working-class families in South Korea were less likely to initiate play than children in the other three groups (Tudge et al. 1995). Children in the United States, irrespective of class, did not differ in their initiation of play, but boys were more likely to initiate play either alone or in conjunction with another person. The mother was the single most likely partner in their children's play in both countries, particularly in the middle class groups, where the mother was not employed outside of the home. Although mothers in South Korea engaged more with their children in play than mothers in the United States, the engagement was of a more passive nature; they were not active participants in the play. American parents tend to take a more active role by suggesting characters and themes.

Beliefs of Chinese and United States teachers in early childhood are similar in overall structure and organization (Wang, Elicker et al. 2001). Both child-initiated learning and teacher-directed learning are emphasized in both countries, with Americans favoring the child-initiated approach. This certainly seems to be reflected in the tolerance for play in American society, where children generally choose the toys and kind of play they enjoy. By contrast, in a cultural-historical examination of social play using cross-age groups of adults, researchers found that a co-rearing system was used to support children during long separations from parents who were on fishing expeditions for their livelihoods. Play was described as hierarchically structured according to the member's age, and that adults and children were segregated from each other as social groups. The function of peer group play experiences for a child to learn about community socialization was constrained by geographical proximity (Sawada and Minami 1997).

We are reminded here of children who are raised in the suburbs or in more rural areas in the United States. These children generally do not go out in the street and find their friends. Parents are constantly making play dates for them and driving them to a friend's house. The group play in the streets that we tend to find in larger cities has diminished somewhat; children are less likely to be out playing stickball, hide and seek, leap frog, or even marbles. When we encounter outdoor play in suburban America, it is likely to be found in the backyards of the homes.

Play with video games and computers is discussed more fully in Chapters 4 and 5, but some cultural differences can be addressed here. Chinese-American mothers and European-American mothers were asked to complete a questionnaire after watching their preschool children play a game on computers. They also completed a questionnaire rating children's playfulness. Chinese-American mothers rated computer play higher than European-American mothers. This finding is not surprising given the number of Chinese-Americans now enrolled in computer science in this country. The involvement in computers is found early in their lives and obviously is encouraged by parents. Chinese-American mothers also rated more fanciful or creative play the lowest, whereas European-American mothers rated more structured play the lowest (Liang 1999). Studies of play among Chinese in Taipei, American Irish Catholic, and African-American middle-class families with comparable education reinforces the notion that the cultural disparities are paramount factors in under-standing the different attitudes toward play among these families. Al-though the Chinese mothers were involved in play with their children, the emphasis was on teaching social skills (Haight et al. 1999).

Even within the same country, differences can be found in the way children play. In a rare study comparing Old Order Mennonite, New Order Mennonite, and non-Mennonite Christian schools in the United States, it was found that these three cultures differed in emphasis on modern technology, media exposure, and encouragement of pretend play. Non-Mennonite teachers were the most positive about encouraging overt pretend play, whereas Old Order Mennonite teachers were most positive in accepting the children's private fantasies including imaginary compan-ions. The children's proportion of pretend play at recess times did not differ across groups, but Old Order Mennonite children's play themes adhered more closely to real-life family roles (Carlson et al. 1998)

The cultural differences found above indicate that we must approach the study of play with sensitivity to these differences and that in many cases it is best not to impose the values of one country upon another. This was dramatically apparent in Thailand when an American speaker suggested that a mirror would be a useful play object in allowing babies to become familiar with their own facial expressions. An educator in the audience who came from a rural district objected to this and explained how in village, looking into a mirror would be summoning spirits. A comment such as this underscores the need for the consideration of family values and cultural norms in the study of play.

Play as Restorative

We have discussed at length the various kinds of play, their differences and how they are influenced by gender and culture. We dealt mainly with the play of "normal" children, but there is an important role for play in the lives of children experiencing undue stress. We wonder how one of the more horrendous toys, called Forward Command Post and featured in stores for Christmas of 2002, could be used by such children. This toy consisted of a bombed out house with 75 soldiers and other military pieces. It was advertised by JC Penney as a "fully outfitted battle zone" house with a figure in military dress holding a weapon on the porch of the second floor (Foss 2002). Was this toy designed to help children in distress act out these feelings through their play, or just to have fun by replaying the scenes they saw in real life or on television? Although, morally, one may be shocked at the proposal of this as a gift for children ages "5 and up," there has been no research on the detrimental effects of playing with such a toy.

Play objects including arts and crafts materials can be helpful when children are faced with disaster. After the destruction of the Twin Towers on September 11, 2001, many children handled their anxieties by building towers of blocks and knocking them down or by drawing pictures of the towers burning (D. G. Singer 2002a). Other children coped in a more positive way by drawing American flags, people hugging each other, and families sitting together.

At an art exhibit in New York City entitled "Shocked and Awed," a display of pictures featuring children's reactions to war was on view. These had been created by children aged seven and eight not long after the combat ended in Baghdad, Iraq. There were pictures of tanks and bombers and one with an American tank with red bullets raining everywhere as women and children lay dead. One more hopeful drawing depicted American and Iraqi flags anchoring smiling clouds at opposite ends of a rainbow (Graeber 2003). There are many ways to handle grief and anxiety, and one can only hope that children who have experienced tragedies, witnessed bombed out homes, or homes destroyed by earthquakes or floods will be able to utilize toys and art materials in a constructive way.

Lois: A Child Who Transcends Grief Through Play

Play is especially useful for troubled preschoolers with their limited ability to express themselves verbally, and for early school-aged children who are afforded the opportunity to use play as part of their psychotherapy (Russ 2004; D. G. Singer 1993). Lois was such an eight-year-old, an only child whose parents had recently undergone an acrimonious divorce and custody battle. Coincident with this traumatic experience came the shock that her mother, with whom who she was especially close, was diagnosed with a rapidly developing, almost certainly fatal cancer. Lois was referred for psychotherapy and moved willingly into regular visits, playing with dolls, plastic horses, and blocks. She decided to write a magical adventure book in secret code, as well. After five months, she had become much involved in play and attached to the therapist, but was also facing the terrible reality that her mother, Jean, was now hospitalized. She was cared for by relatives with occasional visits to her father, who lived with his new family in another state.

Play therapy with Lois gave her the opportunity to express her deep-seated fears about the possibility of loss and the fear that she would be abandoned after her mother's impending death. During play, Lois felt safe and could act out her apprehensions by bestowing her anxieties and fears on the play figures. Gradually, she was able to express these fears in words rather than through play, but play was the first step in allowing her some relief and insight into her troubled being. We are not inferring that play therapy alone can cure a child in such a situation, but it certainly opened the way for Lois to envision other possibilities for her future and to come to terms with the reality of the tragedy facing her.

A session in May began with Lois blurting out, "I'm scared. I can't put it into words . . . I don't know what will happen. If my mom is still in the hospital on Mother's Day, I will visit her. On Mother's Day, I'll give her my book."

Lois seemed very anxious and depressed, could not use terms like "death" and "dying," but went to the block pile and constructed a tightly enclosed box.

Therapist: What are you making?
Lois: It's a tower. I'm playing the princess. Here she is—inside. There are no windows, no doors. No one can come in. No on can go out.
Therapist: Why is that?
Lois: She's safe here. She's protected. This is a palace all around here. Here is a mother, a father, one brother, a husband, a maid. People can come into the palace—but only four at a time. The jewels are locked up. There are four horses—two boy horses and two girl horses. This horse will always save the princess. He gets apples for a reward.
Therapist: Doesn't the princess ever leave the tower?
Lois: No, never. She needs to stay in there always.
Therapist: When will she come out?
Lois: She might go out but in disguise—maybe on a picnic.

Therapist: When will that be?

Lois: I don't know. Everyone is in the palace—all the people are there to protect her, to keep her safe. She is afraid to go out.

Therapist: What will happen to her?

Lois: It's dangerous. She just has to stay in the tower.

(D. G. Singer 1993, p. 28)

This theme became the basis for continuing play during the period that her mother's condition worsened. When Jean was briefly out of the hospital, she and her former husband, Ron, visited the therapist to talk openly of plans for Ron to fit Lois into his new household after Jean's death. Although both were controlled and rational with clear concern about the best interests of their child, Jean could not avoid remarking that the "bad parent" was winning out after all. Some of these feelings, undoubtedly, had been conveyed to Lois, who week after week continued her play as the princess who found safety only in her tower. The therapist encouraged her to consider some options, like going out in disguise and using a magical plastic horse that Lois had conjured up as her protector.

Her mother's condition worsened and Lois spent the summer with her father and his new wife. When she returned from an apparently happy summer in early September, her mother lay dying in the hospital. Despite her misgivings about having enjoyed her time with her father and his family, Lois seemed to be now more able to face her future. She continued playing "house" and donned her princess outfit of play clothes, but now she came out of her enclosed tower and moved around the room. She chose some toys, particularly a small china swan, that represented a new family.

Lois: Look, a newborn bird will come out of this shell. We will have a magic potion and make a baby mouse, too.

Therapist: You want some babies around, I see.

Lois: This will be a game where a witch comes to all these dolls—Lulu, Doo-doo, Pooh-Pooh—and makes all new babies.

Therapist: Why so many babies?

Lois: Well—it's a new beginning.

(D. G. Singer 1993, p. 37)

A few days before her mother died, Lois continued to play using the dollhouse and placing small doll figures in various rooms.

Lois: The mother is in bed. Sh, sh—no noise, please!

Therapist: Where is everybody?

Lois: Well, baby is in the crib, and this doll is the big sister. She's reading a book. She's sad.

Therapist: Why is she so sad?

Lois: 'Cause nothing is the same, that's why.

Therapist: Tell me about what's changing.

Lois: Everyone will leave the house.

Therapist: Is the father still inside the house?

Lois: No, he's in a new house, and the moving truck is coming to take everyone away.

Therapist: Everyone?

Lois: No, they'll leave the mother sleeping in her room.

(D. G. Singer 1993, p. 38)

Finally facing the reality of her mother's passing, Lois had one session in which she briefly regressed to playing a baby herself, sucking her thumb and curling up on the floor on a blanket in a fetal position. She then talked of a dead caterpillar she had buried under a peach tree at her home and said it was no use to dig him up because "it's probably disintegrated by now." She and the therapist (Dorothy Singer) visited her mother, who lay dying in bed, puffy and hooked up to various tubes. Lois sat quietly and then took the therapist's hand and led her out. Lois talked of her dolls, about babies, and her future. Her mother died the next day and after the funeral, which Lois handled well, her father brought her to the playroom for one last session. She thanked Dr. Singer for having gone to the funeral parlor and said, "Mommy looked beautiful and like asleep and not in pain." Then she played house for one last time asking the therapist to be the mother doll and saying, "I'll be the father doll." She talked of building a hideout for use if needed. In time she handed the therapist the baby doll, and kissed her. "It's hard to go away. I can't be that baby, and you can't be my mother—only in our play— isn't that the way?" Then she left with her father to start her new life. Follow-up communication for some period indicated that she was doing well.

Our brief samples from the pretend play of Colin and Lois demonstrate how children assemble bits and pieces from their immediate experience and reshape them through storytelling (or in Bruner's terms, narrative thought) into original miniaturized and personally meaningful forms. How will the exposure to and involvement with the electronic media of the twenty-first century influence children's enjoyment and use of their capacity for imaginative play? Will they be able to use the story elements from television programs and from other electronic media to aid them in the process of intellectual growth and personality formation? The following chapters raise these issues and examine the interplay of the new technology and imagination.

— 3 —

Television and Imagination

More than any other single effect, television places images in
our brains. It is a melancholy fact that most of us give little importance to this implantation, perhaps because we have lost
touch with our own image-creating abilities, how we use them
and the critical functions they serve in our lives

—J. MANDER, *FOUR ARGUMENTS*

A boisterous "Peter Pan" was flying around the daycare center while a
chubby little "Wendy" was pretending to cook supper for Peter and his
lost boys, two other four-year-olds who were busy sorting out blocks, the
pretend utensils for their supper. We watched these children playing their
game and wondered if the teacher had read *Peter Pan* to them that
morning. We were surprised to learn that the children had drawn the
story ideas from a television special that had been aired the previous
evening. This Peter Pan game took place more than thirty years ago and
led to a question we asked of each other at home that evening. Does
television enhance a child's imagination or does it impede the child's
capacity for symbolic play?

Interestingly enough, many years later, Steven Spielberg produced a
movie based on *Peter Pan* called *Hook* and told an interviewer in the
Italian magazine *Ulisse* (2000, p. 128) that he always wanted to fly. "And
from the time I was a kid I have been fascinated by people with a blind-
fold over one eye, a bandana on their head and a knife in their teeth.
For me everything to do with pirates was incredibly exciting and romantic." We are sure that some children who saw *Hook* may have been
inspired to imitate the characters in this movie just as the children who
saw the TV production were, but film is not as frequently experienced a
medium for preschool children as the daily fare of television.

The pretend Peter Pan game, acted out so enthusiastically by the preschoolers we observed, was the impetus for our earliest explorations of

the effects of television on the cognitive, social, and emotional life of children. We realized that television was now an important environmental feature in a child's life and one that surely must be taken into consideration as a contributor to a child's development, especially to a child's capacity for imagination. The provocative quotation from Jerry Mander that heads this chapter exemplifies the point of view we found among many scholars and critics. We could not however, justify the validity of Mander's position concerning the negative impact of television on the basis of any known research at that time.

Other media—radio, films, and books—may influence a person's imaginative potential, but none of these are as pervasive in a child's life as television. Children who are very young do not spend as much time with books as they do with TV or electronic games, and certainly they do not listen to radio or attend movies as frequently as they watch television. The role models, heroes, and heroines portrayed in programs viewed by children are likely to become the characters in their pretend play. Indeed, many preschoolers who incorporate characters in their play use the television figures of Batman and Wonder Woman as their superheroes (James and McCain 1982).

Where Do Children Get Their Heroes?

A survey was administered to 100 adults aged 17 to 83 years, representing pre- and post-television periods, to review how children played and who their heroes were from 1900 to 1980. The participants answered questions about their favorite childhood play themes, heroes, qualities of the heroes, and sources of information about heroes. The participants who had watched television as preschoolers reported more incidents of heroic adventure play and more selections of a fantasy hero from television as the favorite character to emulate. The range of qualities attributed to the television fantasy heroes appeared to be much narrower than those of more realistic models. Stereotypical heroes such as Superman and Spiderman may replace friends, siblings, and parents as the child's primary source of information about play themes (Feuerhahn 1984–1985; French and Pena 1991). Just as we found in Chapter 2 in our discussion about choices of sex-based toys, early elementary school–aged girls will tend to admire the female heroines, and boys at these ages will identify with and admire the male heroes (Hoffner 1996). One might argue, therefore, that early exposure to television and particularly to pure fantasy models may to some degree limit the imaginative range of a child's thought concerning ideal figures to emulate.

A poignant story in the *New York Times* about a young family impressed us because of the power of television on the self-concept and the identity formation of a girl. The child's father was in prison, and the mother, overwhelmed by poverty and raising her three children, attempted to maintain some semblance of a family. She took pictures of her children and brought them to cheer her husband on her visits to him. One photo was of her three-year-old daughter posed in "gansta style, like the Polaroids of her father . . . hands on bent knees, with a menacing look, or standing, arms folded across her chest, her expression intently grim" (LeBlanc 2003, p. 34). Her favorite TV program was *COPS,* an inappropriate program for any preschooler, but her mother encouraged it to keep alive the child's connections to her imprisoned father. The child was already getting into trouble in preschool with her classmates.

With the growth of internet use among children, the electronic media must be taken seriously as an influence upon the consciousness of youngsters. Unfortunately, many researchers in the field of child development fail to include measures of the impact of electronic media in their studies. Until we witnessed that Peter Pan game, our own research studies of play had not included any questions about the television viewing habits of our participants. Currently, there is a substantial amount of research addressing the issue of aggression and violence and the electronic media. Much less research has examined the effects of these media on how children employ their *imaginative* capacities. Excellent recommendations for future research on electronic media are offered by Rideout, Vanderwater, and Wartella (2003). These include suggestions for further study on children's cognitive abilities in general, but not explicit suggestions to study the effect of TV viewing and computer play on children's fantasy and imagination. Our intent in this chapter, therefore, is to focus mainly on the effects of television on a child's imagination. We begin with a discussion on the impact of reading and radio (two media that may be less in use by children than television) on the fantasy life of young children.

Reading and Imagination

Children who have a TV in their bedrooms or who live in households with heavy TV viewing spend significantly more time watching TV and less time reading or playing outdoors than other children do (Rideout et al. 2003). Books like the *Harry Potter* series have encouraged some children to read, but the very young who are not able to read rely on the stories told or read to them for themes to use in their pretend play. And increasingly, television rather than story books is the prime source of material for many children's play scripts (French and Pena 1991).

When we read, a more complicated cognitive process occurs than when we view television. We are engaged in an active process of encoding the words on the printed page by combining discrete letters. From strings of words, thoughts are generated, associations are made, and images are constructed. We can control our reading in many ways: reread a sentence, pause to reflect, ponder over a difficult word, stop to consult a dictionary, flip back in the book to an earlier section, or even peek ahead to see how the story ends if we are impatient. We can skip over sentences that we don't enjoy or understand, or savor a sentence that has particular meaning and beauty for us. We can control our pace when we read, by reading quickly or by reading slowly. We carry books with us and they become a part of our personal baggage. We can read with intent or skim. We can finish reading a book, and then start all over, immediately, if we choose to do so. One of us had just such an experience. After reading a beautifully written book, *The Spectator Bird* by Wallace Stegner, it was difficult to relinquish its hold. How wonderful to simply open to the first page and reread the book with the same intensity and appreciation of the words of this great American writer.

It is true that some television programs and films have depth and beauty and are well worth seeing again. For some of us, however, the magic of books will always remain the medium most favored. As Ray Bradbury wrote in *Fahrenheit 451*, "The magic is in what books say, how they stitched the patches of the universe together into one garment for us" (1967, p. 83). According to Bradbury, books have "quality" and "texture." In attempting to address the issue of imagination and television, it is difficult to find enough programs for children with the quality and texture that can enrich a child's life.

In an excellent discussion of electronic media and reading, Desmond (2001) makes the point that no public outcries have urged parents to reduce their children's reading habits, while we often hear demands for restrictions on television viewing from many parent advocacy groups. Few, if any, studies examine the impact of reading on television. As Desmond says, "It is difficult to avoid labeling book reading as superior to

TV viewing, because the strengths of reading appear to be consonant with academic achievement, a gateway to career and personal success" (Desmond 2001, p. 41) On a more positive note, it seems likely that television viewing can inspire children to read a book after they have seen the story portrayed on TV. Perhaps seeing the Harry Potter films may also inspire children to then read the books.

Radio and Imagination

We know that our own experience with radio was an enriching one. The delightful program *Let's Pretend* was aired on Saturday mornings when we were children, long before the days of television. We were able to envision the fairy tales with their gallant Prince Charming and their golden-haired princesses as if they were in the room beside us. Not so long ago we found these radio broadcasts reproduced on audio tapes and presented a set to our grandchildren. One day, eight-year-old Grace put the tape on, stretched out on the couch and closed her eyes so that she could "see the story better in my mind." This, needless to say, warmed our hearts.

Children do not listen to radio as a major source for storytelling entertainment like they did before the advent of TV. Older children do listen to radio and CDs for access to the latest popular songs. Nonetheless, young children play audio tapes or increasingly listen to CDs (especially in the car on long trips). It seemed worthwhile for some researchers in the 1980s to compare the effects of listening to radio with viewing television on the imagination of children. One study found no difference between the two media in terms of fluency, flexibility, or originality of children's responses after exposure to either radio or television stories (Runco and Pezdek 1984). Other researchers found that radio was a more powerful stimulator of imagination (Beagles-Roos and Gat 1983; Greenfield and Beagles-Roos 1988; Greenfield et al. 1986; Meringoff et al. 1981). These authors agree that details produced in children's drawings are remembered better after exposure to television than after exposure to radio. Children listening to radio also showed significantly more errors in comprehension and memory than those watching television (Hayes et al. 1986).

The images presented on television may interfere with those that viewers try to produce in their imagination when listening to an audio version of a story. Valkenburg (2001) refers to this theory as the visualization hypothesis. She cautions, however, that "verbal presentations, such as radio and print, might elicit more novel responses than television presentations not because verbal presentations are more stimulating for creativity but because they are *remembered less well*" (p. 127). Her subsequent research and our own observations do support the notion that imaginative and creative responses are more likely to follow listening alone or reading a story rather than watching it on TV.

The Properties of Television and Its Formal Features

Aside from the obvious characteristics of television, its availability in the home, its use of picture and sound, its entertainment, information, and social value, television has certain properties that distinguish it from other media (Huston and Wright 1989). These conventions or formal features are:

- *Attention demand*—the continuous movements on the screen that evoke an orienting response from us
- *Brevity of sequence*—the brief interactions among people, brief portrayal of events, the brief commercials (10 to 30 seconds long)
- *Interference effects*—the rapid succession of material that interferes with rehearsal and assimilation of material
- *Complexity of presentation*—the cross-modality presentation of material (sound, sight, and printed word, especially in commercials)
- *Visual orientation*—television is concrete, oriented toward spatial imagery
- *Emotional range*—the vividness of action (special effects, music, lighting).

Further technological properties of television include

- Use of slow-motion or speeded motion
- Juxtaposition of scenes or split-screen technique whereby two scenes are placed side by side on the same screen
- Use of subliminal techniques that allow two scenes to be viewed simultaneously (used often in dream sequences)
- Special effects such as zooming in (the enlargement of a character or object), making things appear small, or making them grow

gradually in front of your eyes (In former Wonder Bread ads, a child grows instantaneously.)

- Production of magical effects involving distortions, changes in figure and ground, the rapid disappearance of a person or object
- Ripple effects of words or scenes and the various fades or dissolves as one scene seems to flow into another
- Use of montage to inform viewers of changes of location or passing of time, and even the particular genre (drama, documentary, cartoon, quiz show)
- Chroma-key, a special camera effect, gives us the illusion that a reporter, for example, is standing in front of a famous landmark, when he or she is really in the studio and the landmark is projected on a screen behind him.
- Instant replay, usually reserved for sports events, may lead children to believe that the person performed the act twice.

Even color, a prominent feature of television, may have an effect on viewers. Research with adults finds that the influence of color appears in the self-reports of emotional experience, but is not apparent in any of the physiological measures such as skin conductance, heart rate, and facial electromyography (Detenber et al. 2000). People simply believe that color pictures are more pleasing and exciting than monochrome versions of the same things.

Formal features such as the visual and auditory (music and funny voices) production techniques described above influence comprehension by selectively guiding attention to content. These formal features appeal to children not only because they make a program more lively, but also because they help the children to make sense of it. A body of research informs us about the conventions or formal features of television that affect children's comprehension. According to Bickham and colleagues (2001), children actively encode the characters, settings, time, and location changes. When research with children was conducted to examine the relationship between fast-paced television and creativity, no significant relationships were found. Overall viewing, however, was associated with less vigilance (attention) to the screen. Children, in general, are apt to shift their attention away from the screen, but the rapid pacing keeps them glued to the set (McCollum 1999).

After more than thirty years, the producers of *Sesame Street* decided that the fast pacing of their program needed a change. The segments on the program are now much longer and more comprehensive, usually 10 segments an hour rather than the 20 to 40 segments that had been typical (Fisch and Bernstein 2001). "The charming but peripatetic skits on *Sesame Street*, designed to keep children watching—and to entertain their parents—actually confused and ultimately annoyed preschoolers" (Salamon 2002, p. 27). This is an issue we have long commented on (J. L. Singer 1980; J. L. Singer and Singer 1979).

Television Viewing Habits

How much television is being viewed in the United States? A prime source of information are the Nielsen ratings that include the television viewing hours of children aged 2 and over. To determine the viewing habits of children below age 2, a study was conducted using a Parent Survey and a Family Information Form to assess infants and toddlers usage of both television and video programs, and the role of parents during such usage. Parents were middle-class suburban families with 104 boys and 117 girls aged one month to 23 months as participants. Results indicated that the average age children began watching videos was 6.1 months, and television was 9.8 months. The average number of hours of watching television per day was 1.12 hours versus 0.41 hours for video (Weber and Singer 2004). There were parents, of course, who had the TV set turned on even before their babies reached 9 months. In one study children as young as 11 months were already found to be viewing television, and between the ages of 18 and 36 months, children became regular TV viewers. One 32-month-old was watching 2 hours and 40 minutes per day (Schmitt 2001). In a national telephone survey of 1,065 parents of children ages six months to six years, children averaged about an hour a day of TV and an additional 38 minutes of videos. The heavier viewers in this sample watched TV two hours or more per day, with no significant differences between boys and girls. The youngest children, under the age of two, are heavily exposed to TV, and 26 percent have a TV in their own bedrooms (Rideout et al. 2003).

Children aged two to eleven years, according to other researchers, are spending about 3 hours and 7 minutes a day a day watching television, and if they are upper elementary school–aged children, they are among the heaviest viewers in the United States, watching approximately 24 hours per week (Comstock and Scharrer 2001). Television viewing increases to about 30 hours a week among children in the lowest socio-economic level. Poorer children have less access to extracurricular activities, such as music lessons or organized sports that may cost extra money. Thus, television remains a comparatively cheap form of recreation and entertainment for many children in the United States.

Since the late 1940s when *Howdy Doody* and *Kukla, Fran, and Ollie* first appeared on broadcast television, there has been a proliferation of children's programs of varying quality, and children are exposed to numerous shows on a daily basis. About 98 percent of American families own at least one television set. The average household with children has 2.8 television sets that are on about 7 hours and 40 minutes per day (Woodward 2000). Children of parents who work full-time outside the home spend an average of 43 minutes more each day with all media, television, computers, and video games than children whose parents are not working full-time outside the home. Single parents' children spend 47 minutes more with all media each day than children who have one adult caretaker in the home (Woodward 2000).

Although other electronic media are available, such as video games and computer games, television remains the preferred choice for children. Approximately one-third of children from two to eleven years old do not have cable television and access to such quality educational programs as *Blue's Clues* and *Dora the Explorer*. These millions of parents and children rely on broadcast television for their educational programming needs. Of children who are eight years and older, 65 percent have a TV in the bedroom, and 21 percent a computer (Kaiser Family Foundation 1999). Some parents have even purchased entertainment systems for their automobiles so that children can watch television on their journeys instead of playing the usual car games (Kravetz 2002). We even encounter TV sets at the beach and at sporting events. In some luxury hotels, there are TV sets in the bathroom so that guests are never deprived of any programs they might enjoy.

When children aged ten to seventeen were asked about their favorite television programs, they were more likely to include adult-oriented programs or general audience programs rather than specific shows geared for them. One of the reasons for this choice is the placement of child-specific programs. Many are aired at times when older children are in school—daytimes on week days—or early on weekend mornings. One fine program, *Captain Planet,* that deals with a group of young people who try to keep the planet green and are concerned about water, air pollution, and forests, for example, is now aired at 5:30 A.M., hardly a time popular with children (http://www.captainplanetfdn.org 2003). Many programs with less educational value and often a good deal of violent content tend to be aired during late morning hours on the weekend and before and after school hours during the week (Jordan 1996). As a result, a large number of children are exposed to programs that may be of low quality, and these children are vulnerable to the effects of violent and sexually explicit programs.

Television and Imagination

In the 1980s at Yale University we carried out a series of experimental studies, including a longitudinal one, examining the effects of television on preschool children, with a particular emphasis on imagination. We used various measures of imagination with preschoolers, such as eliciting their original images in response to inkblots, recording their answers to a questionnaire dealing with the kinds of play they engaged in, and training assistants to observe the children and rate them independently over several time periods during their free play in the classroom. In addition, we gathered information from the parents about the children's TV viewing and other patterns of child rearing.

We found that children who were heavy TV viewers, watching at least three hours a day, were *less* imaginative than those children who only watched one hour a day. The highly imaginative children tended to watch programs chiefly on the Public Broadcasting System (PBS) and had parents who also valued imagination. The less imaginative children had a history of watching action/adventure TV programs and cartoons, all associated with high levels of rapid activity and violence. Their parents also were less likely to control their children's TV viewing (D. G. Singer and Singer 1981a,b, 1992; J. L. Singer and Singer 1986; J. L. Singer et al. 1984a,b; Tower et al. 1979).

In more recent work studying *Barney & Friends,* a series for preschoolers on PBS, toddlers in experimental and control conditions were rated during their free play periods, pre- and post-TV viewing, by two trained independent observers for ten minutes on two occasions. The experimental group watched ten episodes of Barney daily just before their free play periods, and the control group did not see the program at all. Children in both groups were rated on imaginativeness of play, persistence, and aggression. Parents filled out questionnaires about their children's language abilities, favorite toys and activities and degree of television viewing. The toddlers who were exposed to *Barney & Friends* showed more imagination, less aggression, less anger, and more socially appropriate behavior than the control group (D. G. Singer and Singer 1998). The children viewing Barney were actively involved with the show, as evidenced by their concentration and their tendency to dance along with the characters and to sing the songs and repeat phrases from the dialog. This particular series makes a special point of emphasizing the value of pretend games as well as fostering new vocabulary and good manners.

Educational programs such as *Barney & Friends* and *Mr. Rogers' Neighborhood* include fantasy elements and offer solutions to problems. They have been shown in research to foster imagination and creativity. *Sesame Street,* in contrast to *Mr. Rogers' Neighborhood* with its strong imaginative content, "emphasizes preacademic cognitive, language and social skills" and is "much less consistently related to creativity" (Anderson et al. 2001, p. 77). In a study of 103 preschoolers, exposure to fantastic programming that presented solutions resulted in more realistic and effective solutions than did realistic programming. In addition, the child's age, mother's education, and teacher's evaluations of a child's realism in solving problems were significant predictors of originality in problem solving (Miron 2000). In trying to determine whether or not preschoolers could categorize pretense or other activities, Lillard and Sobel (1999) found that when pretense is about a fantasy character, four-year-olds are significantly more apt to understand the mind's involvement. This makes sense to us since such young children closely identify with fantasy characters. Just think about the popularity of books, films, and television programs dealing with animals (dogs, bears, dinosaurs, aardvarks) or even inanimate figures (trains, tugboats, airplanes) as heroes who are endowed with human characteristics.

Even more than animation, the presence of live actors can help persuade young children that fantasy episodes can really occur (Skeen et al. 1982). Such was the case with the TV program *Power Rangers,* a mixture of fantasy and realism. Older children, five- rather than four-year-olds, have a more mature reality perception of both cartoon and human fantasy television episodes. Nevertheless, on many television programs adult characters talk to the fantasy characters (*Mister Rogers' Neighborhood, Sesame Street, Blue's Clues, Barney & Friends*); this adds to the seeming realism of the puppets or animated characters on the program. We feel that the presence of live figures on a television program is important if they help in clarifying information and in aiding the children to process the story line more easily. The late Fred Rogers was very careful to explain the difference between one's fantasy world and social reality, with the former represented by a trolley traveling to a make-believe kingdom.

Preschoolers do have difficulty separating fantasy from reality when they watch commercials on TV, cartoons, or even programs with fanciful elements. When a cartoon character, for example, is destroyed and then comes back to life, this is confusing for preschoolers who cannot understand that a real person would not be able to recover. The children's advertising review unit (2004) of the Better Business Bureau has established guidelines for advertising directed to children. They caution against commercials that use fantasy characters to sell a product to children. In their research with older children dealing with advertising, Nicolini, Cocchini, and Fara (1992) found that eight-year-olds preferred realistic commercials. They indicated their preference for those that were focused on reassuring the potential buyer about the product rather than fantasy advertisements that presented a false reality.

Many animated television programs are product-based programs or so-called program-length commercials. The toys or characters in the programs are readily available as toys in stores. The combination of product-based television and thematically related toys is most inhibiting to creative imagination, but stimulating to *imitative* imagination (Greenfield et al. 1993). Children who were designated as imaginative gave toys original names, used imaginary symbols, or created actions, feelings, and dialogue of their own that went beyond the events in the preceding cartoon. Children who were imitative used the toy or animated figure in the exact manner as portrayed in the television story.

What are the effects on imagination of different types of programming? Valkenburg and her collaborators describe fantasy styles that appear regularly on violent and nonviolent TV as positive-intense, aggressive-heroic, and dysphoric (distressful) (Valkenburg et al. 1992). A group of 354 children were surveyed three times at one-year intervals beginning when they were in grades two or four. Children's fantasy styles in year one did not affect their TV viewing in year three. Children's viewing frequency in year one, however, did influence their fantasy styles in year three. Nonviolent children's programs led to an in increase in the children's positive-intense fantasy style, whereas violent programs encouraged children's aggressive-heroic fantasy style. TV viewing was unrelated to dysphoric fantasy. Benign, nonviolent programs do not affect fantasy play, whereas programs with high levels of violence reduce fantasy play (Van der Voort and Valkenburg 1994). In a review of the literature concerning the influence of TV on daydreaming and creative imagination, Valkenburg and Van der Voort (1994) state that the weight of evidence suggests that TV viewing stimulates daydreaming and reduces creative imagination. Most of the studies, however, rely on correlations rather than causal data.

Other investigations of the effect of TV violence on children's fear fantasies was carried out by Viemeroe and Paajanen (1992). Using a questionnaire about fantasies administered to a large number of school-aged children, the amount of TV viewing in general, and of violence viewing in particular, was associated with measures of fearfulness and of aggressive fantasies, as well as dreams about actual TV programs. The effects were less significant for girls than for boys. The use of fantasy was also correlated positively with both peer-nominated and self-rated aggression.

Television and Emotion

Not only can television viewing affect children's fantasies, but it can induce fearful anticipation among children. Research on television's effects on children's fears has been summarized by Cantor (2001). As children grow older, they become more responsive to realistic dangers than to those depicted in fantasy programs. Using a telephone survey of 285 parents of kindergarten, second, fourth, and sixth graders, for example, they found that the older children were more frightened by news stories and less frightened by fantastic content (Cantor and Nathanson 1996). In another telephone survey of Dutch children between the ages of seven and twelve, 31 percent of the children reported having been frightened by television in the preceding year of the study. Television-induced fright produced by fantasy characters, fires, accidents, and violence directed towards people declined with age. Programs that showed scenes of war and suffering increased children's fears (Valkenburg et al. 1999).

Sesame Street researchers surveyed 233 children ages six to eleven of diverse backgrounds. Nearly two-thirds of the children indicated intense anxieties about guns, death, and violence (http://www.abcnews.com 2001). The fear engendered by television or film can last for many years. Many college students report long-lasting fear effects of a frightening program that they saw on television or in the movies when they were children (Cantor 1998; Hoekstra et al. 1999). We certainly are aware of how the September 11th disaster affected children who watched the destruction of the twin towers on television. The scenes were replayed on television for many days and even weeks afterward. Visiting a middle school in Connecticut a few months after the disaster, we heard children express their fears of airplanes flying overhead and their worries about taking an airplane trip in the future. Many of the children in the audience had bad dreams, felt anxious, and were advised by their teachers to talk with their parents and counselors to help alleviate their anxieties.

When children are exposed to TV that may frighten them, parents, understandably, may be concerned with how to help them cope with their fears. Preschoolers benefit more from noncognitive strategies than from cognitive strategies (Cantor 2001). The process of visual desensitization or gradual exposure to threatening images in a nonthreatening context can be effective in helping preschool and even older elementary children deal with their fears. For example, if children see scary material, like a spider or lizard, photographs of this material or exposure to a rubber insect or even to a live lizard can be helpful to the child. Offering a child comfort through giving a child his favorite attachment object, or even food or drink may be beneficial in diminishing the fright reaction (Cantor 2001). We remember two of our granddaughters covering their eyes in anticipation of a scene in the film *101 Dalmatians* in which the dogs were treated cruelly. Older children can be offered verbal explanations about the material viewed on TV or in the movies, emphasizing that the scary material was not real.

How can television viewing influence other emotions besides fear? One clue may come from the research of Paul Harris (2000) which indicates that identification with characters in a story will influence a child's feelings. In one such experiment children were asked to involve themselves in a story and to feel sad along with the main character. Later, in retelling the story, they focused on more of the sad elements in the story and performed worse on a standard memory task, compared to children who were asked to remain detached from the story or were left to their own devices. The control children were less sad after the story and performed normally on the memory task. Similarly, it seems to us that children who are deeply involved with characters on a television story will be more affected emotionally than children who do not invest such emotional effort.

Can we moderate children's awareness of their response to television to reduce the impact of negative emotional messages? Various strategies have been employed by researchers to encourage second to sixth grade children to focus on a victim's feelings and to think about them while they watched cartoons. Children who were encouraged to empathize with the victim did not find the cartoons to so funny and enjoyable. Instead, they reported more positive evaluations of the victims and less positive reactions to the perpetrators of violence than did children who had received no suggestions about becoming involved with the victims (Nathanson and Cantor 2000). Cartoons are a large part of children's television fare; at least one channel, Cartoon Network, is devoted to this genre. Interestingly, broadcast authorities in Turkey shut down a television network for showing a popular children's cartoon in which the Pokemon characters inspired two incidents of children jumping from high places (Moore 2000).

One might expect that situation comedies, shown at a time in the evening when children are viewers, would emphasize prosocial and positive feelings in relation to children more than negative ones. However, Weiss and Wilson (1996) conducted a content analysis of the five most popular prime-time family sitcoms among children ages two through eleven years. They found that, although sitcoms featured child characters in the major story line, the emphasis was primarily on negative emotions such as fear and anger. Humor built around "put-downs," sarcastic or degrading comments, generally accompanied the more negative emotions and was artificially enhanced by the laugh track. For very young children who may not grasp the subtleties of sarcasm or parody, what may stay with them are the insults and incivility.

Even infants are affected by the emotional expressions of adults portrayed on videotape. In experiments with infants aged ten to twelve months, the older children showed an increase in negative responses to a toy after viewing an actress who vividly expressed these negative emotions toward the toy (Mumme and Fernald 2003). It appears from this study that by age one, a child is able to process the social information and the emotional state of an adult.

Directors are aware of the importance of facial expressions, exaggerated gestures, as well as music and sound effects to the emotional components of a program for young children. One would hope that producers and writers of programs for children would become more aware of the developmental stages of children and especially the cognitive differences that children manifest at different ages. We would like to see more positive social examples on programming for children, offering opportunities for them to model more positive emotions in their earlier years, along with more upbeat fantasy content.

The Constructive Possibilities of Television

The Public Broadcasting System (PBS) offers excellent programs for children, but mainly for preschoolers. The benefits of television concerning social adaptiveness such as sharing, taking turns, and cooperating with others are reviewed by Mares and Woodard (2001), but these researchers found much less empirical evidence for prosocial effects than about violent content. We do find numerous TV programs, especially on public broadcasting, that are particularly strong in presenting examples of positive social behavior. Parents of children in the four- to six-year range, as reported by Rideout, Vanderwater and Wartella (2003) indicate that their children imitate both positive and negative or aggressive acts seen on TV (87 percent vs. 47 percent, respectively). The authors are careful to point out that the data in the report are correlational, and one cannot automatically assume a causal influence of viewing on overt behavior.

The Children's Television Act of 1990, extended by the adoption of new rules by the Federal Communications Commission (1996), forced broadcasters to offer children up to age sixteen a minimum of three hours a week of educational/informational programming. The definition of educational/informational programming, however, was not clarified for the producers, and even today this remains rather vague. Amy Jordan (1996, p. 14) uses the following criteria to define the quality of programs for children: content that is understandable and age appropriate for the target audience; an enriching or prosocial lesson that is clear and understandable; a lesson that is integral to the story and/or pervasive throughout the program; content that speaks to many children through diversity in its characters; and content that is creative and engaging in its techniques and its storytelling devices.

One study examined the degree to which second to sixth graders may have been affected by the programming stimulated by this Act. Girls and younger children liked educational television programs more than boys and older children. Girls and older children understood the content of the programs, especially those with prosocial messages (Calvert and Kotler 2003). Other research indicates that children who watched educational programs such as *Sesame Street,* and *Mr. Rogers' Neighborhood* entered school with good academic skills and a more positive attitude toward education. When followed into their teens, they performed at a higher academic level in English, math, and science than children who had rarely viewed educational programming (Huston et al. 2001).

Children in family daycare, especially those in the care of relatives who are unpaid, watch more television than those in daycare centers. The kinds of programs they watch are generally not age appropriate and include soap operas, talk shows, dramas, and adventure programs. Home care providers who are paid tend to be more selective and choose programs on PBS such as *Barney & Friends, Sesame Street,* and *Mr. Rogers' Neighborhood* (Mullin-Rindler and Fucigna 1995; J. L. Singer and Singer 1993).

When social class is considered, differences in the attitudes toward television control are found between upper-and lower-class parents. Jordan (1992) proposes that social class has an important but indirect effect on television usage in the family. Higher socioeconomic status (SES) families are more concerned about *time* spent viewing television, whereas lower socioeconomic status families were more concerned about television's *content.* The higher SES families preferred that children engaged in one activity at a time; they should not be reading or playing while watching TV. The lower SES parents used television in combination with other activities. The higher SES families regarded time as something to be managed and carefully allocated. Higher SES families believed that television viewing was also a waste of time, whereas lower SES families did not hold such opinions since they could combine chores such as ironing or reading to their children at the same time the television set was on. One wonders if combining other activities with television viewing interferes with the processing of information. We know from the work of Salomon and Leigh (1984) that when children expend mental effort, called AIME (amount of invested mental effort), while viewing a program, they process the material better than those who view television more passively.

A Global View of Television's Influence on Imagination

Television has the potential of offering its audience glimpses into the culture of other countries and the worlds of art, music, and science. One can find such content mainly on the public broadcasting channels, but the viewership for these channels is relatively small in comparison with commercial television.

The global village described by Marshall McLuhan (1964) has come to pass. From the primitive village of Gorotire, Brazil, in the Amazon rain forest, where naked children view television as the "big ghost" at night (Simons 1989, p. 36) to the most modern cities, children are enthralled by a continuous outpouring of television programs. Our experience in Marseille at a UNESCO conference demonstrated how television plays a role in the social lives of people, even in developing countries. The representatives from Tunisia stated that Saturday night was "*Dallas* night": no one visited neighbors, everyone stayed home transfixed to the set. These delegates lamented the fact that they were missing an episode of this American TV series while attending this conference and hoped their families would tell them what happened when they returned.

Currently, 93 percent of twelve-year-old children in twenty-three countries, from Angola and Argentina to Tobago and the Ukraine, have access to a television set (Groebel 1998, 2001). According to a report sponsored by UNESCO (Groebel 1998), Europe and Canada have the highest distribution of TV (about 99 percent) and Africa the lowest (83 percent). The world's children spend an average of three hours daily in front of the screen, with variations depending on the particular country. Unfortunately, we have no data on the effect of television on these children's fantasy and imagination in this report, since its main purpose was to examine the impact of television on children's aggression. It is interesting to note that the author found that children have a universal fascination with aggressive media heroes who have become global icons, especially for the boys.

In an earlier study in France, children aged nine through twelve in both rural and urban areas were asked to imagine what they could be if transformed by a magician. Their drawings were then categorized by identification with animals, objects, or media personalities. Animals were the most selected theme by both boys and girls, but when humans were selected as the identification theme, they were stereotypical heroes such as Superman (Feuerhahn 1984–1985).

A comprehensive, cross-cultural study looking at children's make-believe worlds found that television plays a significant role in many of the children's fantasies. A sample of 197 children ages eight to ten from four countries—Germany, Israel, South Korea, and the United States—participated (Gotz et al. 2003). The researchers compared the children's fantasies of nature and animals, amusement, travel, supernatural power and other interests in their make-believe worlds. Children of both genders in all countries did mention conflict and fighting in reference to TV stories. The boys' fantasies dealt mainly with such conflict and the desire to use magic powers to conquer their foes. Children also used the media to "symbolize their own perception of themselves" (p. 34) by selecting particular media content and integrating these into their stories. The boys especially incorporated into their fantasy stories and drawings elements of action/adventure films, computer games, documentary programs, and mythical stories where men are heroes.

At one time a village in the western part of Canada had become a television blind spot because of special transmission difficulties. This was a rare opportunity for researchers to find out what the effects of introducing television would be on the community. When television was finally accessible, the life style of the villagers changed significantly. The adults reduced the frequency of some of their social habits, such as going to the local pub or attending sports events. The children relinquished some of their outdoor physical activities. The introduction of television affected adversely their cognitive skills, especially reading and creativity (Harrison and Williams 1986). Just as television had "stolen the night" from the Amazon village of Gorotire, television was now stealing the day from this town as it had from other towns around the world.

More access to television has not created a demand for quality programs, but children do fare better, at least in countries where the government helps to defray the costs of children's entertainment (Kleeman 2001). In many European countries, educational programming for children is similar to the material broadcast on American public broadcasting channels. In Japan, for example, Nippon Hoso Kyokai (NHK) airs eight programs to nursery schools and kindergartens. One program titled *With Mother* has been on since 1959. Another program, *Let's Hear Stories,* available on radio since 1954, is also geared for young children and is considered by educators to be one that fosters creativity.

Although educational television programs are targeted for children of all ages and aired in the schools in Japan, television viewing as well as radio listening rates for these educational programs for preschoolers has declined. Several reasons are cited. There is an increase in the availability of commercial video cassettes as teaching materials for kindergartners. New guidelines issued in 2000 for teachers emphasized the importance of direct, hands-on learning experiences that reduced the reliance on electronic media in the classroom (Kodaira and Takahashi 2001).

Japan may be a generally more conservative society than the United States, but when it comes to television usage among young children, the Japanese people's attitudes are less restrictive, at least among the middle classes. In a study comparing a large number of Japanese and American college-educated mothers' ideas about television and their active involvement with their preschoolers, the Japanese mothers imposed fewer controls on children's television viewing and offered fewer explanations concerning the content viewed (Komaya and Bowyer 2000). The American mothers tended to supervise both the content and amount of television viewing by their children. They also answered more of the children's questions and were more apt to discuss the programs. This active mediation in clarifying the fantasy/reality distinctions in the programs would be beneficial for preschoolers. The Japanese mothers reported that television was an important source of the educational and entertainment value for their children. In spite of their college education, the more relaxed attitudes toward television of Japanese mothers was quite similar to the lower SES American mothers Amy Jordan (1992) interviewed in her study, described earlier.

Chinese families in various cities report that their children watch about 38 minutes of television a day, whereas children in larger cities such as Beijing watch about 49 minutes a day. In general, children use up to eight different media a day—television is used the most—96 percent had watched television in the two weeks of data collection in 1992—ahead of newspapers, radio, comics, books, tapes, magazines. Two hours per day were spent on all media, with rural areas using fewer cassette tapes (Wei 1996). There are different purposes for media use in China, but the main emphases in both rural and in urban areas involve the employment of television for orderliness in the family and for the encouragement of independence and creativity in the children. Wei regards television as a "playmate for entertainment" (p. 205). She states that television is providing the fantasy characters for children and that children are currently learning more values from the medium than from their families.

In Pakistan, Alay Ahmad (1979) tested the hypotheses that television programs with nonaggressive content would be preferred more by females than by males, and that television programs with partial fantasy content would be preferred more than programs with complete reality or with complete fantasy content. Participants were 94 seven- to fifteen-year-old children. Results indicated that the most preferred programs were those that included some fantasy, and that as frequently found in other cultures, males preferred aggressive themes and females chose social drama. One might speculate that these older children are more mature in their thinking than younger children, and do enjoy programs in which there are real characters to identify with as role models. Of course, they still enjoy storytelling, and fantasy is still exciting to them.

Many of the educational programs in the United States, in Western European countries, as well as in Japan, are geared to the preschool child and use animation or puppet figures. Emmison and Goldman (1997) found that, when studying a particular program, children could easily relate to the puppets because of the importance of the language used in transmitting ideas. The conversation in the show was typical of human adult-child interactions and therefore posed no problem for the viewers.

One program that is now aired in over 120 countries is *Teletubbies*, targeted to children one year old. The program was launched in Great Britain by the British Broadcasting Corporation (BBC) in 1997 and has since brought in many millions of dollars to BBC and to the producer, Ragdoll Productions, through the sales of books, videos, computer games, magazines, and toys (Dominus 2004). Of interest in this chapter on television and imagination is the possible influence of this program's content on an infant's ability to make sense of the story. A series of studies appeared in a special issue of *Televizion,* an international periodical, suggesting benefits for preschoolers who watch *Teletubbies* (Lohr 1999). Most of the data have been gathered through observations of children older than one year or through anecdotal data collected from caregivers, mainly because it is extremely difficult to carry out an empirical study with infants and toddlers. The studies report positive effects in the children such as smiling, laughing, and imitating sounds while viewing in Great Britain, Germany, Australia, and Israel. Two studies in this same issue indicate that no empirical data have been found in the United States or in Norway using an experimental and control design (Hake 1999; Stipp 1999).

The American Academy of Pediatrics (1995) recommends that children below the age of two years should not be permitted to watch television and that a program such as *Teletubbies* designed for the one-year-old is not acceptable. As mentioned in the previous chapter, babies do not evidence signs of make-believe play until about eighteen months of age. They need the opportunity to experience their sense of touch, taste, smell, hearing, and seeing through appropriate toys, exposure to books, and parental involvement in their play.

Examination of imaginative abilities and attitudes of West Australian children in relation to their weekly TV viewing habits found that, in a test of imaginative problem-solving, heavy viewers (who watched 50 hours or more a week) earned lower scores on the test than did light or moderate viewers. Attitudes of school-aged children toward imagination, elicited by means of a questionnaire on the nature of imagination, were overwhelmingly favorable and did not vary with frequency of viewing (Peterson et al. 1986). Children of about the same age in Holland and in the United States were questioned to find which program characteristics they valued. Comprehensibility and action were valued by children in both countries, but children in the United States attached more value to realism than the Dutch children. Boys and girls in both countries also put some value on romance. Girls valued innocuous programs more than boys. This may be attributed to the fact the girls in both countries are more often frightened by media depictions of danger and violence (Valkenburg and Janssen 1999).

Teaching about the Media

What emerges from this brief global review is the pervasiveness of television around the world and how similar are the effects of the medium on children's imagination in different countries. Various curricula have been developed to help children understand the formal conventions and special effects of television and to help mitigate the violence depicted (Brown 2001). When children have been exposed to television literacy lessons, they learn significantly more about how programs are constructed, are better able to understand the difference between reality and fantasy on television, and engage in less in violent behavior than children who have not received such training in critical viewing, (Davies 1997; Rosenkoetter et al. 2004; D. G. Singer and Singer 1998). Older children exposed to media literacy instruction were shown to improve in reading comprehension, writing, and critical thinking skills compared to children who did not receive such instruction (Hobbs and Frost 2003).

Media literacy curricula are generally based on the premise that children adopt society's values, attitudes, and norms through their exposure to popular media. Curricula include such goals as understanding how programs are made using the technical properties discussed early in this chapter. Programs are deconstructed so children can understand how messages on TV can affect them emotionally, influence their cognitive processing, and even change their beliefs. Stereotypes, violence, news programs, commercials, and even programs dealing with morality, sex, drugs, and alcohol are presented and discussed as segments of various curricula (Brown 2001; D. G. Singer and Singer 1998). Television curricula developed for use in United States schools generally offer suggestions to help parents gain control of television through choosing age-appropriate programs, setting rules for the number of hours their children watch, and initiating discussion after viewing programs. Parental guidance can also help reduce media consumption (Van den Bulck and Van den Bergh 2000).

Great Britain, Canada, and Australia have been involved with television literacy for many years, and more recently other European countries have followed suit. Japan is currently developing curricula that will deal not only with understanding television but also with computer use. By the year 2005, computers will be installed in every classroom around the country, providing high-speed Internet access to schools and promoting the development and use of Web content (Kodaira and Takahashi 2001). In Japan, for example, 52.5 percent of elementary schools, 41.9 percent of junior high schools, and 37.9 percent of senior high schools take some measure to foster media literacy. The most popular technology employed for media literacy education are computers and the Internet in all of the schools (Kodaira and Takahashi 2001).

A curriculum combining video and print material was developed for elementary school children using a playful puppet to help viewers understand the content on television and how to become critical viewers (Komaya 2004; Komaya and Muto 2002; Muto and Komaya 2003). The puppet, Ukkie, presents information about television (e.g., how violence is portrayed on TV) to the children, and the children in turn discuss the concepts and prepare their own materials in their classrooms about the subject matter shown on the video.

Research concerning the use of media in the classroom demonstrates that the newer electronic technologies can be used to encourage creativity (Bruce 1989; Reeves and Atkinson 1977). Many teachers, however, are reluctant to introduce television as a teaching tool, fearing this might encourage more television viewing at home. Nonetheless, when teachers do try to use television along with critical viewing discussions, it can be a powerful source for ideas and can motivate children to learn and increase their academic skills. Children who were asked to write a commercial to present on closed circuit television in the classroom found that they needed to spell correctly, use good grammar, and make their scripts lively and original to hold the interest of their classmates (D. G. Singer et al. 1980). One child in the study made a commercial trying to sell old shoelaces. She had to think of novel uses for this product, and her classmates were convinced of the value of this product by her creative approach.

Rehearsal before a TV presentation, which includes role-playing, writing scripts, and imagining positive experiences, can help students overcome any apprehension about appearing before a camera (Hortin 1982). The children in the study by D. G. Singer and colleagues (1980) rehearsed their commercial presentations numerous times before they actually appeared on camera in the classroom. Visual rehearsal, according to Hortin, also helps students and teachers in decision making, self-image, and teaching experiences.

The use of television is effective in teaching science if content is high, rich in facts. In a presentation of eight science TV programs content was varied in both TV and print material. High content material significantly outscored low content on measures of possibility and curiosity, regardless of media presentation. Content more than type of medium, affects creativity and attitude. Low content (use of images), however, outscored high content presentation on tests of visual originality. It may be that dense text interfered with visual productivity (Rubenstein 2000).

The Potential of the Television Medium

We regularly urge the writers and producers of children's television programs to offer stories with more imaginative content and to reduce the violence or aggressive acts in programs geared for children. It is interesting to examine the impact of the Federal Communications Commission (1997) regulations regarding educational programs for children. Representatives from twenty-eight stations were interviewed to assess local broadcasters' reactions to the new rules, their understanding of them, their implementation strategies, and any constraints that enter into the selection of educational programs for children (Sullivan and Jordan 1999). All participants in the interviews responded that they would comply with the three hours of educational programming required of them and would meet the reporting and public file obligations. Many of the respondents, however, were concerned about the financial implications, stating that the numbers of viewers were not high enough to balance the costs of such educational programming. Many children were turning to cable shows, and the three major networks were complaining about financial losses. In many Western European countries, the government helps to finance children's programming, whereas in the United States, commercials are the main source of revenue for children's productions.

The respondents in the Sullivan and Jordan study wanted further clarification of the definition of educational programming. Many of the programs selected would not be considered educational by many child development specialists. The networks argue that parents do not direct their children to view the programs that they have selected, nor do they communicate with the local broadcasters about such programming, and as a result children's programming is not profitable.

Television has the power to be both an entertaining and educational medium; unfortunately, it is much maligned. It is not the *technology* that is to blame for its failure to stimulate children's imagination and creativity. It is the *content* and the *excessive viewing* that truly matter. Many years ago television was called the "early window on the world" (Liebert and Sprafkin 1988). When used along with reading, family discussion, and curricula involving critical thinking, this medium has the potential to give us information about other cultures, dress, food, art, and music. It can offer us programs about nature, science, and the composition of our universe. We can learn about medicine and new ideas in education. We can learn social skills and ways of solving conflicts other than reverting to aggression and violence. Documentaries give us historical information, and panel discussions offer us insights that can broaden our tolerance of other people. Finally, television, if used in moderation, can provide us with experiences that have the possibility to inspire our fantasy life and imagination to soar beyond the here and now.

— 4 —

Violent Themes in Play, TV Content, and Video Games

We had occasion to follow a boy named Philip over a twelve-year period. He had been a participant as a preschooler in one of our studies, and his parents contacted us on a number of occasions subsequently asking us to observe him in free play or to have someone from our staff do home observations. They were increasingly troubled by his over-emphasis on violent themes in his television viewing, comic book collections, and the posters he hung on his walls, which reflected heavy metal music groups in aggressive postures. Philip had showed no imaginative play as a pre-schooler and was somewhat rambunctious in the daycare setting. He was already a steady viewer of action TV shows. Visiting his room when he was seven or eight, one could observe signs of imaginative play specifically focused on violent action figures, which he simulated in "bone-breaking" violent combat while listening to extremely cacophonous heavy metal or rap chanting. A party his well-to-do parents gave for his twelfth birthday was held in a restaurant, which also featured a video game arcade. Philip chose to play the most violent video games with his boy guests and took the prerogative of extra turns and of artificially boosting his scores. While he could occasionally be affable, his interest patterns and choice of friends were extremely narrow and focused more and more on violent video games over the next few years. At first, his parents somewhat minimized these involvements, but when by age fifteen he had engaged in several risky, aggression-simulating behaviors leading to his own broken bones, fights during hockey matches, and then actually threatening his parents, they arranged for extensive psychotherapeutic and social help.

Philip seems a somewhat extreme example of possible media influence. Research evidence shows that growing up in a household in which parents are themselves aggressive and use physical punishment to control children is a consistent predictor of subsequent unwarranted aggressive behavior in children (Barron 1977; Bushman and Huesmann 2001). Indeed, an impressive body of research evidence indicates that the most effective psychological treatment for children and adolescents who are severely aggressive and antisocial is parent-management training (Kazdin 2004). Such therapy focuses on helping parents control their punitive approaches and learning to use reward and understanding of the child's behavior patterns so that they can reinforce more constructive responses by the child. Philip's parents, although somewhat negligent about his TV viewing and video game playing, were not significantly physically punitive, either by their own accounts or by the boy's report. Clearly, then, his aggressive and risky behavior seemed to some extent to reflect the kinds of imaginings and the mental schemas and scripts he had formed from his early media viewing.

How serious is exposure to violent themes in literature or the media, and how much do they influence children's imagination and overt behavior? There seems little question that direct participation in terrible scenes of war or acts of harm to family will have lasting effects upon children. Even when such witnessing of real events occurs only through news reports on the television screen, the impact can be very serious for children, as accumulating research following the September 11, 2001, destruction of New York City's Trade Center buildings has demonstrated (Kaiser Family Foundation 2003). Repetitive exposure seems to have worsened the impact, arousing fears of personal endangerment, nightmares, and other symptoms of post-traumatic stress disorder (PTSD; Shuster et al. 2001).

Adults are often concerned lest their children experience such events even in the safety of their homes. We ourselves remember our response to learning from the news of a terrible airline crash at the same airport minutes after we had met our nine-year-old granddaughter, who was arriving from California to spend a week with us in New England. Since she was resting at our home when we put the TV news on, she was unaware of this event. We made a point of keeping her active and busy enough so she never watched TV or saw the newspapers for her entire enjoyable stay. Even when our drive back to the airport a week later was delayed and detoured (as we afterwards realized because President Clinton was meeting with the families of crash victims), she assumed that normal construction work was the cause.

As we discussed in Chapter 3, even fictional stories of violence and danger vividly presented on television can create distressing emotions that may recur periodically for years. What of the effects of violent themes on the child's thoughts about aggressive acts, hostility, or even overt aggressive behavior? From the earliest days of film, television, and even of comic books, many voices have been raised in alarm. The response of a majority of parents, media industry representatives, and literary artists has been to decry such concerns as excessive since, after all, so many could say, "I watched dozens of cowboy and adventure movies when I was a kid and I've been a peaceful person to this day!" Theatre industry workers also drew heavily on interpretations derived from the psychoanalytic theory of *catharsis,* the at-least partial reductions of aggressive drive energies by vicarious experiences of violence in fictional novels, fairy tales, plays, or film (Bettelheim 1966). Watching real or simulated boxing or wrestling presumably helps one to purge one's instinctual aggressive urges.

In this chapter we will explore the relevant research evidence and scientific theoretical bases for concerns about the possible impact of violent themes upon children's thoughts and overt behavior, first in imaginative play, then in games, then in film and television as well as in electronic video games. We must begin by looking first at children's floor play, derived as it is from the legends of one's culture or religion, peopled often by dolls and figurines of mythical or historical heroic figures.

Playing with Toy Guns or Action Figures in Warlike Settings

Playing with toys and games is one of the oldest of human activities. The first dice can be traced to nearly prehistoric times and were found in the Indus Valley in what is now Pakistan. Relatively complex, elegant games in which pieces (often with animal or bird names) were moved around an elaborate board inlaid with shell and lapis lazuli can be found in ancient Mesopotamia, now Syria, Israel, and Gaza, dating back over four thousand years. In Ur of the Chaldees, later Babylon, these games involved opposing sides. The first dolls and occasionally warlike sets are traceable to ancient Egypt, and a competitive board game was played by women in the Jewish communities settled in Cochin, Southern India (Hallo 1993).

The simulation of warfare in games is thus as old a tradition as one can find in the history of play. Some of our earliest persisting games like checkers or the Japanese game Go are more abstract conquest games. The most widely played and respected of board games, of course, is Chess, in which part of the game's pleasure, at least for beginners, is in the elaborately carved kings, queens, fortress towers or rooks, knights on horseback, mitred bishops, and even the more plainly garbed foot soldiers, the pawns. Although the game seems always to have been popular with royalty, nobility, and military leaders—and we know that Napoleon played chess—there is little evidence of any murders or physical battles fought afterwards between winners and losers. Chess-playing children or even fiercely competitive members of the school Chess team are usually among the most mild mannered of youngsters in their playgrounds or homes. Toy soldiers made of tin, wood, or lead, along with dolls, are some of the oldest extant playthings. From our earliest records we know that children were reared with biblical or other religion-derived accounts, historical references concerning one's culture, myths and legends of great adventures—all forms by which even the humblest parents in a society socialized their offspring into their particular clan, caste, linguistic group or nation. Many of these accounts, and whatever playthings were available to represent them more palpably, involved dangers, conflicts, and feats of great strength or heroism. Our modern superheroes seem prefigured in the Greek Herades, Roman Hercules, or the Hebrew Samson. We know from art history that children were given miniature versions of adult statuary or painted representations of heroes. These included scenes of combat like the Biblical David and Goliath or the god Krishna driving the chariot of Prince Arjuna in the Hindu epic of fratricidal war, the *Mahabharatra.*

Certainly providing children with playthings that reflect old wars, violent heroes, or legendary or historical weaponry and settings promotes the continuity of the prejudices, snobberies, or antipathies of a culture. In any progressive society, one must be constantly reexamining the implications of using particular toys or playthings to sustain actions that we may now recognize as ambiguous, if not heinous. Millions of European Christian children have played at warfare games glorifying the Crusaders of the eleventh century A.D., like Geoffrey of Boulogne or Richard the Lion-Hearted, who sought for several hundred years to drive the Muslims out of the Near East and restore Jewish and Christian rule. We know much more today about the corruption, villainy, and violence of many crusaders and of the comparable violence by the somewhat better educated and, in those days, more religiously tolerant of the Islamic conquerors. And what of the Cowboys and Indians toys of American child-hoods? Should we be encouraging children from the once Confederate States to be reenacting the brilliant war tactics of their ancestors, who fought heroically to preserve the genteel plantation society, built on the cruel enslavement of millions of African workers? These are profound issues of values we must confront as parents and as a society.

The research on violent themes in toys and games has a much more limited role; it cannot usually address the deep controversies of social philosophy implied in the values emphasized by particular advocacy groups. In theory we could track the belief systems and prejudices or conscious and unconscious social or racial stereotypes of children who have regularly played with toy soldiers, pirate ships, or Robin Hood's Merry Men (who were, after all, forest thieves). What of the current action figures who employ massive violence in their battles against ene-mies, who still often have dark-skinned or Asian facial features? Such studies have rarely been attempted, in part because much of education and the arts to which growing children are exposed consists of "de-bunking" or clarifying our earlier beliefs through presenting more his-torical detail or alternative viewpoints and interpretations. As early as in ancient Greece, we know that the tragic plays of Euripides presented critical views of the treatment of women or showed the great hero Her-acles as a somewhat oafish, drunken, but well-meaning fellow. Euripides' contemporary, the brilliant playwright Aristophanes, sought in his poetic comedies to undermine the dangerous military adventurism of the Ath-enians by satirical exposures of the foolhardiness of war. To go from the ancient sublime to the modern ridiculous, consider a publication for the nine- to fifteen-year-old crowd such as *Mad Magazine*. It is designed to question many of children's assumptions about the perfect judgement of one's parents, the seamless "rightness" of our historical or legendary war-riors, the profound intelligence of our political leadership in any gener-ation.

What are the implications of children's play with violent themes if their parents or other socializing influences do not provide counterinformation or value judgements questioning or depreciating the violence? In ad-dressing this topic we need to consider important differences between the forms of play and the possible mediating role of imaginative structures in the play. Children who watch a great deal of television involving fic-tional but relatively imitable violence (fisticuffs, knife fights, gun usage) are more prone to engage in overt acts of aggression. They seem less likely to play out more elaborately plotted pretend games that require building forts and landing strips or defining specific personalities for their toy soldiers, dolls, or other action figures. Instead, even when they initiate a pretend game, they may simply don a superhero cape and dash through the play area knocking over other children's block setups, seizing their toys, or initiating actual fights (D. G. Singer and Singer 1990; J. L. Singer et al. 1984).

We once observed a televised news report in which nursery school children were exposed to a half-hour of either *Barney & Friends* or *Power Rangers*. In the benign, albeit lively, Barney episode the children watched quietly, occasionally singing along with the children on the show or laughing and smiling. The children watching *Power Rangers* were more restless, some actually standing to imitate the punches or karate chops and kicks by the children on that show. After the viewings, the children were provided with a free play period outdoors. Those who had just seen the Barney episode, which included some demonstrations of construction equipment, played at peaceful building games with blocks or toy steam shovels. The children who had just watched *Power Rangers* scattered around the yard, climbing and running; they did not seem to organize any pretend games. Several actual fights began between them during recess period. This "natural" experiment clearly supported the observational learning theory of Albert Bandura (1977) and the dozens of experiments pointing up the aggressive risks for children of watching violent television.

In a controlled study of *Power Rangers,* children were given a choice to resolve ten different scenarios either in a socially acceptable manner or in an aggressive manner. In one scene, a child who has brought his favorite toy to school finds that while he was out of the room another child has taken his toy. Children were asked to choose among five possibilities, from aggressive to nonaggressive, describing what the aggrieved child would do. Children who were heavy viewers at home of *Power Rangers* chose the more aggressive responses, such as punching or calling the other child nasty names, compared to less frequent viewers of the show. This was the case even when the researchers took into account the influences of gender, parental regulation, and interest in programs other than *Power Rangers* (Rosenkoetter and Singer 1995).

What then of other forms of child activity or play? There is almost no research evidence that children who engage in make-believe play with fairly well-developed plots will show later aggressive behavior, even when such games involve stories of piracy, historical battles, or fantasy combat with space aliens, prehistoric dinosaurs, or mythical beasts. If anything, such players seem less prone to engage in acts of unwarranted aggression with peers (D. G. Singer and Singer 1990; J. L. Singer 1973).

What then of play with toy guns? Advocacy groups like *Teachers Resisting Unhealthy Children's Entertainment* (TRUCE) or The Lion and the Lamb have taken strong stands against the sale and advertising of toy weapons and have urged parents to avoid purchasing such weapons or encouraging their use by children (Levin 2000–2001). As citizens, we are repelled by the variety of realistic-looking guns, rifles, or automatic weapons now on sale for children. Yet we are unable, as social scientists, to draw conclusions that such playthings will have the same demonstrable influence on children's aggression that is clearly evident for frequent television viewing of violent content. The actual research evidence is sparse and less definitive, but it does point in the direction of an unhealthy impact for younger children. Surveys of parental concerns about their child-rearing indicate that as many as 67 percent of respondents object to toy gun play and resist purchasing such playthings (Cheng et al. 2003; Smith 2003). Parents of African American background seem especially concerned in this respect.

Almost thirty years ago a study by Turner and Goldsmith (1976) conducted with preschoolers showed that play with toy guns (in contrast to play with action-oriented nonviolent toys, cars, trucks, or airplanes) evoked more antisocial behaviors by the children. The toy airplanes did evoke somewhat more aggressive behavior, however, than did other nonviolent toys. We may wonder today if the September 11, 2001, terrorist attacks in New York City or the daily evidence of warplane bombing by our military in the Iraq War would not suggest to children an even more aggressive role for toy airplanes than may have been apparent to them in the 1970s.

A more recent, carefully done study by Malcolm Watson and Ying Peng at Brandeis University represents the best evidence we have of how play with toy guns may effect preschoolers. Thirty-six preschoolers were observed during free play periods at daycare centers, and their parents filled out questionnaires describing their home play, their use of toy guns, the degree to which they watched television programs, and the extent to which the children experienced disciplinary physical punishment by the parents. Statistical analyses underscore our earlier contention: for both boys and girls, parents' use of physical punishment predicted aggressive behavior at school. In addition, the extent to which boys played at home with toy guns also independently predicted how often they would manifest aggressive actions outside their homes. The children who also engaged in make-believe games of aggression with toy gun play at home were especially associated with such play at daycare. As it turned out, children who played more with toy guns were in general less likely to engage in nonaggressive imaginative play. Both gun play and physical parental punishment seemed less conducive to children's likelihood to engage in more general forms of pretending and nonviolent play (Watson and Peng 1992). More recently, Watson and collaborators (1999) studying older children found that focused aggressive fantasy play was associated with more instances of overt aggressive behavior. Gun play may indeed exemplify the specifically oriented imagery that spills over into overt action.

As we shall see when we turn to a consideration of play with video games of violent themes, fantasy play does not serve any cathartic or release function in itself. It may be a precursor for thoughts of a hostile nature when one is frustrated or interfered with by others. In the case of more elaborate storylike fantasy play involving unrealistic weapons, such as historic jousting lances or the magical implements of a *Lord of the Rings* or *Harry Potter* quasimythical plotline, no comparable weapons are available to a child. Indeed the whole attraction of such legendlike stories is in their long-ago, far-away quality. Toy guns or the increasingly realistic "play" assault weapons marketed by some toy companies in the past decades seem only a hand's reach away for many young children. As Dr. Stevanne Auerbach, founder of the San Francisco International Toy Museum, has written:

> I was shocked to learn that more than 25,000 children are injured annually with toy guns. Injuries are caused by caps or shooting projectiles. Another 200 children are killed when they mistake a real gun for a toy. (1991, p. 7)

There have been numerous accounts in the newspaper of new, realistic war toys and of their conscious linking by toy company designers and advertisers to the extensive television coverage of American military war games and to the actual war in Iraq (*The New York Times* 2002, 2003;

Herbert 2002; Lubell 2002; Hamilton 2003; Harmon 2003). In addition, the more general "gun culture" in the United States, documented in Michael Moore's award-winning documentary film *Bowling for Columbine* (Moore 2002), must be given serous consideration as an influence on children's play, thoughts, and action tendencies. Newspaper accounts and even "live" television coverage of shooting incidents at schools involving quite young children and early adolescents are so widely known and publicized that they need not be elaborated here. We find one instance especially chilling—the case of two boys, thirteen and fourteen years old, who obtained their grandparents' weapons from an unlocked rack and set up a sniping position from a small hill overlooking their elementary school entrance. The younger boy was dispatched to set off the school's fire alarm and then rejoin the older boy in shooting at children and teachers as they emerged from the school.

There seems little doubt among parents, educators, and observers of children's play that those children who focus on play with realistic toy guns may be less likely to develop more complex play plots, but may be more at risk for engaging in overt acts of aggression.

Watching Violent Television Shows

Themes of violence have been a part of theater from its the earliest days. The ancient Greek tragedies, which were viewed in their open-air semi circular theatres by almost the entire citizenry of the various city-states during festivals for the god Dionysios, involved many incidents of violence and often culminated in the deaths of the leading characters. Agamemnon, after returning as the victorious conqueror of Troy, is murdered in his bath at home by his wife Clytemnestra and her lover. In another play Clytemnestra is killed in revenge by her son Orestes, egged on by his sister Electra. In Euripides' play, *Medea*, the protagonist, a woman now scorned by her husband Jason, kills her children and painfully poisons her rival. In the most famous surviving Greek tragedy, *Oedipus*, on learning that he had unknowingly murdered his father and married his own mother, the hero scratches out his own eyes after she has hanged herself. The Greeks did not, however, portray violent acts on stage before the audience; the awful scenes were *narrated* to the chorus or to other characters by witnesses. The great Greek philosopher-scientist Aristotle used the *Oedipus* drama to propose his theory of catharsis, the presumed emotional identification and purging of feelings by the audiences, who often wept openly during the performances.

The power of these ancient dramas persists. We heard a radio presentation in the 1930s of Euripides' antiwar play, *The Trojan Women*. It was so moving that the announcer, a well-known critic, couldn't control his weeping as he came on the air after the show. We also witnessed a live performance in 1946 of *Oedipus* with the great actors Lawrence Olivier and Ralph Richardson. The American audience was gasping and visibly shaken—a clear confirmation of old Aristotle's proposals.

A thousand years after those ancient tragedies, William Shakespeare and his English contemporaries portrayed many violent scenes *on stage*—Romeo and Juliet's suicides, numerous scenes of dueling, Julius Caesar's assassination, and the drowning of an imprisoned English lord in a cask of wine by the hirelings of the villainous King Richard III among them.

But even the cascading violence that concludes Shakespeare's *Hamlet* cannot match the car chases, the gun battles, and great explosions in movies and on television where millions of children are watching three or four hours daily. Although movies were full of action scenes and depictions of violence through the first third of the previous century, family concerns in America, sufficiently strong to influence the industry to institute a self-censorship system, were focused much more on sexuality than on aggression. It was only by the 1950s and 1960s, with the increasing penetration of television into the American home, that parents began to express concerns that exposing young children to aggression might provoke fear or attempted imitation.

It is a curious quirk of history that while the pretelevision generations witnessed many cowboy and Indian, world war, monster, or swashbuckling pirate movies, there was little research evidence to implicate such viewing in overt aggressive behavior by children or adults. Social science research and particularly psychology had not matured in theory or methodology sufficiently to evaluate comic book, radio, or theatre movie violence, even if some mental health specialists and parents decried their impact. By the early 1960s, however, *coincident with the vast proliferation of television,* social learning theory emerged in psychology, sociology, and communication studies. Experimental, large-scale survey and content analysis methodologies were being perfected and applied to evaluate this new medium. Social learning theory as elaborated by Albert Bandura at Stanford University emphasized how much of a child's development is based on imitation or modeling of adult behavior and on observation of the responses of others. Aggressive reactions in cartoons or action adventure programs that are regularly approved by adults or are shown to lead to rewarding results may also be modeled. The cowboy shoots down the "bad guy," the police officer beats up or shoots the crime perpetrator, the superhero hurls a crowd of evil ones in all directions. The real life *consequences* of violent behavior by police or even other heroic figures are rarely seen, and the extremely unpleasant, often tragic social and personal results of acts of aggression are rarely shown. Bandura and others tested this theory in literally scores of experimental studies. They showed that children will imitate aggressive behavior they have seen on a TV screen not only in the laboratory but also in daily life settings (Bandura 1977; Bushman and Huesmann 2001; Huesmann 1998).

Why should television watching be so troublesome? In Chapter 3, we reviewed the various children's shows that may enhance imagination or stimulate cognitive and social skills. The problem is that the amount of violence presented on daily television is simply overwhelming. George Gerbner, the sociologist and former Dean of the Annenberg School of Communication of the University of Pennsylvania, directed a series of studies that demonstrated dozens of acts of violence in fictional television day after day with no abatement over many years (Gerbner et al. 1994; Kaiser Family Foundation 1998). The action, movement, and simplistic comprehensibility of fighting scenes can hold children's interest even when the more subtle features of character, motivation, or ethical issues are well beyond their grasp.

This combination of repeated exposure to high levels of media violence in one's home, the scientific support for social learning theory, and other accumulating research evidence have gradually reached the American public. Nearly 90 percent of parents surveyed very recently believe that the popular media, especially television, video games and popular music, encourage materialism, coarse language, early sexual encounters, and aggressive behavior in children (Kaiser Family Foundation 2003; Penn and American Viewpoint 2003). The result has been a widrespread hue and cry for more evidence, for better ratings on films, network, and cable TV, and for other control systems like the V-chip that parents can use to block violent or sexually provocative material from child viewers.

Some media critics, entertainers, industry representatives, and civil rights advocates have argued that much of the uproar about TV violence, sexuality, or vulgar language is largely an effort to get parents off the hook when their own talk, dysfunctional actions, and aggressive behavior at home may be the major contributors to what they decry in their children. We certainly agree that in our gun-oriented society and with our national historical and current involvement in civil and international warfare, it would be absurd to lay most of the blame for aggression in children and youth on TV or on video or computer games. With respect to television, however, the research evidence almost universally points in one direction: heavy viewing by the young is consistently associated with greater tendencies to get into fights, to use weapons if available, and to engage in obstreperous behavior over and above familial influences. Young Philip's trouble is just one illustration of a tendency that is statistically strong enough to constitute a national public health problem.

How strong is the evidence? There are by now numerous reviews of the scientific literature. We will briefly note the accumulated indications from various kinds of research (Bushman and Huesmann 2001; Paik and Comstock 1994). International research has generally supported the findings of American studies (Groebel 2001; von Feilitzen and Carlsson 2002).

What of the argument about the cathartic effect of vicarious experiences evoked by some psychoanalysts and widely quoted by actors, producers, and entertainment industry participants? Will watching *World Wide Wrestling*, so popular with children and even more with adults, or seeing violent movies on TV with Bruce Lee, Arnold Schwarzenegger, Bruce Willis, or Sylvester Stallone purge onlookers of at least some of their presumed instinctual attacking tendencies? There are very few questions to which social science research gives so overwhelming a response: experimental laboratory studies of the type initiated by Bandura, now numbering in the scores, all point to the negative—rather than having a cathartic effect, watching violence only increases the chances that a child or adult will subsequently be more prone to acts of aggression (Bandura 1977; Bushman and Huesmann 2003). This is not so surprising if we remember how our imagination operates by playing and replaying scenes so that these gradually are formed into schemas and scripts, those organized belief systems about how one deals with frustrations, denigrations, or insults (J. L. Singer and Salovey 1995). We find a narrowing of the range of our cognitive repertoire, indeed almost a poverty of imagery in the area of conflict resolution other than a constant mental regurgitation of scenes of physical attack or violent revenge.

It has also been argued that the TV connection may be an artifact of the controlled laboratory studies. Correlations between watching TV violence and behaving aggressively may merely reflect the fact that youngsters who are already aggressive simply like to watch such shows or a great deal of television in general. We ourselves had raised questions of this kind when we began our collaborative research on children's play (J. L. Singer 1971). Our first studies were focused primarily on how television viewing was associated with make-believe play and how it might stimulate children's imagination. We were surprised and forced by our data to take much more seriously the issue of TV and aggression in preschoolers. Indeed, our research was the first to show the effect with such young children (J. L. Singer and Singer 1981, 1986; J. L. Singer et al. 1984). Our work on the National Institute of Mental Health's 1982 Report on Television and Children (Pearl et al. 1982) further strengthened our awareness of the seriousness of this issue.

One particular general concern about the research evidence we mentioned above was with the seeming "artificial" nature of the Bandura-style laboratory experiments. Initially, the evidence for aggression in these experiments was that a child modeled an adult's hitting by then attacking a Bobo doll, a large plastic, base-weighted, balloonlike clown figure. In our studies, and others as well, we had a trained staff, who were unfamiliar with the study hypotheses or the children's home TV viewing patterns, watching children in daycare settings during daily free play periods on eight occasions over a year's time. The aggression we recorded was real—hitting, pushing, knocking over others' toys. The parents kept biweekly home records on a number of occasions over a year's time, as well. We took into account children's initial levels of aggression and family physical punishment and found, as had the laboratory studies, strong evidence for a specific causal direction from TV viewing, especially of action-adventure or violent cartoon programming, to subsequent hitting or pushing behavior by children.

Similar data have accumulated widely and, as we mentioned, have been extensively reviewed and analyzed by now. We do want to call special attention to longitudinal research studies, much more extended in time than our own, which clearly point to the serious fashion in which viewing television violence may have restricted the imaginative range of growing individuals, thereby leading them to more aggressive forms of dealing with conflicts and frustrations. Perhaps the most telling studies have been those initiated by Leonard Eron and Rowell Huesmann. The first followed children ages six to ten in rural New York State for ten and twenty years. It demonstrated that even when initial levels of aggression were considered, as well as other influences, the heavy viewers of violent TV, especially the boys, showed greater likelihood of serious acts of aggression, spousal abuse, or other criminal behaviors as men (Huesmann 1986, 1995; Lefkowitz et al. 1977). A second study was carried out in five different countries. It yielded comparable evidence, with girls as well as boys showing the effects of early violence viewing on later aggression (Huesmann and Eron 1986).

The most recent study initiated by Huesmann with a sample of Chicago area first graders in 1977 led to a fifteen-year follow-up. This study was remarkable not only because it was the most thorough in covering parent behaviors and family atmosphere generally, but also because the measurement procedures, statistical analyses, and outcome evidence are the most sophisticated that have ever been accomplished. For example, data were available on the children's imaginative and cognitive patterns, for example, to what extent did they believe TV violence reflected reality, or to what degree did they identify with aggressive characters on TV. The outcome measures were by no means trivial. They included criminal conviction records; hitting or throwing things at the spouse; punching, shoving or choking other people; and moving traffic violations. Results of identification with heroes' violence were stronger for boys. The results make clear that TV violence viewing, identification with aggressive TV characters, and belief in the realistic nature of TV violence all predicted later aggression in men and women, even when the variables of family life initial levels of aggression were controlled. As the authors point out, even though aggressive children did watch more violent TV, that could not explain away the results. Instead, the data suggested that these angry, aggression-prone children were watching violent TV shows because such content made them feel "normal" and seemed to justify their hitting or fighting with others. As they write, "Their subsequent viewing of violence then increases their aggressive scripts, schemas and beliefs through observational learning and makes subsequent aggression more likely" (Huesmann et al. 2003, p. 217).

Another very recent study involved over 700 adolescents followed over seventeen years. Again the data made clear that time spent watching TV in adolescence and young adulthood was predictive of later aggressive actions toward others. This result held up even when childhood neglect, family income, neighbor violent atmosphere, and psychiatric disorders were controlled statistically (Johnson et al. 2002).

It should be clear from this very brief review of a most extensive body of scientific literature that focusing a child's or adolescent's imagination on relying upon physical attack to resolve conflict can be a consequence of merely observing such kinds of behavior on television. This imaginative readiness for using a method for handling frustration that is so limited and so dangerous to self and to society can be even more readily translated into direct action by continual physical practice.

The Emergence of Video and Computer Games

Games involving visual-motor skills have a long history in carnival midways or within the arcades so popular with men and boys from the 1920s to 1970s. These arcades were usually found in resort areas like Atlantic City or Coney Island, but also appeared in many local neighborhood sweet shops, soda fountains, or diners. The most popular of these games were the pinball machines, which combined elements of chance with the dexterity of the person mechanically releasing the metal balls to move through various obstacles amid the colored lights and bells to resting places. Although much of the game depended on chance, players tried gently easing the locked-down machine with subtle arm and leg movements so that one could avoid "hazards" or low-score stopping places. Pushing the machine too forcefully could evoke a raucous horn sound and the mechanical discontinuation of the game with the ominous sign "TILT" flashing on the display board. Pinball machines, colorfully lit and geometrically arranged with hazards and escape chutes, were largely abstract and essentially nonviolent. They were competitive in the sense that high scores obtained over many games could yield free games and accumulated high scores could become features of pride for groups of boys or men, who sometimes were rewarded by cash or other gifts from shop owners.

Other arcade games actually involved mimicry of sporting events such as baseball, soccer, or boxing. At carnival midways one could also find games that were more clearly simulations of shooting or target throwing, including the popular one of hitting a bull's eye squarely and with the effect of dropping a clown-attired boy or local official into a pool of water.

With the advances in electronics associated with the widespread availability of television consoles in almost every American home, toy manufacturers perceived the opportunity to produce similar games that could be widely disseminated at reasonable prices to the broadest segments of society. Japanese industry, which had a long history of developing ingenious miniature mechanical toys or artistic displays, took the lead with Atari's 1972 introduction of *PONG*. Modeled initially on pinball machines and geared for arcades, this electronic game used abstract geometric forms to simulate a Ping Pong game. Other skill games followed and by the later 1970s home consoles were produced by Atari, Bally, and RCA. Whereas video arcades had emerged as a major setting for boys through the 1980s, home play increased dramatically. Games began to feature story elements, but the stories took on an increasingly aggressive, warlike quality. Games were titled *Space Invaders*, *Warrior*, or *Battlezone*, with increasingly representational artwork. *Pac-Man* and *Donkey Kong*, with its super-hero Mario, spread widely around all countries where the display technology was available.

Over perhaps two dozen years into the beginning of this century, the seven-billion-dollar game industry has flourished with remarkable advances in the representational realism of the settings and characters. Although video games may not be as intricately plotted as the violence available on television or movies, they have shown somewhat more complexity. Their "bottom line," however, is still the emphasis on shooting or other forms of destructive violence by the game player. Sports games, teaching games, or more elaborate social games are especially featured on the computer and the internet, but arcade games or home console, "play station" games that have especially been attractive to boys are most likely to involve shooting or other relative realistically structured forms of killing. By 1993 games available for home use included *Mortal Kombat* produced by Genesis and *Super Nintendo*, which included actions as violent as ripping body parts from a videoscreen victim through effective manipulation of the "easy to use" levers. Indeed home players (who often include "tweens" despite industry recommendations for teenagers and above) have complained that the programs of games for home consoles are not as violent as the arcade forms. *Street Fighter II Turbo*, a brawling game of vast popularity in which players can simulate brutally beating the screen characters or can structure the game so they can observe other screen characters in vicious battles, combined both the manipulative and observational features of video games or violent TV. Special pods or codes allowed for increases in violence levels. Professor Marsha Kinder, a California professor who served on review panels for video game ratings, said of such games that they are even more dangerous than watching TV or movies. These games send a message that only through violence can one gain a sense of personal power (Elmer-DeWitt 1993).

Provenzano (1991) in his *Video Kids* conducted a detailed quantitative and qualitative analysis of video games. While recognizing distinctions between sports games, games of adventure and exploration, and games primarily focused on increasing rapidity of a violent targeting response, he points out that the players' individuality and contextual awareness are ultimately limited by the producers' programs. He writes:

> The important point is that humanity and the true self are defined by their connection to culture. We cannot stand outside of the context and connections of culture and be fully recognized as human beings. Videogames in their emphasis on violence and the self as an autogenous being, disregard this truth. (pp. 131–132)

From the standpoint of imagination and its breadth and scope, the violent video games, perhaps like the play with toy guns studied by Watson and Peng (1991), have a limiting function. The link is chiefly to direct aggression rather than to a broader problem-solving or exploratory context. The U.S. Army recognized this twenty years ago in drawing on designers from the Atari Videogame Company to help them develop a realistic gunnery simulation game (Dominick 1984). For practical purposes in the military, one's life depends on extremely rapid response with no time for Hamlet-like consideration of consequences.

In the early spring of 2003, American and British troops battled in Baghdad and Basra, Iraq. At the same time, as described in an article in *The New York Times* (Napoli 2003), a group of boys in the neighborhood village of Orange, Connecticut, were playing one of the newest video games, *SoCom: US Navy Seals*, described as "king of the military shooter genre." The game played on a Sony PlayStation 2 console depicts settings remarkably similar to the real desert scenes of soldiers and tanks presented continuously on television news channels. The fifteen-year-old players of the video game, while listening to sound effects of explosions, press buttons to shoot or evade ostensible enemies.

The real war, as made available to us on television news broadcasts, was in some ways more sanitized than the video game. On the TV news, we see no blood, the agonies of the wounded or dying, and we hear no screams from victims whether they are our troops or our enemies. Some of these consequences of violence are more strongly suggested in the portrayals of the game. The boy players in *The New York Times* article are just a few years younger than many of the soldiers we see on the TV news. These boys shared with each other an awareness of how distant they felt themselves to be in the game from the reality of actual warfare. Alas, many youngsters may not be as astute and may become desensitized to the realities of warfare (Napoli 2003).

We have so far emphasized the violence of video games, but it is also clear that video game play, if focused on driving skill, on sports, and on acquiring academic skills, can have socially valuable uses. A Korean textbook company has collaborated with a software firm to produce games that supplement texts teaching mathematics and science. Yet as the electronic entertainment journalist, Justin Hall, has pointed out, the U.S. Army has been developing games to teach teenage players war tactics. The players engage in realistic military missions that involve fighting with guns and hand grenades. As Hall comments, "Where are the games created to teach Americans civilian skills?" He proposes that just as seven million dollars was budgeted for the "American Army" game, could we not "develop freely available games that teach about math and science, history and citizenship?" (2003, p. A–11).

Theory and Research on Video Game Violence

In the past decade a sufficient body of research has emerged to permit us to move beyond value judgments or anecdotal accounts in appraising the impact of playing violent video games. Sandra Calvert and Siu-Lan Tan at Georgetown University in Washington, D.C., studied the effects on young adults of either playing violent video games or of observing others playing the games. They reported that those participants who had played a vivid violent game showed higher heart rates, more nausea or dizziness, and more angry thoughts (Calvert and Tan 1994). Very recent evidence of an even more subtle physiological effect has emerged as reported by researchers at the University of Indiana Medical School. Teenagers who had a history of exposure to video game play showed lowered activity in the brain's frontal lobes, as measured by a Functional MRI (fMRI, magnetic resonance imaging), following exposure to violent video scenes. The frontal areas of the brain are generally associated with emotional control and effective planful or attentional focusing. The investigators have suggested that these results may reflect desensitization to the consequences of violence (Kronenberger et al. 2004; Wang et al. 2002). Although such physiological results are at present tentative, they are not out-of-keeping with the many more findings from studies behavioral outcomes of violent video game playing.

The studies just mentioned were carried out with young adults or adolescents, who are generally the most consistent video game players. However, there has long been evidence that children as young as four can be influenced by a violent game such as *Space Invaders* to increase their general subsequent arousal levels and aggressive behavior (Silvern and Williamson 1987). Another more recent research with a middle childhood group indicated that, after playing violent video games, these children were more likely than control children to attribute hostile intentions to the actions of others, a likely precursor to potential aggressive behavior (Kirsch 1997).

More recently, Craig Anderson and Brad Bushman at Iowa State University have brought together nearly fifty studies, their own and those of many others, into a meta-analysis or integrated quantitative study totaling nearly four thousand participants. These studies compared players of violent video game with control groups who did not play such games or who played nonviolent video games. They found clear evidence that those children or young adults who played violent video games were more likely to show more angry thoughts, more beliefs of a hostile nature, and more physiological arousal. They also showed more overt aggressive behaviors and, interestingly, less willingness to behave cooperatively or to help others, that is, fewer prosocial responses (Anderson and Bushman 2001; Bushman and Anderson 2001).

In further analyses, Anderson (2002) has shown that the statistical results are as strong when they separate children from adults, indicating a more general impact across age groups. When the specific features of the control games are scored for relative amounts of violent content, the findings are even clearer. The practice of shooting or in other ways harming others carries over from seemingly innocuous gaming into overt actions that can be less helpful to others or actually harmful. From a statistical standpoint these findings are as powerful as those reported for the many studies of heavy viewing of violent television by children. They are of sufficient magnitude to be considered public health problems of almost the same order as the research on smoking and lung cancer, lead exposure and intellectual deficits, or condom use in reducing HIV transmission (Bushman and Huesmann 2001).

The research findings for violent video game playing certainly seem ominous. One would be loath to argue that all of the millions of children (mostly boys) exposed regularly to violent video games will emerge as aggressive, hostile youngsters. If only ten percent are likely to show such effects, we need to be concerned considering the great number of children playing these games. Those children who play for several hours a day are largely practicing rapid response shooting skills or lever manipulation designed very specifically at maiming or dispatching "enemies." Although there are nominal adventure story lines about combating hostile space aliens or terrorists and rescuing curvaceous females, extended comprehension or imaginative elaboration of the plot by players is minimized or not required in most games. Instead emphasis is on rapidity of response and rapid choice of appropriate violent weapons. In currently popular games like *KABOOM* or *Grand Theft Auto*, the player's hostile and often antisocial actions are generally encouraged, but what is mainly practiced is shooting. Remember the macaque monkeys in Chapter 1, who could learn to capture objects on the video game screen with only a mental response? How much more concerned ought we to be about the possibility that boys who have *overlearned* hurtful reactions to seeming threats might later impulsively erupt from thought into overt reactions?

What seems to be happening with excessive violent video game play is the narrowing of one's imaginative range. Such restrictions on the range of imagination are in contrast with other games where ingenuity in detecting escape routes, identifying and discriminating friendly or hostile magical figures, or choosing appropriate wizardry implements may make intellectual or even creative demands on the player. Games like *Myst* or some sword and sorcery or science fiction adventure games derived from the precomputer days of *Dungeons and Dragons* may indeed stretch and nourish one's imagery and ability to use fantasy for more constructive and even aesthetically developed purposes. Research has not yet been carried out to show these positive effects, although we believe they are likely outcomes. Instead we find the narrow focus on attack reactions, and it is these that have become the subject of research theory.

Models of Aggression

Anderson and Bushman (2001) have proposed a General Aggression Model to help integrate the research findings of the various studies of video game responses (see Figures 4.1 and 4.2).

In Figure 4.1 we can envision the circumstances in which an individual faces some obstacle or opportunity. The general circumstances may be menacing or promising and the individual person may bring with him or her expectations or over-learned action-routines, those organized mental structures we call schemas or scripts (J. L. Singer and Salovey 1991). The combination of environmental or situational pressures and the particular schemas of the person may lead to an emotional state characterized by a mix of arousal and information processing. That mix may generate a relatively rapid appraisal of one's circumstances and decisions that result either in nearly immediate impulsive action or, with some delay, in thoughtful action. These responses may then generate a social encounter that might involve attacking or insulting another person with the inevitable complicated consequences or, with more reflection, in discussion, negotiation, and problem-solving.

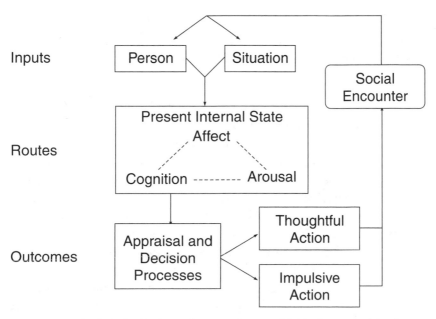

Figure 4.1. Single Episode General Aggression Model (Anderson and Bushman 2002).

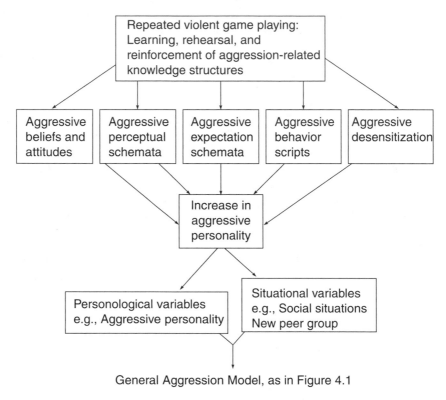

Figure 4.2. Multiple-Episode General Aggression Model: Long-Term Effects of Video Game Violence (Adapted from Anderson 2003).

In Figure 4.2 we spelled out what Anderson and Bushman believe is implied by their actual findings for children or adults who are frequent players of violent games. The specific operations on which players are focused in their continued simulated shooting or maiming activities have led to a repetitive over-learning of schemas or scripts involving aggression. These mental structures are reflected in sets of beliefs or attitudes in which aggression from others is central. Violent gamers' perceptual worlds seem menacing, their repertoire of possible responses is limited to fight or flight, and, to some extent, they exhibit an insensitivity to consequences of aggressive actions. The combinations of these schemas and scripts may then lead to what Anderson and Bushman call an "aggressive personality," an individual of limited imagination who perceives most situations in terms of danger from the violence of others and the values of one's own aggressive actions. Such a person may then seek out others who share this view and become part of a gang or even a member of a criminal subgroup.

Habitual playing of violent video games may therefore serve to drastically inhibit the scope of a child's imagination and increase the risk of developing an aggressive lifestyle. Remember the example of Philip, with whom we began this chapter. We cannot forecast the same negative outcome for children who may, in the course of playing with action figures, blocks or pretend forts, castles or pirate ships, create plots of adventure or occasional violence. Such children seem to develop a broader repertoire of pretend games, from exploration and adventure situations to role-playing doctors, nurses, sports figures, celebrities, musicians. As we shall see below, there are many more opportunities now with computer and Internet games to build a broader repertoire of possible interactions well beyond the limited scope of the violent video game player.

Another way of providing evidence for the unfortunate consequences of violent video game play is to consider what happens when adults intervene and limit children's television viewing or violent game playing. This type of research also points toward a constructive program for parents or schools who wish to counteract the aggressive behavioral consequences of violent themes in games and fiction. Intriguing research by a team led by Thomas Robinson of Stanford University Departments of Pediatrics and Medicine represents one of the first such efforts to counteract the effects of video game play (Robinson et al. 2001). These investigators obtained the cooperation of parents and school administrators in San Jose, California. Identifying two schools that were closely matched in socioeconomic status, cultural backgrounds, and academic quality, they used one school to introduce a systematic intervention designed to modify third and fourth graders' viewing of violent TV and playing aggressive videogames, while the other school remained as an untreated control group.

The intervention was designed to modify children's viewing and game playing through a series of classroom lessons, taught by specially trained teachers, that were designed to help children become critical viewers of television or of gaming and to understand the nature of these media's effects or influences. As indicated in Chapter 3, we had pioneered such a curriculum in the late 1970s and had shown that it had short-term effects at a cognitive level with children from kindergarten through middle school (D. G. Singer et al. 1986; D. G. Singer et al. 1981; J. L. Singer et al. 1984, 1985). Robinson's team carried this approach further by extending the length of time of teaching, and then presenting the children with a variety of encouragements for "intelligent" or selective viewing, time budgeting, and even "enduring" a "TV turnoff" period of ten days.

Even though the intervention did not focus on children's conscious control of their aggressive behavior, the subsequent comparison of the experimental and control school children demonstrated clear effects in the aggressive behavior of the children as reported by their fellow students. The control children continued to watch TV and play video games at a high rate, while the video game play of the experimental group showed a significant decline. The level of aggression directed at other children in the control group continued to rise at almost double the rate of the very small increase for the experimental youngsters. The effects of the intervention were in the same direction for all the other measures, although statistically not as strong. They were also comparable for girls and boys, although in general girls show less peer-related aggression.

This most recent study adds further evidence linking overt aggressive behavior to a combination of watching violent television and playing violent video games. It also points toward a hopeful opportunity for intervention through schools and parents controlling viewing or game use, as well as through teachers and parents mediating video game activity by using the critical viewing skills training methods. These lessons about electronic media are becoming increasingly available for children (Brown 2001; Slaby 2002). They are also taught for secondary school students in a curriculum we designed, which is distributed by the National Academy of Television Arts & Sciences (D. G. Singer and Singer 1998). While parents are also alerted to the risks of violent video game play by industry self-regulation labels of age appropriateness, there are also efforts by advocacy groups and the federal government to prohibit sales of such labeled games to the younger children.

Some Speculations on the Attraction of Violent Video Games

An important implication of the meta-analysis of all the violent video game play is that such play can be shown to stimulate specifically aggressive thought and angry emotionality, physiological arousal as well as actual uncooperative or overtly aggressive behavior. Although boys are the most frequent players, Anderson and Bushman's analyses (2001) make clear that the same results are found for girls, and are evident across the full age spectrum. These findings should thoroughly discount any lingering support for a *catharsis* or a "drainage" of the "aggressive drive" by means of vicarious violent play. They call into question the speculations of Bruno Bettelheim (1966) on the potential psychological value of exposing young children to the frightening and violent fairy tales of the Grimm Brothers. Stories like the "Juniper Tree" are replete with scenes that can terrify very young children, with no evidence that listening to or reading these stories will reduce aggressive behavior.

The hostile cognitions and aggressive mental scripts that are practiced and over-learned by playing video games like *Grand Theft Auto* are also linked to misogynistic attitudes because so often women are represented as victims or evil seducers in these games (Dill and Dill, forthcoming; Dill et al. 2001). For example as a *New York Times* article indicated referring to *Grand Theft Auto*, "all boundaries of civilized behavior have vanished. You get to shoot whomever you want, including cops. You get to beat women to death with baseball bats. You get to have sex with prostitutes and kill them. (And you get your money back.)" (Herbert 2002). As Dill and Dill (forthcoming) have found, boys' playing of violent video games are more likely to show acceptance of demeaning conceptions of women and insensitivity to the harm produced by rape.

Research data indicate that girls who play violent video games or who watch violent TV shows are influenced much the same way as boys, but the facts also indicate that such attraction to violent content in TV watching or game playing is far more frequent in males than in females of any age. One might speculate that boys are inherently attracted more toward aggression because of their constitutional, glandular, and perhaps even brain structure as the hunters and warriors for thousands of years of human evolution. It is also possible that long-standing cultural traditions play a role in the early socializing of boys. They are often encouraged by parents who tolerate rambunctiousness and rough-and-tumble behavior in males, but discourage such behavior in girls. Boys grow up in societies whose legends, folk tales, and histories are replete with tales of males as great warriors and hunters. These include Gilgamesh in ancient Mesopotamia, Samson, Hercules, Achilles, the Samurai in Japan, and the superheroes of American comics. We must also consider those in the armed forces who were visible on television action news film, our infantry and tank fighters in Iraq.

Yet with all these images, it is apparent that our modern industrialized and technological societies are less and less in need of warriors and hunters. One of the most successful males since the last half of the twentieth century is the seemingly unathletic Bill Gates with his high-pitched voice and nerdy looks. The skills needed even for warfare are less and less sheer physical stamina and more and more intelligence and training in mechanical and quasiengineering activities. A woman's finger can press the button or console key that unleashes a powerful missile just as well as a man's, as our new military forces have demonstrated. Even with athletics, which William James called the "moral equivalent of war," we are learning that girls can play quite fiercely and skillfully at basketball, soccer, tennis, or baseball, even wrestling and boxing.

Girls early on are socialized into reading and school readiness skills. Boys, perhaps for both social and constitutional reasons, lag behind them. There is no great abatement in fostering useful social and nurturance activities for girls. Boys, however, are more encouraged to physical play and to extensive enthusiasm and practice of motor skills. Despite hours and hours of practice, only a minuscule fraction of boys will eventually make a living through professional sports. The self-control, social obedience, and cooperative skills encouraged for girls in school are already leading them into developing all the necessary abilities for effectiveness in our increasingly technological societies. Boys, on the other hand, spend longer years playing at large muscle sports. Violent video games, which they play even more than outdoor sports link them to the historic tradition of males as warriors and hunters. This "macho" play offers few skills that will guide them toward the technologies or fine-detail abilities that offer salaries and prestige in modern adult life, as Hall (2003) explains.

The narrow scope of imagination fostered by violent video games may put habitual players at risk not only for developing aggressive personalities or showing antisocial behavior, but also for limiting their imaginative repertoire and scholastic interests. Boys may show less willingness to put in the time needed to master the sequential and focused cognitive and small-motor activities they will need in society, where women will increasingly be their effective rivals. Our world societies are still, of course, largely dominated by men who have grown up with the hunter-warrior self-images. If we can avoid the massive self-destruction of our planet that such outmoded images foster, we may see that men who persist in the warrior image or who are fascinated by violent play become increasingly irrelevant in societies that depend on science, information technologies, health care, and nurturance skills at which women are likely to surpass them. Dare we say it? Perhaps if men are to survive in human evolution as more than a limited number of sheltered studs, as we wrote many years ago (D. G. Singer and J. L. Singer 1977), we will have to teach them from early childhood how to love and nurture, how to play at a broad range of nonviolent games, and how to develop their imaginative repertoires well beyond the warrior themes of the video games that so appeal to them now.

— 5 —

Adrift in Cyberspace:
Children and Computer Play

Since she was just four years old, Phyllis, now ten, has been manipulating her mouse and playing with the family computer. Well before she could read, this intense young girl used the mouse to point at the story icons on the computer screen to listen to the sound effects, to watch the birds or animals pop up, and to "follow the road to Grandma's house." Phyllis is a "late lamb," the last-born of a family of four girls and a boy; her siblings are all more than six years older than she is. Although by now she can read fairly well, she does so only at school and to complete her homework. Much of her time is spent at the computer playing games or cruising the Internet. She has avoided the sickly pallor of a "geek" only because her family's outdoor interests and her exposure to computer games about botany and flowers have led her to volunteer her time at a local garden supply nursery where she devotes several afternoons to plant care. After school, she uses instant messaging to chat in her limited typed vocabulary about the school day with a few friends. Then she shifts her screen to work on her Sim City house, her Sim family, and her Sim alter-ego, a willowy teenager looking somewhat like Britney Spears. She is choosing a wardrobe for "Tiffany" before a foray to a Sim teen hangout. With the newer opportunities for connecting the virtual reality world of Sim identity with the World Wide Web, Phyllis can "enter" a virtual hotel lobby, notice who's around, and engage in conversation with interesting-looking strangers, some of whom are actually English-language speakers from Thailand, Denmark, or Chile. A new form of chat room has emerged for a youngster, a setting in which one's companions have perfect bodies and are attired in wish-fulfillment clothing and, for all one knows, may be other children from far-flung lands or lonely adults, occasionally even sexual predators. In the course of our research, Phyllis allowed us to observe what happens during the fairly extended periods of her involvement in this virtual social world. The conversations and interactions between the characters on the screen, limited as they were by the software, were rather banal. Some of the "balloons" (comic-strip-like conversation spaces) associated with the characters were blanked out, apparently reflecting mutually agreed upon private talk between individuals who had hooked up with each other earlier.

When we asked Phyllis whether she had any special friends, she first mentioned two girls from school and a neighbor boy her age. Then she went on to mention her "really special friends," characters from the Internet and from variations of the Sims games. "You know," she commented, "They don't have colds or make smells or dribble their food. And they're more grown up and look cool." On further reflection she added, "But you know, my computer friends aren't really real. They can't come to my birthday party or invite me to a sleepover. We can't go hunting in the bushes for berries like I do with my real friends."

Let us leave Phyllis with her insight about reality for the present, and examine in more detail how computer games and cyberspace playthings may be influencing cognitive and socially adaptive learning and the important functions of imagination we reviewed in the beginning of this book. Children may indeed be acquiring new psychological tastes, habits, and skills from their play with computers, but are these necessarily of longer-term value to their development? We have reasonable evidence that video game play involving shooting "bad guys" enhances boys' eye-hand coordination and other perceptual motor skills, but at the cost of increasing propensities for engaging in unwarranted aggressive or uncooperative behavior (Anderson and Bushman 2001; Calvert et al. 2002; Subrahmanyam et al. 2001). Familiarization with the use of the mouse or other features of the computer may well ease the child's way toward the uses of a computer that are nearly essential for later school and vocational careers or for selective shopping. But serious concerns can be raised about the ultimate socially adaptive or educational value of early exposure and dependence on such technology (Healy 1998; Oppenheimer 2003). For our purposes we propose to examine in this chapter how computer-related electronic console activities may contribute to or possibly impede the child's development of the great imaginative dimension of our human functions. What options do parents and other caregivers have in a world where rapidly increasing numbers of households now make use of computers?

Reviewing the Developmental Determinants of Imagination

It seems likely that from infancy human beings are "wired up" with a brain capacity for selecting, attending to, mentally reimaging, and then encoding and storing new information, even before language has developed. Such stored information can later be retrieved in response to new stimulation so that it influences how one will selectively attend to novel material and perhaps form the memory structures we call schemas. At its most basic level, memory is evident in the conditioning response first explored by Ivan Pavlov. It is observable even in the learning responses of relatively "simple" organisms like the sea urchins or Aplysia studied by Nobel Prize physiologist Erich Kandel. Conditioning responses are a part of our human memory apparatus, operating often without any conscious or developed linguistic or cognitive components, following a separate brain pathway from the ones reflecting more complex cognitions, as research by LeDoux (1996) has indicated. We experience "nameless" conditioning when we have food aversions, which are possibly traceable to our early prelanguage exposure to unexpected tastes. Moments of dread or sensations of the uncanny have been attributed by clinicians like Harry Stack Sullivan or Sigmund Freud to early psychological shocks experienced in our preverbal years.

A more emotionally positive precognitive experience attributable to early conditioning has been described by Freud as an "oceanic sense" of awe and wonder, perhaps a vestige of an infant's or baby's first awareness of the nonthreatening beauty of nature or of "benign" but "big" faces and voices of parents. Very likely such seemingly indescribable reactions for which we have no verbal labels are early conditioned contributors to the kinds of religious experiences described by William James (1902). At a more mundane level, they are also early conditioned contributors to what may emerge as the "chill up the spine" one feels just by being told about some great feat of personal heroism or athletic prowess or one's recollection of the first hearing of a favorite piece of music.

The more complex, ongoing conscious thought we discussed at the outset of this volume follows more diverse and differentiated brain pathways (Baars 1998; Dietrich 2003). Such thought involves our imagery capacity and our emerging language and labeling skills. The combination of a child's first saying "No!," of taking its first separate steps, of becoming aware of dreams and specific event memories, and making the effort, through play, to create a miniature manageable world with words like "make believe" or "let's pretend" are key features of a *sense of personal autonomy and self-conscious thought*. Visual and motor exploration of one's environment—touching, tasting, and handling—are crucial stages for the child in first moving from vague sensation to perception, and then, with a phase of reflection on such perceptions, storing material for later retrieval. All of these are critical processes for the richness and intensity of our memory system upon which imagination, whether in its retrospective, playful, or planful phases, is drawn.

The narrative or experiential mode of thought begins to bloom in the three- to five-year-old period, as described in earlier chapters. It is further nourished not only by direct physical and social experience, but also by the storytelling or reading of parents or other caregivers. As we have suggested, the electronic media of television, film, and video games now may contribute to the child's development of an autonomous ongoing consciousness but with particular constraints. Looking and listening alone without other sensory involvements can be misleading guides to action. The many physical attacks a child witnesses on television or in playing violent video games without the feel or smell or agonies of real violence can lead to desensitization. As Shakespeare noted, "He jests at scars who never felt a wound."

We emphasized in earlier chapters that the hands-on or sensory experiences of a toddler are critical in shaping a sense of reality that then can balance the fantasy world of storytelling or watching television. In *The Hand,* one of the wisest books of recent decades, the neurologist Frank Wilson (1998) has surveyed the vast role that physical touching experiences have upon the brain. He cautions that we can never be sure what lies ahead in our lives and that we cannot count on "reengineering the brain" to preserve us: "neither will sitting our children in front of computers when they are three years old so that they will skip the 'pointless' experiences of childhood during which they find out what a baseball, or a puppet, or a toy car, or a swing can do to their body or vice versa. We have no idea what will happen to the child who watches eye-catching imitations of juggling over the internet if that child never gets around to trying a three-ball toss" (p. 309).

We are proposing along with Wilson and others (Lewin 1935; Luria 1932; Sutton-Smith 1966; Vygotsky 1978) that the seemingly ephemeral human capacity for conscious reflection, imagery, and fantasy depends in an important way upon a child's real-world experience. The pretend play with blocks or dollhouses and construction toys is such experience in its primordial form. We can then ask how the virtual reality world presented by the computer can further extend our imagination or, perhaps, constrict or distort it.

In just the past dozen years, there has been a flurry of commercial effort to provide babies and toddlers with videos and computer games designed to stimulate brain activity. One needs to take a cautious attitude toward video or computer presentations for infants and toddlers. The available research on babies below one year of age offers no evidence that they can make distinctions between lively but random visual activity on the TV screen and an actual program like *Sesame Street.* By their second year, babies and toddlers can imitate some of the activity they see on the screen. Studies show, however, that they generally cannot follow a video screen adult's actions to find a hidden toy, but will be able to do so when a live adult instructs them or if they see the toy being hidden through a window in the real world. Most careful observers of children under age two are convinced that direct tangible experience is crucial for them in these first years (D. Singer and J. Singer 1990).

A sensible paper by Erik Strommen (2003) examines the possibilities and limits of technology in physical toys. He focuses on palpable play-things that have built-in computer chips so that they can make gestures, sounds, even talk, sing, and count. Interactive Barney, based on the TV series, sings any of a dozen songs if the child squeezes his toe. If one squeezes his hand, he recites nursery rhymes. If one covers his eyes, he plays the early form of a pretend game, Peekaboo. Strommen has observed that this hiding game is a favorite. Children extend the situation by using pillows or blankets to cover Barney's eyes or even turn the room lights on and off to hear how Barney reacts. What has happened is that children can take control of this *touchable* toy. They can move beyond the constraints of the embedded computer chip's software and use the toy for their own pretend games. Along with this extension, however, they may benefit from the words, songs, rhymes, and numbers that Barney speaks. We can only wish that this toy were not so expensive or, better yet, that there was a live adult actively playing the same kinds of games with the child.

What are some of the concerns that emerge from recent research and anecdotal accounts of the risks and worrisome possibilities that attend the increasingly younger and more frequent computer play by young children and adolescents? In our next chapter, when we discuss the constructive possibilities for school readiness, effective learning, or imaginative enhancement using our electronic media, we will also point up the usefulness of certain forms of computer play.

Pretend Play and Virtual Reality on the Computer and the Internet

One of the informants for our examination of computer games and the internet was a 16-year-old named Faith. She reported that she "played so much" on the computer that the game content intruded more and more into her daily spontaneous thoughts, her fantasies, and even into her nocturnal dreams. She described that dream-intrusive experience as "scary," almost "like an addiction that takes away from doing productive activities." She freed herself from that phase by finding a set of real-world friends, by an intensive effort at home schooling that has opened the way for her to start college early, and by working in a medical setting that has provided her with opportunities to serve others directly.

Faith seems to reflect a pattern frequently reported by youths who started early in computer play. Probably most of her age cohort have been able to move beyond "addiction," but there is reason to believe that at least some adolescents and young adults may have built a significant portion of their imaginative worlds and even their social lives around computer play and online interactions. A man in his early 50s whom we interviewed lives alone and works daily in a department store. He spends most of his evenings on the computer, building and reshaping a personal website and seeking friends through chat rooms. He has few "real" friends and does not translate the chat room or website "hits" he gets into face-to-face contacts.

The availability of computers to American children in their homes has been well documented by the most recent report from the Kaiser Family Foundation (Rideout et al. 2003). According to these investigators, as many as thirty one percent of children aged three and younger and 70 percent of four- to six-year-olds have used a computer, almost one-third have played video games, and if one includes TV viewing, as many as two-thirds of children under age two will be exposed to a screen medium for about two hours a day. Parents acknowledge that children in heavy electronic media households are less likely to read. They also indicate that among boys, as many as 59 percent have imitated aggression they saw on TV, and among girls, as many as 35 percent have done so. The parents, on the whole, still believe that TV and computers do have an educational value. We should note, however, that there remains a "digital divide" in home computer availability when income levels are considered, according to the data from a report by the United States Department of Education (Ashby 2003).

Computer based game-playing can contribute considerably to children's imaginative ability in the object-manipulation manner already mentioned in games like *Tetris* (Calvert 1999; DeLisi and Wolford 2002; Ko 2002; Subrahmanyam et al. 2001). Henderson, Klemes, and Eschet (2000) showed that when eight-year-olds approached a narratively organized science simulation game as a learning as well as entertainment opportunity, they made strong gains in thinking skills and science language usage. Transfer of such gains to a broader variety of technical or social problems have yet to be shown. Eugene Provenzano (2003), one of the pioneers in studying children's computer use, has called attention to what may be new forms of literary and social valuation emerging as children play simulation games like *Oregon Trail, Populous,* and *Sim City.* As Oppenheimer (2003) has also pointed out, Provenzano worries that the failure to train teachers in the implications of home and classroom computer use may be leading children to create their own cultures and social values. These values may be driven in part by the commercial orientation of the software producers. Issues of power, authority, morals, and ethics are evident in the structure of the games and in the forms that emerge almost spontaneously in the interpretations that children derive from the narratives they produce in their simulated adventures.

Individual case studies as well as larger-scale research demonstrate that traditional sex role differences continue to be evident in the forms of computer game play of young children. Boys still favor adventure games and sports games and, of course, predominate in their usage of violent themes in computer games as well as in the arcade or console video games discussed in an earlier chapter. The sex differences we observed in spontaneous pretend play as well as in TV program viewing thirty years ago persist in computer game content preferences (Calvert 1999; D. G. Singer and Singer 2001; J. L. Singer and Singer 1981; Subrahamyan et al. 2002).

Girls who, for many decades before the emergence of electronic media, played dress-up games with paper cut-out dolls, now chose Barbie—Fashion Designer as one of the few software, interactive "girls' " games that has proved commercially successful. While there is ample evidence that over the twentieth century girls gradually expanded their play patterns to incorporate "boys' toys," adventure themes and even male imaginary playmates, boys have shown little tendency to adopt traditionally female playthings or themes in their fun repertory (D. G. Singer and Singer 1990; J. L. Singer and Singer 1981). At the preschool level boys do adopt plush toys, such as cloth Barneys or Winnie-the-Poohs, as security blankets or transitional objects. More recently, many even chose to play with electronic nurturant toys like Tamotogotchi or Furby. They do not generally adopt female-appearing dolls at the plush stage, but there is increasing indication from sales reports and surveys that simulation games like *Sim City*, which have a strong appeal to girls, are also drawing male players.

From the standpoint of influences upon imagination, perhaps the strongest impact may come from simulation games, with indications that such play will continue to be a major source of stimulation for the future. We know from play research how often children engage in dress-up or in donning superhero capes, firefighter helmets, or pirate costumes to try out different roles. One of us (JLS) has provided an introspective analysis of how several such simulations were carried on in the privacy of conscious daydreams even through middle childhood, with some influences on personality style, but no apparent deleterious mental health effects (J. L. Singer 1966, 1975). In rare instances some individuals may translate one or two such simulations into overt role playing as adults, a pathological condition known as multiple or dissociative personality. Dr. Jekyll and Mr. Hyde, popularized by Robert Louis Stevenson's novel, or more recently, the kindly, intellectual Dr. Banner and his genetically distorted emergent violent alter-ego, The Hulk, from comics and television, represent extreme fantasy forms of such dissociations to which, in real life, a few severely disturbed individuals are prone.

The attraction of simulation computer games lies in their seemingly harmless interactive opportunities. We know, of course, that some simulations, like the heroic "killer" roles of violent-themed video and computer games such as *Mortal Kombat, KABOOM,* and *Grand Theft Auto* do influence the overt behavior of a statistically significant if, fortunately, modest number of game players to be more aggressive or uncooperative in their behavior. There is no clear evidence of so specific an influence of the simulations from more complex games such as *Sim City, Myst,* or other adventure or sword and sorcery games (the genre of popular series like the *Lord of the Rings, Chronicles of Narnia,* and the *Harry Potter* books). Large-scale correlational studies with teenagers indicate on the whole that such gameplaying is in general not associated with high levels of general emotional disturbance, social isolation, or problems of self-esteem (Durkin and Barber 2002). A more careful study of English youth, while somewhat confirming Durkin and Barber's conclusions, reported that those boys who favored violent theme showed the lower self-esteem and greater aggressive behavior found so regularly in other studies (Colwell and Payne 2000). We do not, as yet, have really solid data about the newest forms of simulation games, but we can speculate on how such play may intrude into the fantasies and even the dreams of repeated players, as our informant Faith reported to us.

Perhaps the most frightening implication from a simulation through computer play is that suggested by the customized version of *Doom* found on the computer of Eric Harris, one of the two boys who carried out the terrible attack on students and teachers at Columbine High School, Colorado. Harris had changed the details of the game to resemble more closely the actual setting and behavior he later showed in reality. The personally and socially malignant potential of violent computer games as forms of interactive practice with potential generalization to real life have been well outlined by Subrahamanyan et al. (2001). These dangers include preemption of time spent on actual schoolwork or on hands-on research and exploration activity. More serious are the involvements through chat rooms with strangers who suggest romantic or educational involvement and then, when real-world meetings are arranged, prove to be older adults, some just lonely, some actually sexual predators.

Perhaps the most complex and subtle implications of imaginative computer game play, especially relating to simulations, have been presented by the MIT sociologist and psychoanalyst Sherry Turkle (1995). Based on direct observations of adolescent and adult computer game play and interviews with committed players, Turkle proposed that one's view of nature and society and one's sense of personal identity might well be changed by the complex and ultimately random nature of Internet interactions. She especially emphasizes what she calls multiuser domains or multiuser dungeons (MUDs). The term "dungeons" she believes is historically reflective of the likelihood that fantasy games like *Dungeons and Dragons,* popular with adolescents in the precomputer game era, have influenced the development of MUDs. In computerized forms these games allow for assuming various adventure or romantic identities. Through the potential for worldwide Internet communication, unknown others and their simulations can join in one's own home computer play. Turkle provides an account of Doug, a college junior, who has devised four different characters that he "sends" to four different domains. In one simulated identity he is a seductive woman, in another a Marlboro Man macho type, a third a friendly rabbit named Carrot, and in a domain in which all the "characters" are animals he plays a "sexual tourist" furry creature (p. 13). The young man recounts how he tries to balance these simulated personalities as he confronts messages that come from RL— real-life friends or college administrators. He feels his RL personality is "just one more window . . . and it's not usually my best one."

Doug exemplifies important ways in which the various "windows" and computer identities can be reshaping our ways of constructing our beliefs about ourselves and our identities. As Turkle writes:

> The self is no longer simply playing different roles in different settings at different times something a person experiences when . . . she wakes up as a lover, makes breakfast as a mother, and drives to work as a lawyer. The life practice of windows is that of a decentered self that exists in many worlds and plays many roles at the same time . . . MUDs . . . offer parallel identities, parallel lives . . . this parallelism encourages treating on-screen and off-screen lives with a surprising degree of equality. (1995, p. 14)

In less than a decade since Turkle wrote this, there has been a vast increase in the quantitative expansion of such multiuser games and in their qualitative features. As she reported more recently, there are now more than 300 MUDs involving more than 13 different kinds of software (Turkle 2002). One can see that games like *Sim City* have created windows or domains for identity variations that are more pictorial and therefore penetrate younger and younger markets.

An even further advance in the Sims series, *Sim2,* began to be marketed on September 17, 2004, to an amazing response from children as well as adults. The Sims games had already sold in multi-millions and the new game was developed to allow the game-derived characters to show a fuller, more human range of emotions. The developers, led by the game's originator, Will Wright, have sought to increase the reality of the characters by introducing more motivations based on psychological research, elements of the occasional inconsistencies that characterize us all, as well as more three-dimensional graphics (Yi 2004). It remains to be seen whether children will become even more involved in attempting to forge more complex personal identities from these play opportunities or, perhaps at younger ages, will be put off by the seeming "willfulness" of the new characters.

The chance encounters that characterize the anonymous, simulated interactions in simulation games or on chat rooms force us increasingly to recognize the essentially random, noncentralized nature of experience that Resnick (1994) has discussed. He is another pioneer from MIT's group of explorers of the implications of artificial intelligence and artificial life, and has elaborated on the new possibilities of social interaction through "allowing" the computer to simulate "spontaneous" group processes. In his work he developed software to represent the groupings and movements of antlike creatures.

We have been associated from its early days with the Santa Fe Institute, a remarkable interdisciplinary scientific center organized by Nobel prize physicist Murray Gell-Mann and former National Science Advisor George Cowan. At this high-level think tank, much attention has been paid to understanding how complex events in physics, biology, economics, and even anthropology show *emergent* properties; that is, new structures and organizations appear from seemingly chaotic, noncentralized or hierarchically guided interactions (Morowitz and Singer 1995, p. 2). Computerized simulations of the flocking and flights of birds (or "boids" as they are called, to indicate their artificial nature) and in Resnick's work with simulated ants point to the possible consequences for real human individuals who adopt multiple identities and come together in cyberspace. There, chance interactions may actually feed back new life possibilities or forms of social encounter to home players. Some of these virtual reality encounters may penetrate fantasies and dreams, as our young informant Faith reported; others may lead to actual daily life changes.

One can begin to discern certain rules that govern how seemingly chaotic, decentralized interactions shift positions or form new structures. In the case of chat room conversations or multiuser domain games, for example, certain conventions begin to appear. Although most contacts and chatter between strangers in a simulated hotel lobby or mall are replete with banalities, a few off-beat, provocative statements may lead to new forms of social intercourse (Evans 2001; Markey and Wells 2002; Pankoke-Babatz and Jeffrey 2002).

Although Turkle's focus was on older simulation game players, our own interviews make clear that even middle-childhood participants like Phyllis, with whom we began this chapter, enter MUD games playing fantasized roles. As we suggested earlier, mental play with pretend alter-egos may be a natural, even adaptive feature of growing up. As the extensive research on social learning has shown, we form our identities by combining early awareness of our own early temperamental characteristics (impulsivity vs. reflectivity, fearfulness vs. assurance, irritability vs. amiability) with modeling ourselves on features of people we admire, beginning with parents or other relatives, teachers, friends, public figures, and even fictional characters from reading or from the popular electronic media. For better or worse many girls draw on Barbie dolls, as Phyllis did, for emulating physical proportions. Many boys focus on athletic heroes or superstrong violent protagonists like those portrayed by Arnold Schwarzenegger or Sylvester Stallone to try to build personal styles. One of us (JLS) early in the 1930s read all Edgar Rice Burroughs' books of jungle and fantasy adventure and would tell so many of the stories to his nine- and ten-year-old playmates that he was given the nickname of "Tarzan," a soubriquet which scarcely matched his scrawny shape and mediocre climbing skills. Tarzan's intelligence (as presented in the books, not the Hollywood films) and the investigative skills of the stories about Sherlock Holmes, Sir Arthur Conan-Doyle's fictional detective, played a role in alter-ego daydreams. These undoubtedly contributed to later "real" career opportunities as a U.S. Army counter-intelligence agent in World War II and as a clinical psychology diagnostician and psychotherapist. The late renowned astronomer, Carl Sagan, has also described in interviews how his childhood reading of Edgar Rice Burroughs' series and novels about John Carter on the planet Mars led him to a career in science and to his lifelong explorations of outer space and the possibility of extraterrestrial life (Sagan, personal communication).

Research on Self-Representation:
A Framework for Approaching Identity

Ordinary reading can influence one's fantasy life to evolve into try-out alter-egos, some of which may go beyond playfulness to actual self-guides that can evoke emotion or motivate career interests. The psychological study of our experiences of one or more senses of self began with an early chapter in William James' classic *Principles of Psychology* of 1890. In the past few decades the self has emerged as an object of increasingly frequent careful scientific research. The beginnings of this recent work can be traced to the efforts of psychologist Carl Rogers (1961) in the 1950s. He began to study the psychotherapy process and actually to track from tape recordings how certain types of counselor-client interactions facilitated the latter's increasing recognition of different beliefs about oneself, some almost forgotten, some avoided in thought because of early family experience. The research data from these studies began to point to the conclusion that increased self-awareness and self-acceptance were associated with improvements in the patient's symptoms or general psychological adjustment. Following up on Rogers' and his collaborators' work, it became possible to set up reasonably precise, quantitative measures of one's self-attitudes or self-esteem (Rosenberg 1979; J. L. Singer and Schonbar 1961).

Since psychoanalytic practice had from Freud's earliest days suggested the importance of individuals' beliefs about their identifications with one or both parents to the organization of their personalities, one could now ask people to fill out attitude questionnaires as their Actual Self, their Ideal Self, and even as they believed their Father or Mother would respond. Then one could look at similarities and differences between Actual and Ideal, Actual and Father, or Actual and Mother, or even score discrepancies or similarities between one's Ideal Self and Actual Self, Father, or Mother. These scores could then be used to make tests of theoretical predictions of how various beliefs about oneself would influence one's moods and emotions, imagination, personality, and overt behavior. Some of these research studies may open avenues for new research that can assess how the alter-egos or pretend selves that children and adults are trying out on the Internet may be shaping MUD users' imaginations and self-representations.

Data from reports, interviews, and questionnaire research suggest that people daydream mostly about themselves in varying situations. Although it is true that most people do not actually picture themselves, since they see themselves ordinarily only in mirrors, they usually actively participate in the plots of their fantasies and dreams (Domhoff 1996). Daydreams about oneself in various social settings may be some of the building blocks for the formation of those organized mental structures that cognitive psychology has labeled *schemas* and *scripts*. We examined whether how people thought of themselves in relation to parental figures might influence patterns of daydreaming and functions such as creativity or achievement motivation. We asked middle-class adults from a variety of ethnic backgrounds to respond to questionnaires as their actual selves, as their ideal selves, and then as they thought their fathers or their mothers might answer the same list of questions for themselves.

By scoring the degree of difference between one's own set of responses and those perceived for the parent, we assessed the degree of identification with a particular parental figure. For people more closely identified with one's mother, we found a somewhat greater tendency for daydreaming in both men and women. This may have reflected the more traditional family style of that period (the 1940s and 1950s), when mothers were more likely to be at home and also more likely to be the family storytellers while fathers went to work and reflected a life of outside action rather than imagination.

We also developed a measure in which the discrepancy between self and father in response to questionnaires was related to the discrepancy between the self and mother, so that when a simple formula—such as $(S-F) - (S-M)$—yields a greater distance from father and greater closeness to mother—a positive relationship to reports of daydreaming or creativity is predicted. Our findings in general supported hypothesized relationships (J. L. Singer and McCraven 1961; J. L. Singer and Schonbar 1961). More recently, Tory Higgins (1987) developed an elaborate and testable theory of self-schemas or, as he termed them, self-guides. The motivational role of the ways in which one conceives of "possible selves" is also shown in other studies by Ruvolo and Markus (1992).

Self-representation may be a critical feature of a life narrative. Explicit memories of how one has been treated by other people, of what one wants in different situations, and of how one behaved in dozens of settings often enough form an extremely dense and complex network for the general memory associative structure. Self-relevance generally yields a powerful effect in studies of memory. A memory study by Kreitler and Singer (1991) demonstrated that young adults were more likely to recall self-relevant lists of words than words relevant to another person. Especially interesting was a personality measure of self-complexity that also correlated with the frequency of word recall under the self-relevant conditions.

It seems likely that, as William James suggested in 1890, that one is more prone to an awareness more of multiple self-representations than of a single "core" self. The experimental research of Markus and Nurius (1986) on possible selves has shown how some of James's conceptions can be translated into operational forms suitable for experimental and clinical study within a social cognition framework. The research program initiated by Higgins (1987) within a social cognition orientation perhaps operationalizes most effectively some key elements of what might be called Freud's superego into the so-called self-guides of actual self, ideal self, ought self, and their relationships. This work has been especially effective in demonstrating how discrepancies between the actual and the ideal self-representations are linked to depression and saddened moods, whereas discrepancies between the actual self and the ought self (or socially obligatory self) are linked to agitation and social anxiety (Strauman 1992, Strauman and Higgins 1988). Even more remarkable are the dramatic findings of Strauman linking these discrepancies between actual and ideal or ought selves to the functioning of the "psychologically silent" immune system of the individual (Strauman et al. 1993).

Our group at Yale collaborated with researchers at the University of California–San Francisco Medical School for several further studies of how people's beliefs and images of them selves were linked to their emotions, to their self-esteem, to their ongoing daily thoughts, and more generally, to their basic personality traits. The studies involved 100 young Yale students who filled out questionnaires including ratings of their Actual Self, Ideal Self, Ought or Socially-Expected Self, and Undesirable Self. They also wore paging devices for a week and were signaled randomly seven times a day, at which point they had to fill out a card with what thoughts, emotions, and activities they were engaged in at that moment. In this way, we could tap into their natural stream of thought and determine how their passing thoughts and emotions were connected with the ways that their Actual Selves were close to or distant from the Ideal, Ought, or Unwanted Selves.

The results of these complex and technical studies seem relevant to the question of identity formation that is very likely linked to the trying out of different personalities through SIM computer games or computer chat rooms. We found that when these adolescents, both male and female, showed greater closeness of their Actual to their Ideal or their Ought Selves, they also reported less depression or anxiety. On a separate measure they showed more self-esteem. If they also showed more overlap between Actual and Ideal or Ought Selves, their scores on a highly respected measure of personality traits revealed that they were more likely to be friendly and outgoing, and they showed less signs of emotional instability. Their Self-scores were also consistently related to the moods and to the thoughts they reported having about themselves during the 49 times we interrupted them through the week. In a further study we found that when individuals were made aware of the differences between their Actual Self ratings and their Ideal or Ought Self scores, their ongoing moods during the week showed greater depression than did the feelings reported by control group participants who were not primed to notice Actual Self and Ideal or Ought Self discrepancies (Hart et al. 1997; J. L. Singer 2003).

We have presented this work on self-representation at some length because we believe that examining the ways we relate our sense of actual to ideal self or even our actual selves to key figures in our lives, like parents, may be a very useful way to approach research on the effects of playing computer multiuser domain identity variation games. Can we hypothesize that when the measures are suitably adapted to middle childhood ages, youngsters who show large discrepancies in their self-representations may be most prone to very frequent simulation play and trying out different identities? Might we also suggest that such trial efforts, while occasionally enjoyable, could lead over time to even greater awareness of the differences between one's Actual Self and Ideal or Ought Selves, and thus to greater depression or anxiety? The players might even show increased desperation or quasiaddiction to try to make the games "come out right." We can see methods of the type we've described as very useful in capturing the implications for imagination, for self-beliefs, for identity formation, and ultimately, for emotional stability or open action as a result of simulated identities in social games or in chat rooms. The image of young Eric Harris, the Columbine School murderer, desperately reshaping his violent computer games to bring his actual and violent ideal selves together, haunts us.

Consider the potential of multiuser domains where one goes beyond the private fantasy to a more interactive quasisocial encounter, often several encounters at a time, as Turkle's informant Doug described. The life span theory of identity formation with its early child beginnings as proposed by Erik Erikson (1968) may serve as a starting point. The great excitement for children of pretend alternative worlds, controllable by the player, may explain children's early attractions to dinosaurs, whether benign like TV's *Barney & Friends* or menacing, as in the movie *Jurassic Park*. Recently, some four-year-olds were telling us about their reactions. For older children exposure through reading to epic fantasy worlds like Tolkien's Middle Earth led to organized games like *Dungeons and Dragons* and undoubtedly influenced the later development of MUD adventure computer games with their wizards, monsters, and dwarves. The amazing popularity of the Harry Potter books and of the Witchery and Magic Academy are being translated not only into more movies but also into simulation games. These will certainly evoke computer play in which many children will establish multiple identities as they do now at *Harry Potter* parties. When played on the Internet, such games may create a virtual reality with strangers and lead to the emergence of confusions in identity and a potential for even more extensive difficulties in separating one's sense of daily reality from cyberspace. They may, of course, also open new opportunities for forming constructive, realizable identity goals for some fortunate players.

It is probably too soon to draw conclusions on how the shifting identities emerging from computer games will play out in the lives in those children and adolescents who are confirmed MUD participants. We need careful follow-up, longitudinal studies that use reasonably matched control groups and that take into account family, educational, and socioeconomic features. Parental monitoring and involvement may minimize negative impacts and possibly even show constructive, socially adaptive outcomes for youth from such trial identities. Clinical studies as well as personality research on self-schemas of the kind we described above may also be useful in providing a richer picture of how such identity variation through Internet games may be influencing children's imagination as well as their overt behavior.

A very recent study conducted by a team led by Sandra Calvert demonstrates that systematic research on how preadolescent children engage in multiuser domain play is possible. This investigation involved 84 children between ages ten and thirteen who were fifth and sixth graders. Under carefully balanced, experimentally controlled conditions, the children played a game in which they could choose a name and a character or costumed avatar to represent them in the game. Under particular circumstances boys played with another boy or with a girl, and girls had similar options. The researchers scored the variables like the names, characters, and costumes they chose, how active their characters were in their screen movements, the language used in creating dialogues (which appeared as overhead bubbles). They also scored the emotional expressions employed, scene changes, role play which involved pretending and having their characters acting out pretend sequences, and finally, creating a game like Peekaboo or Hide-and-Seek in which the avatars or their creators could compete.

The findings are particularly striking in demonstrating gender differences. Boys showed more mythological or pure fantasy tendencies, choosing names like Lord of the Rings. Girls made up names such as Brittany or Shania, which reflected their interest in pop music stars. These eleven- and twelve-year-olds chose characters of the same sex to represent themselves. Generally, both sexes stayed close to real life, with apparently, we believe, some reflection of MTV influences. Boys largely chose to represent themselves in mildly rebellious stances wearing "leather jackets" or with punk identities. Girls seemed more likely to choose as a model of assertiveness soccer costumes. In keeping with findings from studies of sex differences in play, girls used more verbal expression and boys were more playful and engaged in more action. When boy players were pitted against girl players in the MUD, they talked more and were less active. Girls in the mixed-sex play also made adjustments, moving their characters more and talking less (Calvert et al. 2003).

Although this study primarily examined sex differences, it seems clear that the method opens exciting possibilities for understanding self and ideal self conceptions worked out by children in their computer play. Special games created for children or adolescents may be very helpful in exploring the natural developmental issues of identity formation as well as the particular influence of computer play in opening a cyberspace real or fantasy world for a child.

Some Special Hazards of Computer Use

We cannot deny that many computer games continue to involve violent themes. Accumulating evidence indicates that exposure to violent if seemingly heroic models puts a number of children at risk for persisting aggressive fantasies and overt actions. The research reviewed in Chapter 4 and the dramatic instances of school murders suggest that we must remain concerned about what early play with computer games may lead to. While writing this chapter, we had occasion to observe and interview a four-year old boy who was participating in a study we were conducting of children's responses to a nonviolent early childhood television program. In the viewing session the boy, whom we'll call Norman, stood out from the scores of other children we watched by the degree to which he was restless, standing for much of the time while others sat quietly and showing overt aggressive actions, pushing and blocking others from seeing the program. Norman had clearly enjoyed the show, singing along or imitating some of the exercises and dances on the video monitor. In the interview he showed a good understanding of some of the main points of this program, but then voluntarily described some of the computer games he played even at this young age and the violent programs he preferred to watch at home. These programs included *Spiderman* and other superheroes whom he liked to imitate. "I like to put on a cape and I could wonk this one and that one and he could bleed and yell and die! Yeah, he could fall down and die!" This is a dramatic example of the imitation of violence in a four-year-old that conforms to the reports of parents in the Kaiser Family Foundation survey (Rideout et al. 2003). Is Norman already showing the beginnings of an identity formed around a powerful but violent character? In a few years one can envision him adopting killer roles in console and computer video games and perhaps entering cyberspace as several macho heroes, practicing aggressive acts in fantasy and perhaps carrying them into overt actions more serious than his mild obstreperousness as a preschooler. Again, we were haunted by the image of the Columbine School killers.

Constructive and Prosocial Possibilities of Computer Play

We began this chapter by referring to the risks and challenges of computer play for fostering aggressive behavior or identity confusions. How can computer games contribute in constructive ways to children's imagination, creativity, and their development of useful social skills?

One of the children we interviewed in the course of our research was Viola, a bright nine-year-old at the time, who had always been encouraged by her parents to play computer games like *Chill Manor*, which combined exploration, adventure, and even spooky encounters with ghosts or werewolves, along with new vocabulary or world information lessons. Viola found herself stimulated by these games to seek out some of the books they suggested at her local library. Her parents had seen the online comments and a book by Larry Magid (1994), an early advocate for children's safety and intelligent use of the Internet. They had exposed her via Yahoo to some of his suggestions for child users, including avoiding giving out personal information, telling parents if you encounter uncomfortable information, and refusing to meet anyone encountered in a chat room or multiuser domain game personally. Sure enough, one day when Viola was preparing a school report on the U.S. president and his administration, she clicked naturally onto whitehouse.com only to get pornographic material. She was sensible enough to run into the kitchen to ask her parents to come and see what had happened. They figured out that what she needed for her report was whitehouse.gov. One wonders how many children may have been drawn into pursuing the sexual material if they had not had this prior warning or the ready availability of parents.

Viola was initially quite intrigued by the computer games she tried. Soon, however, she found that it was much more satisfying to stretch out on a couch or in an easy chair and lose herself in a book. Her computer play had piqued her interest in girls' detective adventures, and when she encountered the Nancy Drew series she plunged and read every one she could find. Soon she encountered the Harry Potter books and she moved on to books of fantasy adventure. As she grew older she made limited use of the computer for play, mostly focusing again on the mystery games. The computer had become primarily a tool for enhancing schoolwork, whereas books and, of course, rented videos, limited TV programs, and theatre movies remained her primary sources of imaginative stimulation.

One might see Viola as almost an ideal example of cognitive and emotional development with the computer initially as a stimulant. The complexity of reading and Viola's capacity to generate her own images and fantasies about book characters and settings, paced and controlled by her own time and location, proved more enjoyable than sitting at the computer. Perhaps as she moves further into adolescence, instant messaging with real-life friends will be another major online activity. Certainly our Yale College students report to us that instant messaging and burning music CDs have become their chief recreational uses of computers.

Certain computer games such as *Marble Madness* for ten- and eleven-year-olds have proven to enhance children's visualization skills, their ability to manipulate physical objects or geometric figures mentally. This ability was enhanced by using the computer to guide a marble through a virtualized three-dimensional framework, avoiding its tumbling down or being seized by mysterious enemies. College students in Europe and America who played a form of Concentration that emphasized using pictorial representations or semiotic icons, such as road signs of deer crossings, increased their tendency to use diagrams and related representations in analyzing electronic circuits (Subrahmanyam et al. 2000). Clearly, just at the level of pure imaging, computer game play can contribute to an important element of imagination, pictorial representation. In Viola's case computer games further encouraged her use of books to create private images. What other possibilities can we find for enhancing productive or creative imagining and even social skills through computer play?

The possible risks of identity confusion or increased loneliness we mentioned by playing online simulation games may be offset if there is some adult guidance or even peer group support. We do, after all, build our imaginative resources out of our mental simulations of the different roles we need to play in our daily lives. If parents or teachers themselves provide examples and if historical figures, national leaders, or even socially responsible celebrities are available, the simulations one tries out may effectively assist the young person in establishing a repertoire of personal representations suitable for the different roles one must indeed play in daily life.

Subrahmanyam and her colleagues express concern about the confusions between fantasy and reality that may occur as a consequence of playing simulation games or becoming involved in virtual reality settings. They give examples of a child and of an adolescent who see the figures on the computer screen as energized, almost given life, by the plug in the wall. Our own experience over a quarter of a century ago was with child TV-watchers who believed that people on the TV screen lived in the wall and moved through the electric plug wire to the monitor when the set was switched on. Such encounters with children led us to develop a series of school lesson plans in a curriculum on critical television viewing for use by teachers and parents. These lessons provided even kindergartners with information about the TV medium, how shows were constructed, how to understand magical effects like superhero leaps, how to confront the violence and taking a critical stance toward commercials (see discussion of Media Literacy programs in Chapter 3 and in Brown 2001). It seems clear now that both parents and educators have a responsibility to extend such media literacy efforts to include the even more complex impact of computers. They can provide useful information about the unique features of the computer, about spam, about the risks of chat rooms, and about the potential harm from identity confusions. They can also highlight the more enjoyable interactive narrative features of computer play and simulations, once the child recognizes that these are games.

Kathryn Montgomery (2001) has been a leader in promoting media education and in identifying constructive play and educational opportunities for children's interactive use of computers. She has assembled descriptions of nonprofit organization websites, like the American Association of School Librarians ICONnect, that guide parents, teachers, and children to useful links for pleasant narrative play, reading encouragement, and research sites. Laurie Trotta (2001) has also listed extremely helpful names of advocacy groups and their websites. For younger children most of the best PBS or Nickelodeon TV shows have useful websites that afford opportunities for storytelling and games that extend the humor and adventure of these shows. Especially promising, we believe, are websites like MaMaMedia that focus on easing children gradually into technology and fostering creative exploration by enlisting children's healthy curiosity. On the MaMaMedia site children encounter vividly colored, musically appealing play and story-creation opportunities that are increasingly under their control as they gradually master different levels of technology.

We began this book with a discussion of the importance of imaginative play in early childhood. It is clear to us that narrative thought and pretend play have constructive educational and social benefits. It is gratifying to see that computer play can enhance such opportunities for older children. Literally hundreds of websites of commercial companies, TV networks or toy industry sources, subtly interweave storytelling and pretend play opportunities with advertising messages. Montgomery's (2001) Center for Media Education is an organization designed to alert the public to some of the exploitative possibilities of such websites, and she elaborates on risks in her articles. At the same time we believe that—with the dramatic exception of games with violent themes or overly stereotyped toy tie-ins like the sexy Barbie-Chillin' Out dolls that also peddle cell phones—many of these commercially sponsored software, website-fostered playthings do offer children opportunities for interactive computer play. Computer games can be further elaborated with home play figures, doll-houses, block assemblies, or other construction materials like LEGO™ or K'NEX™.

Ian Pearson, working with BTExact, which is associated with the British Telecon company, has indicated that he is not concerned about high-tech toys involving computer chips that can move around and interact with each other. Nor is he fearful of interactive computers if the children who play with them find opportunities to stretch their imagination. As our example from Strommen's discussion of the interactive Barney demonstrates, Pearson envisions that such electronically driven toys will be regular features of children's play rooms. Dolls may soon be able to converse with each other or participate in a party demonstrating both good manners and nasty gossip. He believes this will be a boon to children's imagination and offer "a fantastic life style." Pearson even speculates that such dolls may "begin to have real life consciousness and awareness. The doll ceases to be a toy and will have the same basic legal protections as animals" (cited in Sennott 2003, p. 66).

Sennott writes in *Newsweek* that within a decade it may be possible for special contact lenses to afford children opportunities for playing within three-dimensional virtual worlds. The child may seem to be participating within elaborate fantasy environments ranging from more mundane dancing or athletics to exploration of legendary or fairy tale settings (2003, p. 66). We will of course need considerable research in the future to assess the broader developmental import of computer and virtual reality play in fostering constructive imaginative skills rather than generating reality confusion.

A surprising number of computer science students are turning their attention to devising electronic games, software for computer play, and in some cases combinations of tangible playthings (meeting Wilson's [1998] call for the importance of human touch) along with computer screen imagery. The Media Lab at the Massachusetts Institute of Technology is an exciting center for such efforts. We have already referred briefly to the work of pioneers like Mitchell Resnick in the area of computer science and artificial intelligence. Resnick, along with many other faculty, staff, and students, continue to devise ways to create learning opportunities for children and adolescents that combine software, palpable construction materials, and even Internet communication with play and narrative thinking formats (Resnick 1998). Some of these projects may eventually be available as retail playthings or may inspire commercial manufacturers to apply these principles to widely distributed products. The examples over the next several pages are drawn from the MIT Media Lab website (MIT 2003).

A number of projects are designed to improve technology so that games or information settings can draw upon the user's interactive capabilities more fully. Thus, a project directed by Dan Arieli strives to establish structures to help participants in electronic environments learn to distinguish among various forms of human thought from the rigorously rational through what is plainly irrational in ordinary behavior. Such an approach, we suggest, if simplified and put into storylike form, could be an enjoyable and ultimately instructive tool even for very young children. A group directed by Walter Bender is exploring how to present news efficiently and in a form that allows for an interactive participation by the consumer. Obviously of interest to adults, this could be of tremendous value to children who might, within a playful format, query a real or fantasy newsprovider about the meaning of words like "taxes," "constitution," "mosque," or "founding fathers" and receive answers with history playlets, vivid icons, or other narrative elements. A project directed by Stephen Benton is designed to develop computer-generated 3-D displays without glasses using holography. When applied to children's games involving geography and exploration or even mystery, Benton's technology would have tremendous appeal.

Even more immediately relevant for children are projects led by Bruce Blumberg on building characters who show common sense, learning ability, and even the level of empathy that can be found in animals like dogs. Children could eventually develop their own characters, fantasy figures or animals, whose interactions with them could be surprising and enjoyable. Justine Cassell's group is carrying such notions further in devising computerized or palpable toy figures with some humanlike language or social abilities. Work on communicating robots by Cynthia Breazeall's group and on self-organizing systems in V. Michael Bove, Jr.'s efforts to translate computer content into scripts can serve as foundations for the computer toy play games.

An ambitious effort by Chris Csikszentmihályi is designed to help artists rework computer technology so that it addresses a fuller range of human experience. Glorianna Davenport is seeking to find ways in which an adult or child could use computer methods for more interactive storytelling, whether on video or still photography. Other projects concentrate on how to represent various aspects of physics or ecology. Resnick's "Lifelong Kindergarten" group is a broad-ranging effort to building real and computerized communities of "playfully inventive" learners (1998). This program has led to the building of a LEGO-constructed robot. Groups of teenagers in Britain and Singapore communicate by video and the Internet to combine software and palpable materials to create a direction-sensitive robot. Roz Pickard's work on building computational systems that can sense and understand human emotions may ultimately help children use computer play to enhance their own emotional intelligence. Barry Vercoe's method of building intelligent music systems may carry much further the simpler computerized toys like Leapfrog that provide children with only very slight creative opportunities in music.

Other approaches designed to integrate computer and physical toy play are being developed by commercial as well as nonprofit researchers. Helen Shwe, working at the LEGO's San Mateo Lab, devised an old-time seafaring game that appeared on a computer screen. A child had a similar toy set of sailors or pirates and ships on the floor or table near the computer. Using patented Zowie Power™ sensing devices in the toy figures, a child can put an action figure in the *Redbeard Pirate Quest* near the steering wheel of the toy ship and, by turning the wheel, the child can then see the same ship's maneuvering on the virtual ocean depicted on the screen (Shwe and Francetic 1999). The laboratory was designed to translate the principles and adaptive values of imaginative play and the importance of children's control of the play scene to bring together the vividness and manipulability of the computer with the narrative drive of the child players. Another toy of this type from this group is *Ellie's Enchanted Garden*, with colorful flowers and toy animals that can talk on the computer screen as their counterparts are manipulated on the floor by the children.

At the University of Maryland, Alborzi, Druin, and their group have tried to move beyond the computer to devise electronically driven toys with sensors and other controls that children themselves place in the stuffed animals or other figures around which they are building a story (Druin and Handler 2000). Like Shwe's group, these investigators have emphasized multisensory experience, the ability to control the play so that the learning situation is repeatable, and the importance enjoyment in narrative play. Indeed, they call these playthings Story Rooms.

Of special significance in both the San Mateo and Maryland approaches is the demonstration that shows that these types of play go beyond the solitary, often isolating, quality of much electronic play situations to foster social play between two or three children. We know from our own research the importance of early make-believe play in fostering cooperation and opportunities for group enjoyment. We can only hope that some of these laboratory or "in-development" approaches can move further toward providing useful social experiences for children.

It is impossible at this time to summarize comprehensively the implications of computer use for children's imagination. The development of new software, of interactive "real" toys and computer games, and of virtual reality games is occurring too rapidly. The research necessary to evaluate such activity by children or adolescents is only in the planning stages. The video and computer game industry, already appraised at over $7 billion, is burgeoning. We foresee serious problems for many children who already have family problems or identity confusion if they become overly involved with the rapidly spreading multiuser domain play. At the same time we do see efforts in university laboratories and among some game and toy manufacturers to provide opportunities using computers and associated tangible toys for imaginative and constructive play. One rather impressive effort is the Fifth Dimension after-school curriculum pioneered by Michael Cole (1996) in children's clubs across several countries. Led by volunteer college students, parents, or teachers, these programs combine computer instruction and computer games, including multiuser domains, to introduce children to the adaptive features of electronic media. Research indicates they stimulate playfulness, cognitive advances, and social interaction (Subrahmanyam et al. 2001). The challenge and responsibility falls on parents and educators to guide children into cyberspace in much the same way as their encouragement, reading, and storytelling is critical for aiding children to develop imagination and literacy.

— 6 —

A Role for Play in Early Learning

In our previous chapters we emphasized the importance of play and its role in imagination, and how the electronic media may affect the consciousness of children. We believe that imaginative play can be taught, and along with adult guidance, can lead to the growth of cognitive, social, and emotional skills.

The No Child Left Behind Act of 2001 emphasizes early testing and the importance of emergent literacy curricula including phonological awareness for preschoolers. The pressure on Head Start and other early childhood programs to meet the demands of the Act has led to the substitution of repetitive drill for pretend play in many of these settings, and for standardized yearly assessment in Head Start Centers. As we talk to parents and teachers, we are finding more and more that very young children are becoming tense and anxious as they enter kindergarten. One reason for this is that the cognitive demands have increased to the point where free play has been virtually eliminated from the curriculum. We had the opportunity to look at the requirements for kindergartners in one school system. We were stunned to see that these five-year-olds are expected to create graphs, read high-frequency words, draw pictures accompanied by *written* sentences, and dictate full sentences, among other cognitive demands that research has overwhelmingly shown to be developmentally inappropriate.

In this chapter, we present an argument for the use of guided play as one technique for learning the basic skills suitable for preschoolers. In addition, we stress the need for more open-ended computer software that could inspire greater imagination in children. We also offer a brief overview of our own research projects dealing with play training for caregivers and their children.

First, let us peek in on a child who attends a child care center where free play is valued. Susan is playing "bus." Seated on cushions on the floor are three passengers, Susan's favorite Raggedy Ann doll, a well-worn tiger, and a teddy bear. Before Susan takes her seat in the front of the bus, she asks her passengers for money, counts the pretend dollars out loud from 1 to 10, and says, "Thank you" to each playmate. After Susan puts the money in a little box, she begins to drive. She is making lots of noises and swaying her body, pretending that she is steering around curves and going up and down hills. Susan calls out the names of the places she pretends to pass—"Library!" "School!" "McDonalds!" "Fire station!" "Zoo!" "Bus" is one of Susan's favorite pretend games. She can play it alone or with a friend on a play date.

At our Research Center at Yale University, we have developed a series of imaginative games such as "Bus" that encompass social skills, colors, numbers, shapes, vocabulary, letter recognition, and identification of emotions. These are the skills that the National Association for the Education for Young Children (NAEYC) deems important for readying children for school (Raden 1999). We proposed that children could learn these skills through playing make-believe games, and subsequently they would also show improvement in persistence, cooperation, taking turns, sharing, independence, and controlling aggression. But, most of all, children who play make-believe are having fun. They are also increasing their capacity for imagination and fantasy, the unique human qualities that we discussed at length in Chapters 1 and 2.

The Role of Television as a Teacher

We acknowledge that educational television programs can play a role in helping children with their social and cognitive skills. Chapter 3 discussed in more detail the effects of television viewing on a child's imagination. The late Ernest Boyer (1991), former president of the Carnegie Center for the Advancement of Teaching, recommended that television used judiciously can be a supplemental "teacher" in preparing children for school. *Sesame Street,* a popular children's television program, has for over 30 years been an exemplar of teaching children the names of letters, counting numbers, and modeling social behavior. *Barney & Friends* and *Mister Rogers' Neighborhood* are particularly effective in helping children to accept and develop their imaginative skills. In April 2003, the Nickelodeon cable channel introduced, through Noggin, their commercial-free company, a "connected learning" concept to teach preschoolers lessons that incorporate emergent literacy, language development, mathematics, social sciences, and visual arts (Umstead 2003). Three new programs reflecting these goals are now aired on The Learning Channel (TLC) and on the Discovery Channel as part of the "Ready, Set, Learn" block. Little attention, however, has been paid by these channels to the explicit development of the imaginative potential of children.

We appreciate the relative value of television as a teacher, but it is imperative that parents take a more active role in their children's television use. Unfortunately, the heavy reliance by children on electronic media—video games and computers for recreation as well as television—may displace the time needed to concentrate on perfecting their social skills, playing imaginative games and, of course, practicing their emergent literacy skills. As reported in the 2000 National Assessment of Educational Progress, one-third of our country's fourth graders cannot read and two-thirds of children fall below what is considered the minimum level of reading proficiency (Hunt 2002).

If television is used to help children learn, there are several things a parent or other caregiver can do to enhance its educational use. Probably most important is the judicious selection of programs for the very young child. Previewing the programs by the parent before exposing the child to them can effectively eliminate any programs that contain excessive violence or other inappropriate material. Once a parent decides which programs are best for their children, co-viewing the program is desirable. In this way, the adult can detect if a child is confused, bored, or even scared by a particular event. A parent can discuss the themes of the programs to clarify the meaning. Words that were used on the program that are new or seem difficult can be explained and used by the parent and child in later conversations. Ideas from a TV program can be incorporated into a child's play just as stories read to a child can be used as the impetus for a play theme. Television can motivate a child to use imagination if the parent asks the child to think of different endings for a story, or to make up other characters who could be on the program. Explanation or mediation by the adult, or even by an older sibling, can be effective in helping a child become a more active viewer of television and subsequently draw many ideas from the programs (D. G. Singer and Singer 2001).

Computers as Formal Teaching Tools for Children

As more and more young children are using computers (Rideout et al. 2003), we believe that this medium can also be helpful in enhancing a child's imagination if the writers of the software would become more inspired to stretch their own imaginative capabilities. In preparation for this book, we drew not only on formal research, but also on interviews and observations of children like Susan, our "bus" player, and Diego, a bright, precocious child who was not quite three. Pacific Island–reared parents had exposed Diego very early to brain-stimulating games like *Baby Einstein*, a video cassette they ran on the computer. His father, a computer technician, had access to or could modify a number of such teaching games for the little boy. Diego was able to tell us the names of different geometric forms. He went further and asked his mother to draw a clown for him. He told her to make "an oval for the body," then "a circle for face," then "a triangle for a hat," "two rectangles for legs," and "small circles for buttons on the oval." He chortled with glee after the image she drew was recognizable as a clown.

A very articulate ten-year-old named Helena actually sent us a perfectly typed letter in which she remembered her earliest exposure to computers. She mentioned her parents' complaints of time wasted setting up her computer. They called it a "a modern nightmare!" Helena recalled her first computer games, described as, "little storybooks with animated pictures and learning games. I learned how to distinguish numbers, colors and shapes. When I got to be around seven, my family got a CD to help my sister and me type quickly. My early years of computers were more focused around learning." She goes on to mention that her current uses of the computer, except for homework and research, are centered on instant messaging with friends, entertainment, and especially playing *Sim City* alone or with a friend or two beside her.

The increasing international use of computers for teaching has been carefully documented by von Feilitzen and Carlsson in a UNESCO report (2002). The actual teaching potential for computer games and more formal materials like *Tetris, Millie's Math House,* and the Bruderbund

Company's storytelling approach such as *Where in the World is Carmen San Diego?*, have been extensively reported in recent chapters and books (Calvert 1999; Oppenheimer 2003; Subrahmanyam et al. 2001).

The *Tetris* wall and shape games, in which the player must mentally rotate attached groupings of squares to fit them into openings on a "wall" of squares, relate to our imagery capacities rather than to our linguistic skills. There is no doubt that children and adolescents can learn to improve their performance and visualization skills for similar games from this computer game. Generalization to more day-to-day uses of imagery from playing computer games has not yet been shown (Calvert 1999; Subrahmanyam et al. 2001). Greenfield (1998) does suggest that recent evidence of national improvement in the nonverbal features of intelligence tests may reflect the fact that many children have been gaining these skills from widespread computer game playing.

In an early, creative effort to establish the age-specific capabilities of preschool and early school-aged children for learning to identify, recall, manipulate, and label objects, Calvert (1999) and her group developed the computer games *Park World* and *Talk World*. They exposed children to various stationary (tree) or moving (dog) objects on a computer screen while the teacher read a story and then hid the objects. The children generally preferred to play with the *moving* objects and recalled them better. Action especially helped the younger children to recall objects after they were erased from the screen. The results of these studies support earlier memory research suggesting that by ages six or seven, children are able to use a dual coding system of imagery and verbal labeling for effective recall. An intriguing finding was that using the same content on a felt board manipulated directly by the teacher and, later, the child led to equally effective learning performance at a much lower cost. The children enjoyed their own hands-on activity, a verification of Frank Wilson's insights about the psychological and neurological importance of the hand (1998). One implication of these results is that *movement* of objects is motivating for children and facilitates recall. We would propose that studies of this type support the value of action and narrative along with a "live" teacher in helping children extend their selection, encoding, retrieval, and labeling processes.

Three studies carried out in the early 1990s and using the technique of meta-analysis with students from kindergarten through higher education indicated varying results. The first study examined 120 research reports and found gains in proficiency for those children using computers on only one factor, the *quality* of the computer-assisted instruction that they received (Fletcher-Finn and Gravatt 1995). In a meta-analysis of 254 controlled evaluation studies, Kulik and Kulik (1991) suggested that computer-based instruction had a moderate but significant effect on achievement. In a later analysis of 500 individual studies of computer-based instruction, Kulik (1994) found that students who used such instruction scored higher on achievement tests, learned in less time, and were more likely to develop positive attitudes toward learning. It is evident from these studies that children can benefit from receiving help, reinforcement, and specific instructions that are computer based, but especially if they are of *high quality*.

Another body of research deals with computer-based instruction with children considered to be at risk. One report described inner-city kindergarten children who were exposed to a multimedia environment for language development for a period of three months. They were compared to children in a conventional kindergarten classroom. Results indicate that the experimental group showed superior gains in auditory and language skills. They were able to tell stories better and used tenses more accurately than children in the control group (Mayfield-Stewart et al. 1994). Similarly, in another study, 54 prekindergarten children from unstable home environments were divided into three groups. Two groups used computer-based math activities and the third group participated in noncomputer-based math activities. The children in the computer-based math activities groups scored significantly higher on a test of early math ability compared to the control group (Elliot and Hall 1997). Out of curiosity, we observed a child in a local school using a computer-based math program in the computer room. The boy was very relaxed, moved at his own pace, received good feedback from the computer screen, tried using different ways to solve the math problems, until finally, he was able to arrive at the correct answers. He seemed to enjoy the fact that he was not embarrassed by mistakes he made, as he might have been if he were asked to respond out loud in the presence of his classmates. The teacher was always available in the room to help the children if the computer information was too frustrating or incomprehensible.

There is now good evidence that older children and even college students made stronger gains compared to control groups in math problem-solving, vocabulary, or even comprehension of brain anatomy and function, when the material was embedded in visual and verbal storytelling contexts via video discs or computers (Calvert 1999). The use of such formats in computers seems especially valuable because it can be interactive, with the child capable of controlling pacing and other features via a mouse or joystick.

Jane Healy (1999), who sometimes seems to have "gone overboard" in her critique of electronic technologies at home and in the classroom, seems to us at the same time to be an astute proponent of the crucial role of the human element, the parent or teacher, in managing television and computers. Healy offers suggestions for the adult caregiver or school teacher in making effective use of the computer for adaptive learning. These include paying careful attention to the age-dependent cognitive capacities of children, tying computer activities to the children's interests, emphasizing the hands-on features of an activity before moving to a more cyberspaced modality (Calvert's felt board versus computer game). Healy's suggestions also emphasize that adults should allow time for reflective thought and should encourage expressive reporting by the child of the material. She also urges adults to help the child use different sensory modalities—telling, drawing, writing, constructing—wherever possible. The teachers' or parents' role—explaining, questioning, expressing interest, smiling, showing warmth—are crucial (1999, pp. 246–248). Our own research on parents as mediators of the "real" and television world for children strongly support these suggestions (D. G. Singer and Singer 1990, 2001).

Our frequent interviews and observations of children's learning from computers point strongly to the positive influence of parental or other adult guidance. Recently, we observed a group of four-year-olds in a day care center who were enjoying playing a game on the computer. The teacher sat nearby, constantly referred to items on the screen, and would stop the program to talk about the game and ask questions. This was an excellent use of the computer for young children, very similar to Healy's approach, and one we would like to see carried out by more teachers and certainly by parents in the home.

A recent study of the use of computers in the schools by Todd Oppenheimer (2003) has provided numerous examples of the wastefulness and misuse or ineffectiveness of computer technology when teachers, whether through the inadequacy of their own technological education, insufficient financial and administrative support, or personal indifference, fail to provide the backup and assistance that children need. Oppenheimer makes a strong case for the danger that public funding for computers, may be wasteful and self-defeating if no effort is made to train and motivate teachers to play the critical humanizing role. If teachers network with mentors and with other teachers electronically, they can overcome the isolation often found in the classroom. They can share resources and even strategies for teaching, as well as any new software packages they find.

It is apparent that electronic media are a major part of children's lives, and even very young children are now exposed to videos, television, and computers that have instructional possibilities. At the same time the research points out how crucial is human contact for the child's effective use of these new technologies. We believe that we must help the child make the smooth transition to school and eventually to the electronic media by encouraging parents or childcare workers to establish early rapport with children. A key feature of developing such rapport is in engaging the child's intrinsic interest in narrative thought and play. This has led us to a program that emphasizes, for the very young child, guided play as a means of sustaining the joy of childhood while establishing the building blocks for cognitive and social development.

Teaching Cognitive and Social Skills through Guided Play

Teaching Cognitive Skills

Why is it important to help preschoolers learn some of the cognitive skills they will need in kindergarten? Research indicates that children who have mastered rudimentary skills, such as identifying letters and numbers, are more likely to learn to read, write, and calculate earlier and more proficiently than those who have not (Siegler and Richards 1982). In an excellent monograph discussing the research, theory, and practice relevant to how children learn to read English, the authors state that children who perform well on tasks that involve phonological awareness (deciding if two words rhyme and recognizing that two words start and end with the same letter) do markedly better in early reading than children who have difficulty with these tasks (Rayner et al. 2001). Although we are not advocating teaching *reading* to preschoolers, we are in favor of young children becoming familiar with books, learning the names of letters, and recognizing that these letters relate to words in a book. And of course we strongly favor parents' reading to their children each day and offering encouragement to their children to engage in imaginative play.

What is so striking to us is that during free play periods, many preschool children we observed were wandering around the classrooms from activity to activity in an aimless fashion. We do not think it is necessary for the teacher to be intervening during every moment of a child's play, but certainly some of this guidance could benefit the child who has very little parental mediation at home. Many of the teachers sat on the sidelines and interceded only if aggressive behavior was evident.

Rarely did we see teachers using this free play period as an opportunity to interject some ideas or suggestions that could help the children play more imaginatively and use their play scripts to learn some skills. For example, when we watched some boys building a dog house, there was a chance for the teacher to ask some questions about the size and shape of the blocks, how many blocks were needed, or to introduce some new words, such as leash, dog catcher, kennel, roof, ramp, and collar. During a game of "Store," it would have been appropriate for the teacher to help define the words needed to play the game, such as "customer," "cashier." The teacher might even have had the children identify the items in the game by naming the first letters of each—"b" is for ball, "c" is for car—or encouraged the children to count out play money when they made their purchases, thereby learning one-to-one number and object correspondence. Instead, the teacher sat by passively, interceding only when the children would fight about who was in charge.

In a game like "Store," there is ample opportunity to teach about all the elements needed in shopping—making up a name for the store, setting up the merchandise, choosing the roles for each child, opening the store, buying the items, paying for them, counting out the money and closing the store. In addition, cooperation, taking turns, and using civilities ("please," "thank you," "you're welcome") could be part of this make-believe game. In their later replaying of the game, children might naturally practice new words and appropriate social behaviors while adding in their own variations and novelty.

When the children have a script in mind, the play flows more evenly. Preschoolers' pretend play that involved strategies *implicitly* included in the play scenarios were more successful than when children stopped their play to discuss *explicit* suggestions, as a study by Sawyer (1997) demonstrated. Thus, if the children have an idea before they begin their game (as in "Store"), they tend to play without constant interruptions. A teacher or parent can supply ideas for a game before the game actually begins. If the children have a story in mind based on a book that was read to them or even after exposure to an educational TV program, they are apt to play the game more smoothly and, one hopes, introduce some improvisations as they go along.

Christie and Enz (1992) investigated the effects of two types of intervention on preschooler's play patterns and literacy development. The Materials Plus Adult Involvement condition, in which the teacher used suggestions and modeling to encourage the children to use literacy materials in their play, was more effective in encouraging literacy-related play than a Materials Only condition. Other cognitive skills such as mathematics can be enhanced through play. It has been argued that teaching mathematics in a playful mode led to more enjoyment of the subject and easier learning (Ginsburg et al. 1999).

Play training need not stop when children reach elementary school and can be important for a child's later development, as Williamson and Silvern suggest (1990). Academics such as reading and writing improved for kindergarten and even second grade children when they played together during fifteen hours of play sessions (Stone and Christie 1996). Play training with 75 older primary children who were identified as poor comprehenders was helpful in aiding them to understand stories more easily after these stories were enacted out. Play actually does not decline as children get older and can be useful as a learning tool to help children in their social understanding of reality. In work with dramatic play involving props and with enough time to enact various themes, eleven- and twelve-year-old children were able to learn the skills needed to deal with such issues as confrontations with adults or with their peers, gangs, or bullies (Restrepo and Lucia 1999; J. L. Singer and Lythcott 2002).

Pretend play fosters language use and takes place within social contexts (Bergen 2001). We are not advocating that teachers or parents overwhelm the children with their questions and probing, but certainly in subtle ways a teacher or parent can interject some ideas so that the play becomes richer for the children and some useful learning may follow. Indeed, the adult is instrumental in helping children to keep a game going and to learn from their play, as Parker et al. (1999) found when they examined links between parent-child relationship, home learning environment, and school readiness. The authors also reported that increases in a parent's understanding of play and ability to facilitate a child's learning predicted several positive outcomes in the classroom.

Bert van Oers (1999) suggests that play, which is a complex process, can prepare children for learning, but that a teacher must not disturb the play itself. Teachers and parents can assist children in how to use schematic representations meaningfully and reflectively in their play activities. It is essential that the adult allow the game to flow, and if the child chooses to change the storyline, this is acceptable. The pretend play, by and large, is in the child's control. In her early work in South Africa observing mothers and children during play, Diane Shmukler (1981) found an optimal point for the mother's facilitation. When mothers are too intrusive, the child plays less imaginatively than when the parent makes a suggestion, withdraws, and allows the child to continue on his or her own. Many times we have observed children pulling back from play when their parents intervened too much, took over the play game, or became too silly, moving out of their adult roles.

More recent research by Marcon (2002) suggests how important it is for a preschool curriculum to be child initiated. This means that the teacher facilitates learning by allowing children to actively direct the focus of learning. The teacher in the study was a facilitator who could ask questions and mediate, but the child's interests were paramount in choice of materials. Children who had experienced such a curriculum at a young age did significantly better at the end of their sixth year in school than children who had been exposed to a more academic curriculum in preschool. In a review of the literature from 1908 to 1994 focusing on the relationship between dramatic play and creativity, Mellou (1995) found that most of the of the studies supported the relationship between the two variables. It was suggested that a qualified tutor was helpful in encouraging and fostering children's creativity, especially if nonspecific props were used rather than clearly defined materials. To repeat, we are not suggesting that guided play be carried out continuously by the parent when a child plays at home or even by the teacher in the free play periods in the classroom. In school, it can take place for a few minutes during each play period, and the teacher can use guided play with different children each time. If this were a part of the curriculum over the year, we believe that much incidental learning could take place in an atmosphere of enjoyment so that children would be motivated to repeat the games on their own and, in effect, practice the new words and activities naturally.

Parental involvement in play as a factor in influencing cognitive and social development was demonstrated by Gottfried and Brown (1986). They reviewed a series of longitudinal studies designed to examine which home environment variables correlated with learning. The two most potent factors correlating with cognitive development during infancy and the preschool years were the availability of play materials and the quality of parental involvement. As the child matured, these two variables were found to influence cognitive development even more. Unfortunately, many parents buy the toy of the moment, usually a toy that is heavily advertised, but may not be educationally beneficial or even induce imaginative play.

Teaching Social Skills

We particularly enjoy hearing mothers use pretend language early on with their children. Even if the child is not quite sure of all the words mothers use, the tone of the words signify fun and play. Many parents feel self-conscious when they talk to babies, but the smiles a parent receives from babies exposed to such talk are worth it. Pretend talk encourages pretend play, and pretend lay engenders social awareness. Work by Haight and Miller (1992) examining the effects of mother-child partnering on pretend play with children aged 12 to 48 months found that mothers were the primary partners through age 36 months. After that age, children began to pretend about equally with mothers and with other children. Children engaged in pretend play with their mothers played longer than when they played alone. Children also incorporated their mothers' pretend talk into their subsequent play periods. After 36 months children tended to taper off from mimicking their mothers' pretend talk, and "by age 48 months, pretend play with other children was almost four times as sustained as mother-child pretending" (p. 345). In a more recent study, Katz (2001) corroborated these results. When pretend talk by parents to their preschoolers (talk with pretend elements) was compared to non-pretend talk (a literal orientation to actions and to toys), mothers and children who engaged in pretend talk usually reached a peak duration of play at age four.

Parent-child joint pretense play is linked to children's social competence, and children's emotional knowledge is positively associated with social competence (Lindsey and Mize 2000). In a play setting a child can pretend that a doll is sick and cuddle it, put a bandage on its cut finger, or sing the doll to sleep. All of this play centering on the emotional aspects of the script helps a child to interact appropriately with the peer group even when no pretend game is taking place.

Not only are the parents important in encouraging social competence in play settings, but school behavior is influenced by the nature of a child's play. Coolahan et al. (2000) were interested in whether low-income preschool children's peer play interactions were related to learning and to problem behaviors. Positive interactive play behavior was associated with active engagement in classroom learning activities. When there were breaks in the continuity of sequences during play, these were followed by inattention, passivity, and lack of motivation in the children's other activities. Disruptive children evidenced conduct problems and hyperactivity in the classroom.

Pioneering work in Israel demonstrated that through sociodramatic play intervention, poor children who were recent immigrants to Israel were able to improve reading readiness skills, adjust better to school, and became more sociable (Feitelson 1972; Smilansky 1986). Through play, leadership qualities and social skills emerged. Feitelson (1972) also found that divergent thinking and creativity were encouraged through play training. In the United States, an early study focused on training economically disadvantaged preschoolers in acting out imaginary stories. Children who were trained performed significantly better than a control group of youngsters on a number of measures of social and cognitive development. Fantasy play training was highly related to the incidence of spontaneous sociodramatic play and to higher scores on selected subtests of standard IQ instruments. Children with fantasy training also scored higher on tasks designed to measure story sequence memory and story verbalization skills (Saltz and Johnson 1974).

Imaginative or pretend play in young children has been shown to foster other important skills needed for success in school, such as taking another's perspective, regulating one's emotions, and taking turns with peers (Saarnie 1999; D. G. Singer and Singer 1990; J. L. Singer and Lythcott 2002; J. L. Singer et al. 2004). Additional empirical research has established that children's play experiences are indeed a valuable resource for their social, emotional, cognitive, and language development (Belsky and

Most 1981; Christie 1983, 1985, 1991; Fein 1981; Goleman 1990; D. G. Singer and Singer 1990, 2001; D. G. Singer et al. 2003; J. L. Singer 1973; Yawkey and Pellegrini 1984).

The Adult's Attitude Toward Play

Even though the research data suggest that imaginative play training can be valuable, the attitudes of teachers and parents toward using such training can affect their willingness to engage in guided imaginative play with children. In our project on play training, many of the participants were at first dubious that brief involvement in training and in playing our games would have any effect on the children's imagination. However, when asked about whether our participants had any educational exposure to the role of play in child development, only a small number of teachers had reported that they had taken formal courses, and most of the home care providers and mothers we worked with had no courses at all (J. L. Singer et al. 2004). Many of the teachers and parents who participated in our project also had very little experience in playing imaginative games with their parents or by themselves when they were children. Some of the mothers in our studies, many of whom were economically disadvantaged and lived in inner-city neighborhoods, said their own childhood play had consisted of chasing their siblings, being chased by them, or imitating characters on TV. The people who raised them, usually their mothers or grandmothers, did not engage in imaginative play with them. If they did play imaginatively, it was on their own and not with any parental guidance. Ideas came chiefly from TV or from stories read to them in school. Thus, our approach was rather new for these particular mothers.

Working with 50 African American Head Start teachers in Chicago, Julie Spielberger (1999) found that although these teachers valued pretend play, particularly for language development, they held different views about their roles and displayed a wide range of behaviors in relation to children's play. A majority believed that it was worthwhile to facilitate pretend play, but not to interfere or guide the children. Teacher's social and personal values, their own early play experiences, and their professional training influenced their attitudes about goals for the children's development.

What Children Are Like When Entering Kindergarten

Why do we need to know the strengths and weaknesses of preschoolers when they enter school? Such information is important for government policy and practice. What children know and how they behave in kindergarten are products of their genetic endowment and the child's experiences *before* entering school. School entry behavior and knowledge can "serve as indicators of how well families, child care institutions, and preschool programs prepare children for school" (Zill and West 2001, p. 1). With this information, educators can best understand what kind of curriculum is needed for the first year of school and design materials that are appropriate.

We have presented some of the research that demonstrates the importance of imaginative play in the development of cognitive and social skills. Before we discuss our own studies, we feel that the reader needs to be more fully acquainted with the reasons why we undertook this particular research project with its emphasis on make-believe play. Two important surveys (Boyer 1991; West et al. 2000) were influential in formulating our strategy of using guided play as a way to help very young children prepare for kindergarten. These surveys provided evidence that about one-third of preschoolers, mainly poor children, were not prepared for school entry. Boyer (1991) was cognizant of how much time preschoolers spent in front of television and how this time interfered with their time for play.

In addition to television displacing the time children spend playing and actively learning about their environment, one of the reasons for poor school readiness is the way in which many children are being taught their skills. As one response to the lack of good teaching and unsatisfactory preschool curricula, the report *Eager to Learn: Educating our Preschoolers* was issued by the Commission on Behavioral and Social Science and Education of the National Research Council. This book includes recommendations for the educational development of preschool teachers, for the kinds of material to be used in preschools, for policy, and for research on learning, curricula, and assessment. There are many occasions for a teacher to use such tactics as acknowledging and encouraging children's efforts, modeling and demonstrating, creating challenges, supporting children in extending their capabilities, and providing specific directions or instructions within the context of play and structured activities (Bowman et al. 2000).

Why is it so important to prepare children for kindergarten through using the techniques of guided imaginative play? How well prepared are children in their cognitive, social, and emotional skills when they enter kindergarten? Based on a 1998 study of 19,000 children from a national probability sample of kindergartners attending 940 public and private schools, the good news is that the majority of children (66 percent) who entered kindergarten can recognize letters of the alphabet by name and 94 percent can identify squares and circles and count to 10. Twenty-nine percent of kindergarten children can associate letters with sounds at the beginning of words. Seventeen percent can associate letters with sounds at the end of words. Two percent of children begin kindergarten able to read simple sight words, and one percent are able to read more complex words in sentences. Twenty percent of kindergartners read two-digit numerals, identify the ordinal position of an object in a series, determine the next number in a sequence, and solve simple word problems. Four percent of pupils begin kindergarten able to solve addition and subtraction problems (Zill and West 2001). In this report, the authors offer no information on the imagination of the children surveyed.

Because our research project involved the preparation of materials to help children learn their basics, we were interested in the "bad news," the kindergarten children described in the report who lag behind. For example, 18 percent cannot demonstrate familiarity with the conventions of print; 34 percent cannot identify letters of the alphabet; 42 percent cannot count 20 objects or read more difficult single-digit numerals; and 6 percent cannot count 10 objects and identify simple numerals and shapes. Zill and West state that the differences in children's academic skills arise from such factors as age, sex, family risk factors, and health status. Older kindergartners obviously do better than the younger ones. Because the age at which children are eligible for kindergarten entry varies by state, some children may be as young as four years and eight months, others as old as six years upon entrance.

Sex of the children does not contribute significantly to the development of skills, although girls are slightly ahead of boys in reading. Seventy-two percent of girls know their letters, compared to 62 percent of boys, upon entry into kindergarten. More girls than boys can associate letters with sounds at the beginning and ending of words (32 percent versus 26 percent respectively). Despite the slight lead of girls in these two areas of literacy, about the same small number of boys and girls can actually read by sight at school entry (3 percent of boys and 2 percent of girls). Perhaps the difference between boys and girls in acquiring cognitive skills results not only from structural variations in their brains, but also from the fact that most teachers are female in preschools and in the lower elementary grades. This leads girls to identify more closely with the teacher, and therefore be more willing to pay attention and learn.

Boys tend to have more developmental difficulties in terms of communication skills and paying attention, and they engage in more active behavior. It is fairly easy to note the differences between boys and girls when one visits a typical classroom. The boys fidget more in their seats, are more easily distracted, and when out on the playground tend to be more active, rambunctious, and more easily engaged in hassles over toys than the girls. Boys also display more social problems, such as being less helpful to classmates, less accepting of peer ideas, and less adept at forming and maintaining friendships. This finding was of particular interest to us because one of the major results of play training is a reduction of aggressive behavior and an increase in civility on the part of the children who participated in our imaginative games.

The children who have the most difficulties in kindergarten come from urban America. Two-thirds of children in large cities are considered to be at risk in at least one of four factors: 1) mothers with less than a high school education; 2) an impoverished family that receives food stamps or cash welfare payments; 3) a single-parent household; 4) parents whose primary language is not English. Nearly three-quarters of children from African American or Hispanic families show one or more risk factors, compared with 29 percent from white families. Indeed, in a study of parent's conceptions of kindergarten readiness and home-learning activities, data suggest that African American, Hispanic, and other parents of color were significantly more likely than Caucasian parents to express concern about their child's readiness for kindergarten (Diamond et al. 2000). The proportion of Asian American children, however, with multiple risk factors, 17 percent, is much closer to the proportion of white children. The children who have multiple risk factors do not know their letters and cannot count to 20. These children are more likely to be in fair or poor health compared to other kindergartners (Zill and West 2001).

A serious implication of this study, according to Zill and West, is that many of the children who are not up to par have come from Head Start or from other preschool programs that were not quality programs. There are exceptions, of course. In a study by Gilliam (2004), low-income African American children who attended a school readiness program in Middletown, Connecticut, were found to attain school readiness scores on a developmental screening test that were comparable to white children in general, and higher than low-income African American and white children who did not attend such a program. The study also found that children—across all racial and economic lines—who attended two years of prekindergarten were significantly better prepared for kindergarten than those who attended only one year.

Questions remain concerning the curricula, the methods of teaching young children, and the kinds of training preschool teachers receive in general. As just one example of what needs to be done to remedy the situation of finding qualified teachers, since 1998, Connecticut has been operating a model training program for childcare providers. Supported by the Children's Fund of Connecticut and the Connecticut Department of Social Services, the curriculum, *Training Program in Child Development*, emphasizes child health and development, how to be a more effective provider, early literacy, working with children with special needs, and training in how to access health care for low-income families with children. The courses for childcare workers are conducted in English with 20 percent of the training programs presented in Spanish. Training is under the auspices of the Wheeler Clinic, a nonprofit human services agency, and as of June 2001, 4,156 providers have received training (Wheeler Clinic 2001). Another example of a training program that has worked successfully is the *Teach* program, which started in North Carolina in 1990 and has now been adopted by seventeen states. This program provides scholarships to workers to attend school and bonuses or raises from employers when students finish their programs (Manzo 2002). Perhaps one of the best trainers for preschool teachers is our military establishment. Teacher turnover is low, and the 800 centers that serve more than 170,000 children are accredited by the National Association for the Education of Young Children (Manzo 2002).

A Special Role for Play in School Readiness

Obviously we are in need of drastic changes in our preschool programs. The current administration has budgeted $75 million toward preschool programs with an emphasis on using the money for reading (Schemo 2002). The government also has instituted a yearly testing program for all Head Start centers. This program will test 908,000 four-year-olds nationwide. Some education experts are protesting that these children are too young to be evaluated by a standardized examination. This testing program will be under the direction of Westat, a research company that will be paid $1.8 million to help develop the assessment (Strauss 2003). If the goal is to raise standards in childcare centers throughout the country, as is claimed, monies would be better spent on more preschool teacher training, development of quality curricula, and universal preschool education.

Our efforts to introduce play into preschools stems from the concerns raised by the above discussion. We believe that poor, at-risk children are capable of learning more than Zill and West's study showed (2001). Currently, 313,000 preschool children are considered to be educationally disadvantaged (U.S. General Accounting Office 2000). In 1989, the Even Start literacy program was established with federal funds to improve the educational opportunities of children and adults in the United States by integrating early childhood education and adult education for parents into a unified program (Riedinger 1997). Literacy training was to be provided for adults, and they were to be considered full partners in their children's education.

Even Start children must participate in an early childhood education program. Curricula are varied and must be developmentally appropriate. Many of the children in Even Start are at-risk children. All of the programs are receptive to parents visiting and volunteering in the classrooms. One of the most important techniques used by teachers to help parents become more sensitive to their children's needs is through modeling behaviors. The staff focuses on positive, supportive interactions with children to convey to parents that such behavior will yield more healthy relationships between parent and child. Some constraints that impede the work with parents are poor attendance at some of the parent meetings, the multitude of problems the parents face on a daily basis, such as economic stress, and the challenge of drug abuse, which is evident in many of the homes (Riedinger 1997). Of interest to us is the fact that even in this federal program, very little is mentioned about guided play as a technique for reaching the children and helping the parents prepare them for kindergarten. We can only address the concerns of a small number of at-risk children with our methodology, but our hope is that our work will motivate a movement to incorporate imaginative games and guided play in the curricula of preschools around the country.

Teaching Imaginative Play to Enhance School Readiness: The Research Project

We agree with this description of our task as educators and parents:

> To see our children as active learners, to see the world as a virtual school yard of interesting lessons, and to find a play medium that allows us to teach children and to retain the unprogrammed benefits of childhood. This occurs when the teaching is incidental and part of play (as opposed to drill) and the learning is embedded in an emotionally supportive context. (Hirsh-Pasek and Golinkoff 2003, p. 251)

The materials used in training parents and teachers in guided play with their preschoolers include ready–to-learn skills embedded in imaginative games. Encouragement and modeling (the scaffolding alluded to in Chapter 2) are essential aspects of the program. We reviewed the curricula of various benchmark preschool programs in Connecticut and Georgia, Jumpstart (a national preschool enrichment effort), Head Start, the military, and the federal guidelines for preschoolers to determine whether or not these approaches utilized guided play as a way to learn. There was considerable emphasis on literacy, science, language arts, and physical components such as fine and large motor skills. It was rare in these sample curricula to find strong recommendations for the use of guided play as a method to help young children develop the fundamentals needed for entrance into kindergarten (D. G. Singer et al. 2003). Because the federal guidelines are intended to guide teachers in preschools throughout the nation (Dwyer et al. 2000), this omission of play is especially troublesome.

In an effort to demonstrate techniques for enhancing pretend play skills in children, *Learning Through Play*, a short-term early childhood education intervention program, was created to improve children's preparations for formal schooling (J. L. Singer et al. 1998; J. L. Singer et al. 2004).

Phase One: The *Learning Through Play* Games

Our first participants were 103 low-socioeconomic status parents whose preschoolers children attended childcare centers in an urban setting. The parents were recruited through by directors of schools that included Head Start and child development centers and were either city supported or privately owned.

Parents attended two training sessions, where they were shown a video of the games and where we reviewed the training manual with them to be sure that they understood the procedures. Rather than actors, the people in the video were parents, teachers, and children who were not part of the research study and who were of comparable socioeconomic and ethnic backgrounds as our participants. A professional producer, Harvey Bellin, and his staff from the Media Group of Connecticut filmed and edited the videos used in all our studies. We developed rough scripts based on games in our book and on make-believe games, and Bellin later refined them (D. G. Singer and Singer, 2001).

The video began with an introduction about the value of play for pre-school children and included a total of six games. The games included Restaurant (described below); Mirror about feelings and emotions; Bus to the Zoo that taught the children about their neighborhood, sequencing, social skills, physical movement, names of different animals, and colors; Submarine that emphasized colors, shapes, counting, sequencing; Puppet that dealt with counting discrete objects; and Camping that taught about the seasons, colors, counting, and social skills.

The Restaurant game, the favorite of adults and children, is a story about a birthday party at a pretend restaurant designed to enhance skills in vocabulary, sequencing, social skills (cooperation, sharing, taking turns), shape and color recognition, counting, and fine motor skills. The children followed a simple story whose text the parent had previously read in the training manual. It set up the steps needed to play the game and described the materials involved and the learning goals of each game. The parents viewed the story on the video about going to the restaurant to celebrate a birthday. The simple materials could be found in any household. Children and their parents took turns acting as waiter or waitress, birthday child, and guests. Stuffed animals became guests if no other children were available. The children set the table first using placemats that they had designed with various colored shapes, circles, squares, triangles, and either paper or plastic dishes and utensils. A menu was prepared, and children pretended they could read it as they ordered their food. The waitress took their orders and scribbled on a pad. A birthday cake made out of clay with clay candles was brought to the table at the end of the meal. The birthday song was sung, the birthday child counted the candles, made a wish, and blew them out. At the end of the meal, the waitress brought the bill, and the child carefully counted out play money and presented it to the server. The next time the game was played, roles were changed.

We asked parents to play the games over a two-week period, to keep records of which games they played, how long they played each game, and their own and their children's reactions to the games. Parents also rated the usefulness of the video and the manual as methods for encouraging play and for the teaching of the skills emphasized in each game. All children were pretested using measures that contained the concepts embedded in the imaginative games we designed.

A control group of parents and children did not receive this training. After the trained parents played the games on a daily basis with their children over the two-week period, we again tested all the children in both groups to determine if any gains were made. (After the experimental phase of the study was completed, we trained the control group of parents using similar methods and materials.)

Trained research assistants who were unaware of the purpose of the study or of the control or experimental condition observed and scored the children at two different times during their free play periods at school. The observers, in pairs, visited the children's classrooms two times each, before and after the caregiver training sessions, to independently rate children's play behavior during free play times. Four aspects of children's play behaviors—persistence, imaginativeness, positive emotion, and cooperation—were rated for frequency of occurrence during the observation period. In addition, a school readiness test was created to assess the skills that children would learn following the caregiver training (J. L. Singer et al. 2002). These test items were selected based on recommendations from the NAEYC, which derived from kindergarten teachers' feedback. The test was administered to each child before and after the training sessions and included domains such as cognitive, social, and emotional development (that is, knowledge of shapes, numbers, colors, vocabulary, and manners). Practitioners and researchers alike have identified the concepts assessed by these items as important skills for preschool children to have when they begin school (Peth-Pierce 2000).

Children whose parents received the training showed significant improvement in overall scores on the school readiness test, compared with children whose parents received no training. Modest increases were also found in subcomponents of the overall test, including vocabulary, knowledge about nature, general information, and knowledge about manners. Once the control group of parents were trained and played the games with their children, similar improvements were found for those children.

Although the records kept by the parents indicated that the children played the games on their own at home from time to time, we did not see evidence that the children were playing these particular pretend games during school hours. The teachers were not involved in the study and did not know which games we were training the parents to play. Therefore, teachers tended not to encourage the children to play these games during classroom free play periods. Since the children spend much of their day in preschool centers, we decided we would need to train teachers as well as parents.

Phase Two: Training Teachers and Parents

Consequently, the next phase of the study involved training both low-income parents and the teachers in the childcare centers where their children were enrolled; 107 children were involved. The design included three groups of four-year-old children's caregivers who received training: parents only, teachers only, and parents plus teachers. A fourth group in which neither teachers nor parents received training served as a control.

A new training manual and video were developed and adapted into a two-part program to demonstrate examples of games that could foster children's pretend skills. A facilitator at each site explained the purpose of training to the parent and teacher groups and used the video to illustrate how each game could be played. Parents and teachers were requested to use the video and manual for their own reference and teach the children the games. They were to keep records during the two-week training program of which games they played and the time spent playing each game. Forms were provided that asked for an evaluation of gains that children made and for comments about the training materials. The same procedures were employed for assessment as in the earlier study.

The important finding in this phase was that training *both* parents and teachers resulted in the most improvement in the children's performance. Gains were made for all three training groups, compared to controls, in knowledge of shapes and general information. Those children who had been given the opportunity to play the games with either parent alone, teachers alone, or with parents and teachers showed more imagination, persistence, and cooperation. These behavorial indications of change in play were positively correlated with higher levels of school readiness, as demonstrated from the posttest assessments of the children.

Phase Three: Extending the Study to Atlanta and Los Angeles

Would we find similar results if we carried out the study with a different staff focusing mainly on teachers, and in different parts of the United States? We chose two cities: Atlanta, Georgia, where we worked in 19 childcare centers with 104 teachers and 837 children, and Los Angeles, California, in 10 centers with thirty-two teachers and 475 children as participants. These centers were comparable in socioeconomic status to the earlier test sites. Fifty-three teachers in Atlanta and 24 teachers in Los Angeles were actually trained. We hired psychology graduate students under the supervision of faculty consultants for each site. They explained the purpose of the study and reviewed the materials with the directors of the participating centers. In addition, we visited some of the sites in both cities during the training phase to observe the progress of the study.

Directors offered the training to teachers and to five parents who wished to receive training as well in two training sessions, with the written materials reviewed and the video shown each time. Teachers then played the games with the children over a two-week period averaging 30 minutes a day. Directors and teachers at all participating centers filled out a questionnaire at the end of the project stating their reactions to the video and to the written materials. Directors and teachers also recorded whether or not they observed any changes in the children in the following areas: imagination, cooperation, persistence, positive emotions, and school readiness skills.

The data from both Atlanta and Los Angeles indicate that the training materials were easy to understand, that teachers and children enjoyed the games, and that teachers and daycare center directors were eager to continue using the learning games as a means of strengthening children's ready-to-learn skills. Children in both cities should improvement in their readiness and social skills on rating scales that the teachers filled out based on their observations of the children. The teachers and directors rated the materials as very useful for themselves, as well as potentially for parents. Center directors reported that parents who saw the videos were extremely positive in their response to the program. All directors expressed a desire to use the video and manual to train future children in these imaginative games.

After two years of testing demonstrated that the program produced measurable gains in childrens' readiness skills and could be replicated in geographically diverse sites, we then distributed 2,700 free copies of the video and manual, *Learning Through Play*, to agencies that serve low-income families across the United States. These included Head Start centers, Connecticut training centers for low-income parents and other caregivers, Public Broadcasting Service's Ready-to-Learn station directors, public libraries, and the United States Department of Education (J. L. Singer et al. 1999).

Circle of Make-Believe: A Training Program for Adults and Children

Would it be useful to make videos directly aimed at children rather than just use them to train the adults, as we had been doing in previous studies? Would this motivate the children to want to get up and play the games, and would this be of help to the adults when they played with the children? for the next phase of the project, called *Circle of Make-Believe*, we prepared new videos involving more direct talking to and modeling of play behaviors for the child viewer by adults and children, who were the actors. In this electronic age where children are exposed all the time to at least some learning opportunities on television and on videos, it seemed appropriate to present our games in a playful format for our audience of preschoolers. A new video and printed manual were prepared, and the manual was simplified so that any adult could use the materials without the need to attend a workshop for training.

Five imaginative games were introduced. Two had been used previously, Restaurant and Puppet. A new game, Nature Island, dealt with politeness, taking turns, safety, practicing names of letters with words, animal names, and practicing animal sounds and movements. Readiness skills such as identifying emotions, cooperation, sharing, and numbers were in Grumbles Makes Friends. Concepts such as near, far, above, below, under, and over were embedded in Where's My Kitten? The manual provided materials to use along with the games, a numbers page for the counting game, an alphabet page, pictures of animals used in the nature game, and play money. A resource page for adults included a summary of developmental stages, names of children's books related to the particular readiness skills we emphasized, and phone numbers to call for educational materials.

Since an enormous number of children in the United States are in the care of home care providers, individuals who tend small numbers of children in their homes, we included these adults in this study. Over one hundred child care teachers, home care providers, and parents in nearly equal in numbers from lower socioeconomic groups filled out a consent form and a questionnaire. The questionnaire included such background information as their level of education and whether they had taken courses in child development. As in the former studies, adult participants kept records of the games played and which games they and the children liked best. Children were to play the games guided by the parent, teacher, or home care provider over a two-week period with a minimum of 10 minutes per day. At the conclusion of the training period, the participants evaluated the video and manual on a five-point scale, and the children again were rated (as they had been before the intervention began) on their imagination, persistence, self-help/independence, and social skills (cooperation, sharing, taking turns). The parents, teachers, and home care providers, also rated the children on the school readiness skills (numbers, colors, shapes, and letters) to discern any improvements. Participants attended focus groups at the end of the study to share their impressions of the materials and the outcomes of their efforts.

Results

The three groups—parents, teachers, and home care providers—did not differ very much in time spent playing the games. The adult records indicated that they played the games with the children in their care on the average of a little more than four times per week, averaging 30 minutes per day, with no significant differences among the groups. The strongest effects tended to be for children who were trained either by parents or by home care providers. The home care group had very little in the way of structured curricula, so they had more time to spend playing and encouraging imagination in the children. Even our parents who worked found ample time in the evenings and on weekends to play the games.

Forms kept by the adults demonstrated that children in all three groups showed significant increases in spontaneous imaginativeness and in pro-social skills, cooperation, sharing, and taking turns. There were increases in children's persistence on tasks, concentration, and displays of positive emotions (smiling, laughing, interest/excitement). These findings are generally similar to those of our earlier studies following child training, or after the combination of viewing particular TV shows along with training in more controlled experimental studies discussed in Chapters 2 and 3.

Although we found an increase in the children's ability to identify letters, there were no significant effects for numbers, colors, or shapes in this sample. This may be because the children in his study were already well along in their ability to count to 10 and recognize colors and the more common shapes such as squares, triangles, and rectangles.

Qualitative data from the questionnaires and from the focus group sessions suggest that parents, teachers, and home care providers enjoyed the materials and found them easy to use. The children "loved" the video and wanted to view the games repeatedly. The participants claimed that they would continue to play these games with the variations outlined in the manual and with their own improvisations. They offered us many ideas for new games, and some of these were incorporated in the last phase of our project. Many of the adults found less aggressive play and more constructive social interactions among the children as a result of playing these imaginative games.

Additional Sites for the *Circle of Make-Believe* Training Project

A final phase of the project included eight test sites around the country— Alabama, California, Connecticut, Ohio, Maryland, Minnesota, Wisconsin and Wyoming. The number of participants in these sites were 38 lower socioeconomic parents, 35 teachers and 32 home care providers. Children reached by the parent and teacher trainers in this project numbered 242. We improved the video and manual after reviewing our results from the previous phase of the study and added the Store game suggested by parents in our focus groups. In this game we introduced sounds of letters to comply with the mandate of the No Child Left Behind Act. To foster imagination and to encourage expressive language, we added Make a Story, a game that motivated a child to tell an original story about any object retrieved from a paper bag.

Results of this final phase of the *Circle of Make-Believe* project reinforced our belief that children can learn their readiness skills through the use of imaginative games. In all nine areas assessed—imagination, social skills, persistence, self-help, independence, and number, letter, color, and shape recognition—children rated higher on average on their posttest scores compared to their pretest scores. The three groups of parents, home care providers, and daycare center teachers rated both the video and the manual's usefulness very highly. Home care providers gave the highest rating to both video and manual. We believe that they were extremely appreciative of new materials that would keep the children interested and involved while in their care. These providers who usually worked in isolation from other caregivers also were most in need of materials, and gave us much positive feedback on their forms. The Restaurant and Store games were the clear favorites of both adults and children.

Final Thoughts about Guided Pretend Play Training

Our review of the literature and our own research suggest that one way to teach children the skills that will lead to readiness for school is through guided imaginative play. When a teacher or a parent offers a child an incentive through a story, a song, or just a few sentences, or becomes an active participant in a child's television or computer use, these prompts inspire the child to construct, elaborate, and enter into a world of imagination where learning and play combine in a pleasurable way.

We began this book by considering the special role in our human imagination and our ability to relate ourselves not only to the present but also to the future and, indeed, to *possible* futures. We tried to suggest that our adult consciousness, imagery, and potential creativity could be traced to the emergence in childhood of pretend or make-believe play. In this chapter we have examined in more detail some of the contingent factors that can foster the adaptive development of such play in early childhood. Play training involves time, materials, opportunity, and especially, the dedication of adults who can encourage and nurture play. Children now develop in an environment that goes much beyond the physical objects, the toys and the words, touches, and smiles of parents and other adult caregivers. We have described how to use the electronic media, the television set, video games, and computers constructively as a part of children's daily experience in the home and in other settings. We especially focused on how parents and other adults can foster and encourage the natural love of play that very young children share and extend such play in the service of school readiness. Our own willingness to become a child's play guide can harness the joy of imagination and fantasy in our children to the necessary goals of improving their cognitive and social skills.

Epilogue

A central theme featured in this book is that an adult's stream of thought bears a strong resemblance, even if it is more elaborate, to the "talking out loud" one hears from preschoolers engaged in pretending or make-believe play. Make-believe games emerge naturally as part of early development, but their flowering is encouraged and fostered by parents and other adult caregivers who tell stories, read aloud, or interact playfully with children. The new electronic "members of the family," television, video games, and computers, may also shape and direct the imaginative and creative potential of the children's thought.

Pretend play, the foundation for later adult imaginative processes, can be understood as an effort of the very young to deal with the large objects and people around them by trying to match new stimulus complexes with preestablished schematic mental structures drawn from memories of earlier experiences. A key feature of make-believe play, observable as early as 18 months of age, involves an effort to enhance positive emotions and to reduce negative emotions by seeking to cut down the large things around them to manipulable proportions. This can be accomplished by assigning meanings to dolls, blocks, soft toys, and other objects that roughly match the real objects in the environment. Needless to say, such efforts arise when the complexities confronting children are not only properties of the physical world, but also situations of a more social nature. These social novelties may involve the departure of a parent, arguments or fighting among family members, and situations of teasing or humiliation by parents, siblings, or peers.

Children strive to incorporate new material, either from direct contact in the physical and social environment or from print and the electronic media, into their previously formed mental organizations that we call schemas or scripts. When they can match the new experiences with these prior expectations, they are likely to feel the positive emotions of affirmation and joy. Children take pleasure in linking, through repetition, novel material with familiar material in the fairly controlled setting of pretend play. Similarly, in the course of make-believe games, they may find opportunities to express a full range of emotions, from excitement to fear, sadness, or anger, all in a framework that they control. Children may pretend that a doll or toy cowboy is in danger, angry, or frightened, but then may think of a way to resolve the situation by some previously learned script of heroic action or escape. The excitement of discovery and the joy of the solution may follow vicarious negative emotions. Make-believe play thus becomes a critical stratagem by which children learn to make sense of their world: the nursery, the family, the neighborhood, television, video games and computer play, and the ever-broadening social and physical settings that they confront as they grow older.

We cannot, however, overlook the hazards presented by growing up in the new worlds of electronic media. Some forms of play with realistic toy weapons, overexposure to imitatable aggression portrayed on television, and practice of violent behavior in videos or computer games may actually narrow one's imaginative breadth and result in impulsive and maladaptive social behavior. Some children may also be heavily caught up in using computer play to generate multiple grown-up selves that run the risk of serious identity confusion. Parents and educators face an important new responsibility to monitor and mediate their children's electronic game involvement. With such guidance, children may be able to take more effective advantage of the positive and constructive possibilities inherent in the new technology. Just as reading opened the way for children to internalize information about the world, the judicious use of computers and multitasking by children may begin to lead to subtle changes in brain capacities.

The complexity of the frontal lobe of our human brain is likely what distinguishes us most strikingly from other animal species, and the special features most associated with this area are language and conscious thought. Over millions of years humans evolved with the ability to reproduce from memory, or through those elaborations of memory that we call imagination, the great cave paintings of leaping animals drawn on the walls of caves in Spain and France. We can now go beyond the simple cave paintings and use the computer to perform complex animation and elaborate simulations. Scientists have even directed the robots, Spirit and Opportunity, to explore and photograph the terrain on the planet Mars. And these images are now easily accessible to children via television and the Internet.

We believe that a key principle of adaptive thought lies in the conception of *what might be*, when the child in play moves beyond the concrete shapes of blocks or toys—the *what is*—to *what was, what could have been, what can be tried, what might happen*. This path to realms of purest fantasy may be the route to that miracle of human experience, the creative imagination. Making up little plots and transforming blocks into spaceships or nondescript rag dolls into parental figures must call for some effort on the child's part to generate private images or to recombine earlier memories of individuals or scenes with new, projected mental representations. Certainly, we can expect that exposure to television, video games, and computer play should potentially contribute to a richer internal life for the child. The active involvement called for by video and computer games should increase the child's learning ability and incorporation of play material into consciousness.

Correlations between play and imagery or divergent production (a forerunner of creativity) might well be common to children who are imaginative players. There is good reason to believe, as we discussed in Chapter 2, that increased opportunities to engage in imaginative play encouraged by adult caregivers and by computer surrogates may actually enhance the later occurrence of divergent thought, imagery capacity, or storytelling abilities in children. In effect, then, we can see indications that imaginative play either through live or electronic interaction can have an array of adaptive benefits that might themselves lead to the kinds of imaginative leaps—a willingness to tolerate divergent mental operations—that often characterize adult creativity.

Even if watching television or playing computer games may sometimes foster the imaginativeness of children, we should be cautious in predicting an increase in the number of writers like Goethe, Ibsen, and Woolf, or inventors and scientists like Einstein, Edison, Watson, or Crick. Nor can we anticipate, on the negative side, a dumbing-down of the nation. We can hope, however, that through an increased awareness of the constructive uses of the media to enhance children's imaginativeness, we can establish an atmosphere that will allow for greater everyday creativity and at least set a tone for the rare surfacing of major genius.

Preschool pretend play predicts positive emotionality and more creative forms of thought in later childhood (Russ 2004; Russ et al. 1999). The attitudes of peer cooperation, positive emotionality, and exploratoration we find in children who are active pretend players at early ages have been shown to persist in children through the high school years as the basic traits of agreeableness and openness (Hair and Graziano 2003). Even twenty years beyond childhood, as research by Shiner, Masten, and Roberts (2003) has shown, the behavioral correlates of youthful pretend play we described in Chapter 2 are evident in adults in the form of agreeableness, mastery motivation, and academic achievement. We hope that future researchers will go beyond the hands-on make-believe play we have stressed to long-term follow-up of the persistence of traits associated with constructive and imaginative computer play as well. We also have stressed "creativity in the small," the kind of self-developing, self-healing shown by children in our earlier vignettes. Will we find more research evidence in the future that childhood computer explorations of multiuser domains or of games of adventure and simulation predict a richer employment of imagination in later years?

Certain personality styles, as discussed in Chapter 1—most especially openness to experience, which is related to curiosity, tolerance for ambiguity, and the preference for challenge and complexity—are critical in laying the basis for affective pleasure. Although openness may be in part constitutional, it may also be influenced by early experience, parental values, and modeling. The reinforcement of continuing positive feedback from emotional enjoyment and from successful achievement, and the social bonding among children playing together with toys or with adventurous or nonviolent video games and computer explorations can also strengthen the trait of openness.

Paul Harris (2000) has conducted very careful research to examine in detail how children first demonstrate signs of imaginative activity. He explored how emotion enters into this process, and then how the combination of increased language skills and imagery produce a rich and fertile human capacity for moving beyond the here and now into a region of subjunctive mental cognition. Although our nearest animal cousins, the Bonobo chimpanzees, certainly engage in rough and tumble play, Harris argues that they show no sign of going beyond concrete givens or directly present objects in their behavior.

The social features in the environment of the growing child can foster a rich and flexible mental capacity for considering alternatives and for enhancing one's access and control of imagination. How can parents and other adults continue to stimulate a child's imagination? What space and time considerations are important for a child? We need much more study of the conditions under which exposure to such media as books, film, television, video games, and computers contributes to or suppresses our children's imaginative development. We have attempted to answer some of these questions in this book. It is very likely that nonviolent computer games, simulations, and Internet chat rooms will become incorporated into the average child's stream of thought. We need more study to determine how we can help children move beyond the passive experience of ongoing thought toward reflection and effective control of their virtual reality exposures. We can anticipate a tremendous increase in children's interactions with artificial electronic worlds in the coming decades. With proper adult guidance, we believe such exposure can stimulate the brain's capacity for evoking that great human miracle of imagination through which we conceive of possibilities and generate originality in our thoughts and actions.

References

Prologue

Bruner, J. 1986. *Actual minds, possible worlds.* Cambridge, MA: Harvard University Press.

Dickinson, E. 1929. I dwell in possibility. In *Further poems of Emily Dickinson,* ed. M. Bianchi and A. Hampson, 30. Boston: Little, Brown.

Lapham, L. 1984. Old relics in new bottles. *Harper's Magazine* (March): 105.

LaSpina, J. A. 1998. *The visual turn and the transformation of the textbook.* Mahwah, NJ: Erlbaum Associates.

Norman, D. A. 1993. *Things that make us smart: Defending human attributes in the age of the machine.* Reading, MA: Addison-Wesley.

Singer, J. L., and D. G. Singer. 1981. *Television, imagination, and aggression: A study of preschoolers.* Hillsdale, NJ: Erlbaum Associates.

Singer, D. G., and J. L. Singer, eds. 2001. *Handbook of children and the media.* Thousand Oaks, CA: Sage Publications, Inc.

Wolf, D. P., and S. H. Grollman. 1982. Ways of playing: Individual differences in imaginative style. *Contributions to Human Development* 6:46–63.

Zigler, E. F., D. G. Singer, and S. Bishop-Josef, eds. 2004. *Children's play: The roots of reading.* Washington, DC: Zero to Three Press.

1. Our Conscious Imagination

Antrobus, J. S. 1993. Dreaming: Could we do without it? In *The functions of dreaming,* ed. A. Moffitt, M. Kramer, and R. Hoffman, 200–222. Albany, NY: State University of New York Press.

Antrobus, J. S. 1999. Toward a neurocognitive processing model of imaginal thought. In *At play in the fields of consciousness: Essays in honor of Jerome L. Singer,* ed. J. A. Singer and P. Salovey, 3–28. Mahwah, NJ: Lawrence Erlbaum Associates, Publishers.

Blakeslee, S. 2003a. Imagining thought-controlled movement for humans. *The New York Times*, October 14.

Blakeslee, S. 2003b. In pioneering Duke study: monkey think, robot do. *The New York Times*, October 13.

Bruner, J. 1986. *Actual minds, possible worlds*. Cambridge, MA: Harvard University Press.

Carmena, J. M., M. A. Lebedev, R. E. Crist, J. E. Doherty, D. M. Santucci, D. F. Dimitrov, P. G. Patil, C. S. Henriquez, and M.A.L. Nicollels. 2003. Learning to control a brain-machine interface for reaching and grasping by primates. *Public Library of Science, Biology* 1 (2):1–16.

Ciba Foundation. 1993. *Experimental and theoretical studies of consciousness.* Symposium 174. Chichester, UK: Wiley.

Costa, P. T. and R. R. McCrae. 1995. Domains and facets: Hierarchical personality assessment using the revised NEO Personality Inventory. *Journal of Personality* 64: 22–50.

Csikszentmihalyi, M. 1990. *Flow: The psychology of optimal experience.* New York: Harper & Row.

Epstein, S. 1999. The interpretation of dreams from the perspective of Cognitive-Experiential Self-Theory. In *At play in the fields of consciousness: Essays in honor of Jerome L. Singer,* ed. J. A. Singer and P. Salovey, 51–82. Mahwah, NJ: Lawrence Erlbaum Associates, Publishers.

Frank, G. 2003. Triebe and their vicissitudes: Freud's theory of motivation reconsidered. *Psychoanalytic Psychology,* 20 (4):691–697.

Freud, S. 1911/1948. Formulations regarding two principles in mental functioning. In *Collected Papers,* trans. J. Riviere, Vol. IV, 13–21. London: Hogarth Press.

Harris, P. 2000. *The work of the imagination.* Malden, MA: Blackwell Publishers.

Humphrey, R. 1954. *The stream of consciousnes in the modern novel.* Berkeley and Los Angeles: University of California Press.

Hurlburt, R. T. 1990. *Sampling normal and schizophrenic inner experience.* New York: Plenum Press.

Hurlburt, R. T. 1993. *Sampling inner experience in disturbed affect.* New York: Plenum Press.

Jackson, H. 1932. *Selected writings.* J. Taylor, ed. London: Hoddler and Stoughton.

James, W. 1890/1950. *Principles of psychology.* New York: H. Holt & Company.

James, W. 1892/1958. *Talks to teachers on psychology: And students on some of life's ideals.* New York: Norton.

Johnson, M. K., and K. Multhaup. 1992. Emotion and MEM. In *Handbook of emotion and memory,* ed. S. A. Christianson, 33–66. Hillsdale, NJ: Erlbaum.

Joyce, J. 1934. *Ulysses.* New York: Modern Library.

Klinger, E. 1999. Thought flow: Properties and mechanisms underlying shifts in content. In *At play in the fields of consciousness: Essays in honor of Jerome L. Singer,* ed. J. A. Singer and P. Salovey, 29–50. Mahwah, NJ: Lawrence Erlbaum Associates, Publishers.

Lewin, I. 1985–1986. A three-dimensional model for the classification of cognitive products. *Imagination, Cognition and Personality* 6 (1):43–54.

McAdams, D. 1990. *The person.* San Diego, CA: Harcourt, Brace, Jovanovich.

McCrae, R. R. 1993–1994. Openness to experience as a basic dimension of personality. *Imagination, Cognition and Personality* 13 (1):39–55.

Panek, R. 2004. *The Invisible century: Einstein, Freud, and the search for hidden universes.* New York: Viking.

Pope, K. S. 1978. How gender, solitude, and posture influence the stress of consciousness. In *The stream of consciousness: Scientific investigations into the flow of human experience,* ed. K. S. Pope and J. L. Singer, 259–299. New York: Plenum Press.

Root-Bernstein, R., and M. Root-Bernstein. 1999. *Sparks of genius.* New York: Houghton-Mifflin.

Runco, M. A., ed. 1994. *Problem finding, problem solving, and creativity.* Norwood, NJ: Ablex.

Runco, M. A. 2004. Everyone has creative potential. In *Creativity: From potential to realization,* ed. R. Sternberg, E. Grigorenko, and J. L. Singer, 21–30. Washington, DC: American Psychological Association.

Shiner, R. L., A. S. Masten, and J. M. Roberts, 2003. Childhood personality foreshadows adult personality and life outcomes two decades later. *Journal of Personality* 71 (4):1145–1170.

Singer, D. G., and J. L. Singer. 1990. *The house of make-believe: Children's play and the developing imagination.* Cambridge, MA: Harvard University Press.

Singer, D. G., and J. L. Singer, eds. 2001. *Handbook of children and the media.* Thousand Oaks, CA: Sage Publications, Inc.

Singer, J. L. 1966. *Daydreaming: An introduction to the experimental study of the inner experience.* New York: Random House.

Singer, J. L. 1975. *The inner world of daydreaming.* New York: Harper & Row.

Singer, J. L. 1978. Experimental studies of daydreaming and the stream of thought. In *The stream of consciousness: Scientific investigations into the flow of human experience* ed. K. S. Pope and J. L. Singer, 187–225. New York: Plenum Press.

Singer, J. L. 1995. William James, James Joyce and the stream of thought. In *Seven pioneers of psychology: Behavior and mind,* ed. R. Fueller, 21–48. London and New York: Routledge.

Singer, J. L. 1999. Imagination. In *Encyclopedia of creativity,* ed. M. Runco and S. Pritzker, Vol. 2, 13–25. San Diego, CA: Academic Press.

Singer, J. L., and G. A. Bonanno. 1990. Personality and private experience: Individual variations in consciousness and in attention to subjective phenomena. In *Handbook of Personality*, ed. L Pervin, 419–444. New York: Guilford Press.

Singer, J. L., and S. L. Brown. 1977. The experience-type: Some behavioral correlates and theoretical implications. In *Rorschach psychology*, ed. M. A. Rickers-Orsiankina, 325–374. Huntington, NY: Krieger.

Singer, J. L., and K. S. Pope. 1978. The use of imagery and fantasy techniques in psychotherapy. In *The power of human imagination*, ed. J. L. Singer and K. S. Pope, 3–34. New York: Plenum.

Singer, J. L., and P. Salovey. 1991. Organized knowledge structures and personality: Person schemas, self-schemas, prototypes, and scripts. In *Person schemas and maladaptive interpersonal patterns*, ed. M. S. Horowitz, 33–79. Chigago: University of Chicago Press.

Sternberg, R. 1999. The theory of successful intelligence. *Review of General Psychology* 3:292–316.

Sternberg, R., E. Grigorenko, and J. L. Singer, eds. 2004. *Creativity: From potentiality to realization.* Washington, DC: APA Books.

Wordsworth, W. 1980. The pedlar. In *The selected poetry and prose of Wordsworth*, ed. G. Hartman, 69. New York: New American Library.

Zhiyan, T., and J. L. Singer. 1996. Daydreaming styles, emotionality and the Big Five personality dimensions. *Imagination, Cognition, and Personality* 16 (4):399–414.

2. Play: Its Beginnings and Stages

Almquist, B. 2002. The childcare institution: A significant subculture in an international perspective. Paper presented at the Symposium on Toy Culture in Preschool Education and Children's Toy Preferences: Common Features and Differences in Europe and Across the World. World Congress—Toys, Games, and Media, London, UK, August 19–22.

Aronson, J. N., and C. Golomb. 1999. Preschoolers' understanding of pretense and presumption of congruity between action and representation. *Developmental Psychology* 35 (6):1414–1425.

Azar, B. 2002. The power of pretending. *Monitor on Psychology* 33 (3):46–51.

Bagley, D. M., and C. Chaille. 1996. Transforming play: An analysis of first-, third-, and fifth-graders' play. *Journal of Research in Childhood Education* 10 (2):134–142.

Barnette, M. 2001. Tech Toys: How are they really affecting your child? *Child* 92:94–95.

Bell, N., and W. Carver. 1980. A reevaluation of gender label effects: Expectant mothers' responses to infants. *Child Development* 51:927.

Bruner, J. 1986. *Actual minds, possible worlds.* Cambridge, MA: Harvard University Press.

Caldera, Y., A. Huston, and M. O'Brien. 1989. Social interactions and play patterns of parents and toddlers with feminine, masculine, and neutral toys. *Child Development* 60:70–76.

Carlson, S. M., M. Taylor, and G. R. Levin. 1998. The influence of culture on pretend play: The case of Mennonite children. *Merrill-Palmer Quarterly* 44 (4):538–565.

Chase, R. A. 1994. Toys, play, and infant development. *The Journal of Perinatal Education* 3:7–19.

Cherney, I. D., L. Kelly-Vance, K. Gill Glover, A. Ruane, and B. O. Ryalls. 2003. The effects of stereotyped toys and gender of play assessment in children aged 18–47 months. *Educational Psychology* 23 (1):95–106.

Cobb, N. J., J. Stevens-Long, and S. Goldstein. 1982. The influence of televised models on toy preference in children. *Sex Roles* 8 (10):1075–1080.

Csikszentmihalyi, M. 1982. Does being human matter? On some interpretive problems of comparative ludology. *Behavioral and Brain Science* 5:166.

Dunn, J., and N. Dale. 1984. I a Daddy: Two-year-olds' collaboration in joint pretend play with a sibling and with a mother. In *Symbolic Play*, ed. I. Bretherton, 131–158. New York: Academic Press.

Edwards, C. P. 2000. Children's play in cross-cultural perspective: A new look at the six cultures study. *Cross-Cultural Research: The Journal of Comparative Social Science* 34:318–338.

Eisenberg, N., K. Tryon, and E. Cameron. 1984. The relation of preschoolers' peer interaction to their sex-typed toy choices. *Child Development* 55:1044–1050.

Erikson, E. H. 1968. *Identity: Youth and crisis.* New York: W. W. Norton & Co.

Fabes, R. A., C. L. Martin, and L. D. Hanish. May/June 2003. Young children's play qualities in same-, other-, and mixed-sex peer groups. *Child Development* 74 (3):921–932.

Farver, J. M., Y. K. Kim, and Y. Lee-Shin. 2000. Within cultural differences: Examining individual differences in Korean-American and European-American preschoolers' social pretend play. *Journal of Cross-Cultural Psychology* 31:583–602.

Farver, J. M., and Y. Lee-Shin. 2000. Acculturation and Korean-American children's social and play behavior. *Social Development* 9:316–336.

Fein, G. G. 1981. Pretend play in childhood: An integrative review. *Child Development* 52:1095–1118.

Foss, K. 2002. All I want for Christmas is a bombed-out dollhouse. *Common Dreams News Center* http://www.commondreams.org/views02/1123-01.htm. Accessed September 2004.

Gelman, R., and J. Lucariello. 2002. Role of learning in cognitive development. In *Steven's handbook of experimental psychology,* 3rd ed., Vol. 3, *Learning, motivation and emotion,* ed. H. Pashler and R. Gallistel, 395–443. New York: John Wiley & Sons, Inc.

Goencue, A., J. Mistry, and C. Mosier. 2000. Cultural variations in the play of toddlers. *International Journal of Behavioral Development* 24:321–329.

Golomb, C., and R. Kuersten. 1996. On the transition from pretense play to reality: What are the rules of the game? *British Journal of Developmental Psychology* 14:203–217.

Graeber, L. 2003. Not enemies, but children. Family Fare, *The New York Times,* December 26.

Haight, W. L., X. Wang, H. H. Fung, K. Williams, and J. Mintz. 1999. Universal, developmental, and variable aspects of young children's play: A cross-cultural comparison of pretending at home. *Child Development* 70:1477–1488.

Harris, P. 2000. *The work of the imagination.* Malden, MA: Blackwell.

Hartmann, W. 2002. Toy culture in preschool education and children's toy preferences in Viennese kindergartens (Austria) and in German-speaking kindergartens in South Tyrol (Italy). Paper presented in the Symposium on Toy Culture in Preschool Education and Children's Toy Preferences: Common Features and Differences in Europe and Across the World. World Congress—Toys, Games, and Media, London, UK, August 19–22.

Howes, C., and A. G. Wishard. 2003. Revisiting sharing meaning: Looking through the lens of culture and linking shared pretend play through proto narrative developent to emergent literacy. In *Children's play: The roots of reading,* ed. E. Zigler, D. G. Singer, and S. Bishop-Joseph, 143–158. Washington, DC: Zero to Three.

Hughes, F. P. 1991. *Children, play, and development.* Boston: Allyn and Bacon.

Ivory, J. J., and J. A. McCollum. 1999. Effects of social and isolate toys on social play in an inclusive setting. *Journal of Special Education* 32(4):238–243.

Jenvey, V. and H. Jenvey. 2002. Toy culture in Australian preschools and Australian children's toy preferences. Paper presented in the Symposium on Toy Culture in Preschool Education and Children's Toy Preferences: Common Features and Differences in Europe and Across the World. World Congress—Toys, Games, and Media, London, UK, August 19–22.

Kazura, K. 2000. Father's qualitative and quantitative involvement: An investigation of attachment, play, and social interactions. *Journal of Men's Studies* 9:41–57.

Kinzer, S. 2003. Dolls as role models, neither Barbie nor Britney. *The New York Times,* November 6.

Kishimoto, T. M. 2002. Toys and public policy for child education in Brazil. Paper presented in the Symposium on Toy Culture in Preschool Education and Children's Toy Preferences: Common Features and Differences in Europe and Across the World. World Congress—Toys, Games, and Media, London, UK, August 19–22.

Lee, J. 2002. Making toys for children too mature for most toys. *The New York Times,* February 12.

LEGO Learning Institute. 2002, April. *Cross-cultural comparison of parental attitudes toward play, learning, and time.* Billund, Denmark: LEGO Learning Institute.

Leslie, A. 1987. Pretense and representations: The origin of theory of mind. *Psychological Review* 94:412–426.

Liang, P. H. 1999. Playing with computers: Multiple correlates of young children's computer play behaviors. *Dissertation Abstracts International,* 59, 2844.

Maccoby, E. E. 1980. *Social development: Psychological growth and the parent-child relationship.* New York: Harcourt Brace Jovanovich, Inc.

Manning, M. L. 1998. Play development from ages eight to twelve. In *Play from birth to twelve and beyond,* ed. D. P. Fromberg and D. Bergen, 154–161. New York: Garland Publishing, Inc.

Mead, R. 2001. Wizards in training. *The New Yorker,* December 24.

Mischel, W., Y. Shoda, and M. L. Rodriguez. 1989. Delay of gratification in children. *Science* 244:933–938.

Murphy, L. B. 1956. *Colin: A normal child.* New York: Basic Books, Inc.

Nabokov, V. 1951. *Speak memory: A memoir.* London: Gollanz.

O'Brien, K. 1999. New toy ideas dance in the heads of precocious inventors. *The New York Times,* December 9.

Pennell, G. E. 1999. Doing gender with Santa: Gender-typing in children's toy preferences. *Dissertation Abstracts International,* 59(8-B).

Phillips, A. T., H. M. Wellman, and E. S. Spelke. 2002. Infants' ability to connect gaze and emotional expression to intentional action. *Cognition* 85 (1):53–78.

Piaget, J. 1962. *Play, dreams, and imitation in childhood.* New York: W. W. Norton.

PR Newswire. 2003. The nation's state of play for our children. London, September 2, 2003. http:/media.netpr/PressOffice/print_version_jsp?prs_id= 6391.

Pulaski, M. A. 1973. Toys and imaginative play. In *The child's world of make-believe,* ed. J. L. Singer, 74–103. New York: Academic Press.

Repetti, R. 1984. Determinants of children's sex stereotyping: Parental sex-role traits and television viewing. *Personality and Social Psychology Bulletin* 10:457–468.

Rochat, P. 2001. *The infant's world.* Cambridge, MA: Harvard University Press.

Roopnarine, J. L., M. Ahmeduzzaman, Z. Hossain, and N. B. Riegraf. 1992. Parent-infant rough play: Its cultural specificity. *Early Education and Development* 3:298–311.

Rosen, C., D. Schwebel, and J. L. Singer. 1997. Preschoolers' attributions of mental states in pretense. *Child Development* 66:1133–1142.

Russ, S. 2004. *Play in child development and psychotherapy: Toward empirically supported practice.* Mahwah, NJ: Lawrence Erlbaum Associates.

Russ, S. W., A. L. Robins, and B. A. Christiano. 1999. Pretend play: Longitudinal prediction of creativity and affect in fantasy in children. *Creativity Research Journal* 12 (2):129–139.

Sawada, H., H. Minami. 1997. Peer group play and co-childrearing in Japan: A historical ethnography of a fishing community. *Journal of Applied Developmental Psychology* 18 (4):513–526.

Schwebel, D., C. Rosen, and J. L. Singer. 1999. Preschoolers' pretend play and theory of mind: The role of jointly-conducted pretense. *British Journal of Developmental Psychology* 17:333–348.

Serbin, L. A., L. Moller, K. Powlishta, and J. Gulko. 1991. The emergence of gender segregation and behavioral compatibility in toddlers' peer preferences. Paper presented in symposium *Gender differences in relationships* at the Society for Research in Child Development, Seattle, WA, April.

Shiner, R. L., A. S., Masten, and J. M. Roberts. 2003. Childhood personality foreshadows adult personality and life outcomes two decades later. *Journal of Personality* 71 (6):1145–1170.

Singer, D. G. 1993. *Playing for their lives: Helping troubled children through play therapy.* New York: The Free Press.

Singer, D. G. 2002a. Peace and healing. *Child Art* 5 (January–March): 6–7.

Singer, D. G. 2002b. The power of playing together. *Scholastic Parent & Child* 9:43–47.

Singer, D. G. 2002c. Team building in the classroom. *Early Childhood Today* 16:37–41.

Singer, D. G., P. Cohen, and R. Tower. 1978. A developmental study of animistic thinking: Preschoolers through the elderly. In *Piagetian theory and the helping professions: Seventh annual conference*, vol. 1, ed. R. Weismann, R. Brown, P. J. Levinson, and P. A. Taylor, 237–243. Los Angeles, CA: Children's Hospital of Los Angeles.

Singer, D. G., and T. A. Revenson. 1996. *A Piaget primer: How a child thinks.* Rev. ed. New York: Penguin.

Singer, D. G., and J. L. Singer. 1990. *The house of make-believe*. Cambridge, MA: Harvard University Press.

Singer, D. G., and J. L. Singer. 2001. *Make-believe: Games and activities for imaginative play*. Washington, DC: American Psychological Association Books, Magination Press.

Singer, J. L., and D. G. Singer. 1981. *Television, imagination, and aggression: A study of preschoolers*. Hillsdale, NJ: Lawrence Erlbaum, Publishers.

Smilansky, S. 1986. *The effects of sociodramatic play on disadvantaged preschool children*. New York: Wiley.

Smith, L. J. 1994. A content analysis of gender differences in children's advertising. *Journal of Broadcasting and Electronic Media* 38 (3):323–337.

Spelke, E. S., C. von Hofsten, and R. Kestenbaum. 1989. Object perception in infancy: Interaction of spatial and kinetic information for object boundaries. *Developmental Psychology* 25:185–196.

Stayna, H. J. 2000. Maternal differences in doll play behavior with male and female toddlers. Ph.D. diss. *Dissertation Abstracts International*, Section B, The Sciences and Engineering, Vol. 60(8-B).

Sutton-Smith, B. 1982. The epistemology of the play theorist. *Behavioral and Brain Science* 5:170–171.

Thornburg, H. D. 1979. *The bubblegum years: Sticking with kids from 9–13*. Tucson, AZ: H.E.L.P. Books.

Tower, R. 1984–1985. Preschoolers' imaginativeness: Subtypes, correlates, and maladaptive extremes. *Imagination, Cognition and Personality* 4:349–364.

Toy Industry Association. 2004. http://www.toy.tia.org. Accessed September 12, 2004.

Tudge, J., S. Lee, and S. Putnam. 1995. Young children's play in socio-cultural context: South Korea and the United States. Paper presented at the biennial meeting of the Society for Research in Child Development, Indianapolis, IN.

Vandenberg, B. 1982. Play: A concept in need definitions? In *The play of children: Current theory and research*, ed. D. J. Pepler and K. H. Rubin, 15–20. Basel, Switzerland: Karger.

Vandenberg, B. 1998. Real and not real: A vital development dichotomy. In *Multiple perspectives on play in early childhood*, ed. O. Saracho and B. Spodek, 295–305. New York: State University Press.

von Hofsten, C., Q. Feng, and E. S. Spelke. 2000. Object representation and predictive action in infancy. *Developmental Science* 3:193–205.

von Klitzing, K., K. Kelsay, R. N. Emde, J. Robinson, and S. Schmitz. 2000. *Journal of the American Academy of Child & Adolescent Psychiatry* 39 (8):1017–1023.

Vygotsky, L. S. 1976. Play and its role in the mental development of the child.

In *Play: Its role in development and evolution*, ed. J. S. Bruner, A. J. Jolly, and K. Sylva, 537–554. New York: Basic Books, Inc.

Vygotsky, L. S. 1978. *Mind in society: The development of higher mental processes.* Cambridge, MA: Harvard University Press.

Wang, J., J. Elicker, M. McMullen, and S. Mao. 2001. *American and Chinese teachers' beliefs about early childhood curriculum.* Poster presented at the biennial meeting of the Society for Research in Child Development, Minneapolis, MN, April.

Weber, D. W., and D. G. Singer. 2004. The media habits of infants and toddlers: Findings from a parent survey. *Zero to Three* 25 (11):30–36.

Weissman, D. 1999. Gender of preschoolers' preferred play partners: Children's perspectives. Ph.D. diss. *Dissertation Abstracts International*, 59(12-B).

Wellmann, H. M. 1990. *The child's theory of mind.* Cambridge, MA: Massachusetts Institute of Technology Press.

Whiting, B. B. 1963. *Six cultures: Studies of child rearing.* New York: Wiley.

Wood, S. 2001. The way we play and what it teaches our children. *Nick Jr. Magazine* 11:36–45. August/September.

Wyver, S. R., and S. H. Spence. 1999. Play and divergent problem solving: Evidence supporting a reciprocal relationship. *Early Education and Development* 10 (4):419–444.

Young, R., and E. Davies. 2000. Teddy vies with LEGO in play-off for toy of century. *The New York Times,* January 29.

3. Television and Imagination

ABC News. 2001. Fearful kids: Report from Sesame Workshop. June 4, 2001. http://www.abcnews.go.com.

Ahmad, A. 1979. Television programme preference of Pakistani children. *Pakistan Psychological Studies* 3:25–57.

American Academy of Pediatrics. 1995. Children, adolescents, and television (RE 9538), Statement by the Committee on Communications. *Pediatrics* 96 (4), 786.

Anderson D. R., A. C. Huston, K. L. Schmitt, D. L. Linebarger, and J. C. Wright. 2001. Early childhood television viewing and adolescent behavior: The recontact study. *Monographs of the Society for Research in Child Development* 66 (1)1–147.

Beagles-Roos, J., and I. Gat. 1983. Specific impact of radio and television on children's story comprehension. *Journal of Educational Psychology* 75:128–137.

Bickham, D. S., J. C. Wright, and A. C. Huston. 2001. Attention, comprehension, and the educational influences of television. In *Handbook of children and the media*, ed. D. G. Singer and J. L. Singer, 101–119. Thousand Oaks, CA: Sage Publications, Inc.

Bradbury, R. 1967. *Fahrenheit 451*. New York: Simon and Schuster.

Brown, J. A. 2001. Media literacy and critical television viewing in education. In *Handbook of children and the media*, ed. D. G. Singer and J. L. Singer, 681–697. Thousand Oaks, CA: Sage Publications, Inc.

Bruce, R. 1989. Creativity and instructional technology: Great potential, imperfectly studied. *Contemporary Educational Psychology* 14 (3):241–256.

Calvert, S. L., and J. A. Kotler. 2003. Lessons from children's television: The impact of the Children's Television Act on children's learning. *Applied Developmental Psychology* 24:275–335.

Cantor, J. 1998. *"Mommy, I'm scared": How TV and movies frighten children and what we can do to protect them*. San Diego, CA: Harcourt Brace.

Cantor, J. 2001. The media and children's fears, anxieties, and perceptions of danger. In *Handbook of Children and the Media*, ed. D. G. Singer and J. L. Singer, 207–221. Thousand Oaks, CA: Sage Publications, Inc.

Cantor, J., and A. I. Nathanson. 1996. Children's fright reactions to television news. *Journal of Communication* 46 (4):139–152.

Captain Planet Foundation. 2003. Captain Planet Foundation: Back by popular demand. February 7, 2003. http://www.captainplanetfdn.org.

Children's Advertising Review Unit. Self-regulatory guidelines for children's advertising. www.caru.org/guidelines/index.asp. Accessed September 19, 2004.

Children's Television Act of 1990. Publ. Law No. 101–437, 104 Stat. 996–1000, Codified at 47 USC Sections 303a, 303b, 394.

Comstock, G., and E. Scharrer. 2001. The use of television and other film-related media. In *Handbook of children and the media*, ed. D. G. Singer and J. L. Singer, 47–72. Thousand Oaks, CA: Sage Publications, Inc.

Davies, M. M. 1997. *Fake, fact, and fantasy: Children's interpretations of television reality*. Hillsdale, NJ: Lawrence Erlbaum Associates, Inc.

Desmond, R. 2001. Free Reading. In *Handbook of Children and the Media*, ed. D. G. Singer and J. L. Singer, 29–45. Thousand Oaks, CA: Sage Publications, Inc.

Detenber, B. H., R. F., Simons, J. E. Reiss. 2000. The emotional significance of color in television presentations. *Media Psychology* 2 (4):331–355.

Dominus, S. 2004. She speaks 3-year-old. *The New York Times,* January 4.

Emmison, M., and L. Goldman. 1997. "The Sooty Show" laid bear: Children, puppets, and make-believe. *Childhood: A Global Journal of Child Research* 4 (3):325–342.

Federal Communications Commission. 1996. *Policies and rules concerning children's television programming: Revision of programming policies for television broadcast stations*. MM Docket No. 93–48.

Federal Communications Commission. 1997. Policies and rules concerning children's television programming: Revision of programming policies for television broadcast stations, 73. 671(c)(6).

Feuerhahn, N. 1984–1985. Social representation of an image of self in drawing: Study of 9 to 12 year old children in two contrasting sociocultural milieux. *Bulletin de Psychologie* 38 (4–7):267–273.

Fisch, S. M., and L. Bernstein. 2001. Formative research revealed: Methodological and process issues in formative research. In *"G" is for growing,* ed. S. M. Fisch and R. T. Truglio, 39–60. Mahwah, NJ: Lawrence Erlbaum Associates, Publishers.

French, J., and S. Pena. 1991. Children's hero play of the 20th century: Changes resulting from television's influence. *Child Study Journal* 21 (2):79–94.

Gotz, M., D. Lemish, A. Aidman, and H. Moon. 2003. The role of media in children's make-believe worlds. *Televizion* 16 (1): 28–39:28–39.

Greenfield, P. M., and J. Beagles-Roos. 1988. Radio vs. television: Their cognitive impact on children of different socioeconomic and ethnic groups. *Journal of Communication* 38 (2):71–92.

Greenfield, P. M., D. Farrar, and J. Beagles-Roos. 1986. Is the medium the message? An experimental comparison of the effects of radio and television on imagination. *Journal of Applied Developmental Psychology* 7:201–218.

Greenfield, P. M., E. Yut, M. Chung, D. Land, H. Kreider, M. Pantoja, and K. Horsley. 1993. The program-length commercial: A study of the effects of television/toy tie-ins on imaginative play. In *Children and television: Images in a changing sociocultural world,* ed. G. L. Berry and J. K. Asamen, 53–72. Newbury Park, CA: Sage Publications.

Groebel, J. 1998. *The UNESCO global study on media violence.* A joint project of UNESCO, the World Organization of the Scout Movement, and Ultrecht University. Paris: UNESCO.

Groebel, J. 2001. Media violence in cross-cultural perspective: A global study on children's media behavior and some educational implications. In *Handbook of Children and the Media,* ed. D. G. Singer and J. L. Singer, 255–268. Thousand Oaks, CA: Sage Publications, Inc.

Hake, K. 1999. Not without research! The "Teletubbies" in Norway. *Televizion* 12 (2):13–14.

Harris, P. 2000. *The work of the imagination.* Oxford, UK: Blackwell Publishers, Ltd.

Harrison, L. F., and T. M. Williams. 1986. Television and cognitive development. In *The impact of television: A natural experiment in three communities,* ed. T. M. Williams, 87–142. San Diego, CA: Academic Press.

Hayes, D. S., S. B. Kelly, and M. Mandel. 1986. Media differences in children's story synopses: Radio and television contrasted. *Journal of Educational Psychology* 78 (5):341–346.

Hobbs, R., and R. Frost. 2003. Measuring the acquisition of media-literacy skills. *Reading Research Quarterly* 38 (3):330–355.

Hoekstra, S. J., R. J. Harris, and A. L. Helmick. 1999. Autobiographical memories about the experience of seeing frightening movies in childhood. *Media Psychology* 1 (2):117–140.

Hoffner, C. 1996. Children's wishful identification and parasocial interaction with favorite television characters. *Journal of Broadcasting & Electronic Media* 40 (3):389–342.

Hortin, J. A. 1982. Innovative approaches to using media in the classroom. *Educational Technology* 22 (5):18–19.

Huston, A. C., and J. C. Wright. 1989. Children's processing of television: The informative functions of formal features. In J. Bryant and D. R. Anderson, *Children's understanding of television: Research on attention and comprehension*, 37–68. New York: Academic Press.

Huston, A. C., D. R. Anderson, J. C. Wright, D. L. Linebarger, and K. L. Schmitt. 2001. "Sesame Street" viewers as adolescents: The recontact study. In *"G" is for growing*, ed. S. M. Fisch and R. T. Truglio, 131–143. Mahwah, NJ: Lawrence Erlbaum Associates, Publishers.

James, N. C., and T. A. McCain. 1982. Television games preschool children play: Patterns, themes, and uses. *Journal of Broadcasting* 26:783–800.

Jordan, A. B. 1992. Social class temporal orientation, and mass media use within the family system. *Critical Studies in Mass Communication* 9:374–386.

Jordan, A. B. 1996. *The state of children's television: An examination of quantity, quality, and industry beliefs.* Philadelphia, PA: The Annenberg Public Policy Center of the University of Pennsylvania, Report Series #2. pp. 3–45.

Kaiser Family Foundation. 1999. *Kids and media at the new millennium: A comprehensive analysis of children's media use.* Menlo Park, CA: Kaiser Family Foundation.

Kleeman, D. W. 2001. Prix Jeunesse as a force for cultural diversity. In *Handbook of children and the media*, ed. D. G. Singer and J. L. Singer, 521–531. Thousand Oaks, CA: Sage Publications, Inc.

Kodaira, S. I., and Y. Takahashi. 2001. New developments in media use in schools. *Nippon Hoso Kyokai Broadcasting Culture & Research*, 17:5–18.

Komaya, M. 2004. Media literacy practices for Japanese elementary schools. In *Invitation to media literacy*, National Institute for Educational Policy research (ed.). ISSN 4-491-01948-7, pp. 49–64. Tokyo: toyokan Shuppansha.

Komaya, M., and J. Bowyer. 2000. College-educated mothers' ideas about television and their active mediation of viewing by three-to five-year-old children: Japan and the U.S.A. *Journal of Broadcasting & Electronic Media* 44 (3):349–363.

Komaya, M., and T. Muto. 2002. Media education/media literacy: Media literacy for Japanese third graders. *News from The UNESCO International Clearinghouse on Children, Youth, and Media* 6 (2):7.

Kravetz, S. 2002. 'Are we there yet?' becomes 'Where's the Barney tape?' *The New York Times*, May 31.

LeBlanc, A. N. 2003. Prison is a member of their family. *The New York Times*, January 12.

Lillard, A. S., and D. Sobel. 1999. Lion king or puppies: The influence of fantasy on children's understanding of pretense. *Developmental Science* 2 (1):75–80.

Lohr, P. 1999. The world of the "Teletubbies." *Televizion* 12 (2):2, 60.

Mander, J. 1978. *Four arguments for the elimination of television.* New York: William Morrow & Company, Inc.

Mares, M., and E. H. Woodard. 2001. Prosocial effects on children's social interactions. In *Handbook of Children and the Media*, ed. D. G. Singer and J. L. Singer, 183–205. Thousand Oaks, CA: Sage Publications, Inc.

McCollum, J. F., Jr. 1999. Children's consumption of fast-paced television as a predictor of their creativity and vigilance. *Dissertation Abstracts International*, 59(9-A).

McLuhan, M. 1964. *Understanding media: The extension of man.* New York: McGraw-Hill.

Meringoff, L. K., M. Vibbert, H. Kelly, and C. Char. 1981. *"How shall you take your story, with or without pictures?" Progress report on a program of media research with children.* Paper presented at the biennial meeting of the Society for the Research in Child Development, Boston, MA.

Miron, D. 2000. The relationship between fantasy in children's television and preschooler's creativity in solving problems. *Dissertation Abstracts International* 60(11-A).

Moore, M. 2000. Turkish broadcast board finds *Pokemon* unfit for children. *The Washington Post*, December 12, 2000. http://washingtonpost.com/wp-dyn/articles/A57842_2000Dec11.html.

Mullin-Rindler, N., and C. Fucigna. 1995. Television use in home-based child care at 24 months. Paper presented at the biennial meeting of the Society for Research in Child Development, Indianapolis, IN, March-April.

Mumme, D. L., and A. Fernald. 2003. The infant as onlooker: Learning from emotional reactions observed in a television scenario. *Child Development* 74 (1):221–237.

Muto, T., and M. Komaya. 2003. *TV mysteries: Ukkie goes behind the scenes!*

Video tape and Guide book. Tokyo, Japan: The Japanese Ministry of Pubic Management, Home Affairs, and Posts and Telecommunications.

Nathanson, A. I., and J. Cantor. 2000. Reducing the aggressive-promoting effect of violent cartoons by increasing children's fictional involvement with the victim: A study of active mediation. *Journal of Broadcasting & Electronic Media* 44 (1):125–142.

Nicolini, C., A. Cocchini, and G. Fara. 1992. Fantasy, reality, humour: Children and adolescents facing television spots. *Eta Evolutiva* 43:3–11.

Peterson, C. C., J. L. Peterson, and J. Carroll. 1986. Television viewing and imaginative problem solving during preadolescence. *Journal of Genetic Psychology* 147 (1):61–67.

Reeves, T. C., and F. D. Atkinson. 1977. Stimulating creativity in the media center. *Audiovisual Instruction* 22 (10):34–35.

Rideout, V. J., E. A. Vanderwater, and E. A. Wartella. 2003. Zero to six: Electronic media in the lives of infants, toddlers, and preschoolers. Report, The Kaiser Family Foundation, Menlo Park, CA.

Rosenkoetter, L. J., S. E. Rosenkoetter, R. A. Ozretich, and A. C. Acock. 2004. Mitigating the harmful effects of violent television. *Journal of Applied Developmental Psychology.* 25–47.

Rubenstein, D. J. 2000. Stimulating children's creativity and curiosity: Does content and medium matter? *Journal of Creative Behavior* 34 (1):1–17.

Runco, M. A., and K. Pezdek. 1984. The effect of television and radio on children's creativity. *Human Communication Research* 11:109–120.

Salamon, J. 2002. Children's TV catches up with how kids watch. *The New York Times,* June 9.

Salomon, G., and T. Leigh. 1984. Predispositions about learning from print and television. *Journal of Communication* 34 (2):119–135.

Schmitt, K. M. 2001. Infants, toddlers, and television: The ecology of the home. *Zero to Three* 22 (2):17–23.

Simons, M. 1989. The Amazon's savvy Indians. *New York Times Magazine,* February 26.

Singer, D. G., and J. L. Singer. 1981a. Television and the developing imagination of the child. *Journal of Broadcasting* 25 (4):373–387.

Singer, D. G., and J. L. Singer. 1981b, March. Television and reading in the development of imagination. In *Children's Literature* Vol. IX, 126–136. New Haven, CT: Yale University Press.

Singer, D. G., and J. L. Singer. 1992. Television influences. In *Encyclopedia of early childhood education,* ed. L. R. Williams and D. P. Fromberg, 374–377. New York: Garland.

Singer, D. G., and J. L. Singer, 1998. Developing critical viewing skills and media literacy in children. In *The Annals,* ed. K. H. Jamison and A. B.

Jordan, 164–179. Philadelphia, PA: The American Academy of Political and Social Science.

Singer, D. G., D. M. Zuckerman, and J. L. Singer. 1980. Helping elementary school children learn about TV. *Journal of Communication* 30 (3):84–93.

Singer, J. L. 1980. The powers and limitations of television: A cognitive-affective analysis. In *The entertainment function of television,* ed. P. Tannenbaum and R. Abeles, 31–65 Hillsdale, NJ: Erlbaum Associates.

Singer, J. L., and D. G. Singer. 1979. Come back, Mr. Rogers, come back. *Psychology Today* 12:56–60.

Singer, J. L., and D. G. Singer. 1986. Family experiences and television viewing as predictors of children's imagination, restlessness, and aggression. *Journal of Social Issues* 42 (3):107–124.

Singer, J. L., and D. G. Singer. 1993. *A role for television in the enhancement of children's readiness to learn: In preparation for a report to the Congress of the United States.* New Haven, CT: Yale University Family Television Research and Consultation Center.

Singer, J. L., and D. G. Singer. 1998. "Barney & Friends" as entertainment and education: Evaluating the quality and effectiveness of a television series for preschool children. In *Research paradigms, television, and social behavior,* ed. J. K. Asamen and G. Berry 305–367. Beverly Hills, CA: Sage.

Singer, J. L., D. G. Singer, and W. Rapaczynski. 1984a. Children's imagination as predicted by family patterns and television viewing: A longitudinal study. *Genetic Psychology Monographs* 110:43–69.

Singer, J. L., D. G. Singer, and W. Rapaczynski. 1984b. Family patterns and television viewing as predictors of children's beliefs and aggression. *Journal of Communication* 34 (2):73–89.

Skeen, P., M. H. Brown, and D. K. Osborn. 1982. Young children's perception of "real" and "pretend" on television. *Perceptual & Motor Skills* 54 (3):883–887.

Stipp, H. 1999. Under fire from American programme criticism. *Televizion* 12 (2):26–27.

Sullivan, J. L., and A. B. Jordan. 1999. Playing by the rules: Impact and implementation of children's educational television regulations among local broadcasters. *Communication Law and Policy* 4:483–511.

Tower, R., D. G. Singer, J. L. Singer, and A. Biggs. 1979. Differential effects of television programming on preschoolers' cognition and play. *Journal of Orthopsychiatry* 49 (2):265–281.

Ulisse. 2000, Spring. Interview with Steven Spielberg, p. 128.

Valkenburg, P. M. 2001. Television and the child's developing imagination. In *Handbook of Children and the Media,* ed. D. G. Singer and J. L. Singer, 121–134. Thousand Oaks, CA: Sage Publications, Inc.

Valkenburg, P. M., J. Cantor, and A. L. Peeters. 1999. *Fright reactions to television: A child survey.* Paper presented at the meeting of the Instructional and Developmental Communication Division of the 49th Annual Conference of the International Communication Association, San Francisco, CA, May.

Valkenburg, P. M., and S. C. Janssen. 1999. What do children value in entertainment programs? A cross-cultural investigation. *Journal of Communication* 49:3–21.

Valkenburg, P. M., and T.H.A. Van Der Voort. 1994. Influence of TV on daydreaming and creative imagination: A review of research. *Psychological Bulletin* 116 (2):316–339.

Valkenburg, P. M., M. W. Vooijs, T. H. Van der Voort, and O. Wiegman. 1992. The influence of television on children's fantasy styles: A secondary analysis. *Imagination, Cognition, & Personality* 12 (1):55–67.

Van den Bulck, J., and B. Van den Bergh. 2000. The influence of perceived parental guidance patterns on children's media use; Gender differences and media displacement. *Journal of Broadcasting & Electronic Media* 44 (3):329–348.

Van der Voort, T.H.A., and P. M. Valkenburg. 1994. Television's impact on fantasy play: A review of research. *Developmental Review* 14 (1):227–251.

Viemeroe, V., and S. Paajanen. 1992. The role of fantasies and dreams in the TV viewing aggression relationship. *Aggressive Behavior* 18 (2):109–116.

Weber, D. W., and D. G. Singer. 2004. The media habits of infants and toddlers: Findings from a parent survey. *Zero to Three* 25 (11):30–36.

Wei, B. 1996. Chinese families and media communications. *International Play Journal* 4:201–207.

Weiss, A. J., and B. Wilson. 1996. Emotional portrayals in family television series that are popular among children. *Journal of Broadcasting & Electronic Media* 40 (1):1–29.

Woodard, E. H., IV. 2000. *Media in the home 2000: The fifth annual survey of parents and children.* Philadelphia, PA: The Annenberg Public Policy Center of the University of Pennsylvania, Survey Series No. 7.

4. Violent Themes in Play, TV Content, and Video Games

Anderson, C. A. 2002. Violent video games and aggressive thoughts, feelings and behaviors. In *Children in the digital age,* ed. S. L. Calvert, A. B. Jordan, and R. R. Cocking, 101–119. Westport, CT: Praeger Publishers.

Anderson, C. A., and B. J. Bushman. 2001. Effects of video games on aggressive behavior, cognition, aggressive affect, physiological arousal, and prosocial behavior: A meta-analytic review of the scientific literature. *Psychological Science* 12 (5): 353–359.

Auerbach, S. 1991. The dangers of war toys. In *WarChild Monitor International,* Spring: 7. Eureka Springs, AR: Center on War & the Child.

Bandura, A. 1877. *Social learning theory.* Englewood Cliffs, NJ: Prentice Hall.

Barron, R. A. 1977. *Human aggression.* New York: Plenum.

Bettelheim, B. 1966. *The uses of enchantment.* New York: Random House.

Brown, J. A. 2001. Media literacy and critical television viewing in education. In *Handbook of children and the media,* ed. D. G. Singer and J. L. Singer, 681–698. Thousand Oaks: Sage Publications, Inc.

Bushman, B. J., and C. A. Anderson 2001. Media violence and the American public: Scientific facts versus media misinformation. *American Psychologist* 56:477–489.

Bushman, B. J., and L. R. Huesmann. 2001. Effects of televised violence on aggression. In *Handbook of children and the media,* ed. D. G. Singer and J. L. Singer, 223–254. Thousand Oaks: Sage Publications, Inc.

Calvert, S. L., and S. L. Tan. 1994. Impact of virtual reality on young adults' physiological arousal and aggressive thoughts: Interaction versus observation. *Journal of Applied Developmental Psychology* 15:125–139.

Cheng, T. L., R. A. Brenner, J. L. Wright, H. C. Sachs, P. Moyer, and M. Rao. 2003. Community norms on toy guns. *Pediatrics* 111 (1):75–79.

Dill, K. E., D. A. Gentile, W. A. Richter, and J. C. Dill. 2001. *Violence, race, sex, and age in video games: A content analysis.* Paper presented at the annual meeting of the American Psychological Association, San Francisco, CA, August.

Dominick, J. R. 1984. Video games, television violence, and aggression in teenagers. *Journal of Communication* 34 (2): 136–147.

Elmer-DeWitt, P. 1993. The amazing video game boom. *Time,* September 27.

Gerbner, G., L. Gross, M. Morgan, and N. Signorielli. 1994. Growing up with television: The cultivation perspective. In *Media effects: Advances in theory and research,* ed. J. Bryant and D. Zillman, 17–41. Hillsdale, NJ: Lawrence Erlbaum.

Groebel, J. 2001. Media violence in cross-cultural perspective: A global study on children's media behavior and some educational implications. In *Handbook of children and the media,* ed. D. G. Singer and J. L. Singer, 255–268. Thousand Oaks: Sage Publications, Inc.

Hall, J. 2003. Professor play station. *The New York Times,* January 4.

Hallo, W. 1993. Games in the Biblical world. *Eretz-Israel* (24):82–88. The Israel Exploration Society.

Hamilton, W. L. 2003. Toymakers study troops, and vice versa. *The New York Times,* Sunday Styles, March 30.

Harmon, A. 2003. More than just a game, but how close to reality? *The New York Times,* April 3.

Herbert, B. 2002. The gift of mayhem. *The New York Times,* November 28.

Huesmann, L. R. 1986. Psychological processes promoting the relation between exposure to media violence and aggressive behavior by the viewer. *Journal of Social Issues* 42 (3):125–140.

Huesmann, L. R. 1995. *Screen violence and real violence: Understanding the link* (brochure). Auckland, New Zealand: Media Aware.

Huesmann, L. R. 1998. The role of social information processing and cognitive schemas in the acquisition and maintenance of habitual aggressive behavior. In *Human aggression: Theories, research, and implications for policy*, ed. R. G. Geen and E. Donnerstein, 73–109. New York: Academic Press.

Huesmann, L. R., and L. Eron 1986. *Television and the aggressive child: A cross-national comparison.* Hillsdale, NJ: Erlbaum Associates.

Huesmann, L. R., J. Moise-Titus, C. L. Podolski, and L. Eron. 2003. Longitudinal relations between children's exposure to TV violence and their aggressive and violent behavior in young adulthood: 1991–1992. *Developmental Psychology* 39 (2):201–221.

Johnson, J., P. Cohen, E. Smalles, S. Kasen, and J. Brook. 2002. Television viewing and aggressive behavior during adolescence and adulthood. *Science,* March, 29 295:2468–2471.

Kaiser Family Foundation. 2003. *Key facts: Parents and Media.* Menlo Park, CA: Kaiser Family Foundation.

Kazdin, A. 2004. Psychotherapy for children and adolescents. In *Bergin and Garfield's handbook of psychotherapy and behavior change*, ed. M. Lambert, 543–589. New York: Wiley.

Kirsh, S. J. 1998. Seeing the world through Mortal-Kombat-colored glasses: Violent video games and the development of a short-term hostile attribution bias. *Childhood: A Global Journal of Child Research* 5:177–184.

Kronenberger, W. G., V. P. Mathews, D. W. Dunn, Y. Wang, E. Wood, M. E. Rembusch, A. M. Giauque, J. T. Lurito, and M. J. Lowe. 2004. Media violence exposure in aggressive and control adolescence: Differences in self- and parent-reported exposure to violence on television and in video games. In *Aggressive Behavior* (in press).

Lefkowitz, M. M., L. D. Eron, L. O. Walder, and L. R. Huesmann. 1977. *Growing up to be violent: A longitudinal study of the development of aggression.* New York: Pergamon Press.

Levin, D. 2000–2001. *Toy action guide.* West Somerville, MA: Teachers Resisting Unhealthy Children's Entertainment.

Lubell, S. 2002. Suicide bomber game tests the boundaries of taste. *The New York Times,* December 5.

Moore, M. 2002. *Bowling for Columbine.* Alliance Atlantis and United Artists presentation; Salter Street Films and VIF 2 production; A Dog Eat Dog Films production.

Napoli, L. 2003. War by other means: Drawing a line with real combat, video game commanders press on. *The New York Times,* March 27.

Paik, H., and G. Comstock. 1994. The effects of television violence on anti-social behavior: A meta-analysis. *Communication Research* 21 (4):516–546.

Pearl, D., L. Bouthilet, and J. Lazar. 1982. *Television and behavior: Ten years of scientific progress and implications for the eighties.* Rockville, MD: National Institute of Mental Health, US Dept. of Health and Human Services, DHHS publication (ADM) 82–1196.

Penn, Schoen, and Berland Associates and American Viewpoint. 2003. The 2003 Common Sense Media Poll of American Parents. May 2003. http://www.commonsensemedia.org/about/press/ParentspollMay212003.ppt. Accessed June 6, 2003.

Provenzo, E. F., Jr. 1991. *Video kids: Making sense of Nintendo.* Cambridge, MA: Harvard University Press.

Rapaczynski, W., D. G. Singer, and J. L. Singer. 1982. Teaching television: A curriculum for young children. *Journal of Communication* 32 (2):46–55.

Robinson, T. N., M. L. Wilde, L. C. Navracruz, K. F. Haydel, and A. Varady. 2001. Effects of reducing children's television and video game use on aggressive behavior: A randomized controlled trial. *Archives of Pediatric Adolescent Medicine* 155:17–23.

Rosenkoetter, L. I., and D. G. Singer. 1995. Answering the Power Rangers question. *Better Viewing,* 10–11, 16. Nov/Dec.

Schuster, M. A., B. D. Stein, L. H. Jaycox, R. L. Collins, G. N. Marshall, M. N. Elliot, A. J. Zhou, D. E. Kanouse, J. L. Morrison, and S. H. Berry. 2001. A national survey of stress reactions after the September 11, 2001, terrorist attacks. *New England Journal of Medicine* 345 (20):1507–1512.

Silvern, S. B., and P. A. Williamson. 1987. The effects of video game play on young children's aggression, fantasy, and prosocial behavior. *Journal of Applied Developmental Psychology* 8:453–462.

Singer, D. G. and J. L. Singer. 1977. Raising boys who know how to love. *Parent's Magazine,* Lii (12).

Singer, D. G., and J. L. Singer. 1980. Television viewing and aggressive behavior in preschool children: A field study. *Forensic Psychology and Psychiatry,* Annals of the New York Academy of Science, 347:289–303.

Singer, D. G., and J. L. Singer. 1990. *The house of make-believe: Children's play and the developing imagination.* Cambridge, MA: Harvard University Press.

Singer, D. G., and J. L. Singer. 1998. Developing critical viewing skills and media literacy in children. In *The Annals,* ed. K. H. Jamison and A. B.

Jordan, 164–179. Philadelphia, PA: The American Academy of Political and Social Science.

Singer, D. G., J. L. Singer, and D. M. Zuckerman, 1981. *Teaching television.* New York: Dial Press.

Singer, J. L., ed. 1971. *The control of aggression and violence.* New York: Academic Press.

Singer, J. L., ed. 1973. *The child's world of make-believe.* New York: Academic Press.

Singer, J. L., and P. Salovey. 1991. Organized knowledge structures and personality: Person schemas, self-schemas, prototypes, and scripts. In *Person schemas and maladaptive interpersonal patterns*, ed. M. S. Horowitz, 33–79. Chicago: University of Chicago Press.

Singer, J. L., and D. G. Singer. 1981. *Television, imagination, and aggression: A study of preschoolers.* Hillsdale, NJ: Erlbaum Associates.

Singer, J. L., and D. G. Singer. 1986. Family experiences and television viewing as predictors of children's imagination, restlessness, and aggression. *Journal of Social Issues* 42 (3):107–124.

Singer, J. L., D. G. Singer, and W. Rapaczynski. 1984. Family patterns and television viewing as predictors of children's belief and aggression. *Journal of Communication* 34:73–89.

Slaby, R. G. 2002. Media violence effects and potential remedies. In *Securing our children's future: New approaches to juvenile justice and youth violence*, ed. G. Katzmann, 305–337. Washington, DC: The Brookings Institution.

Smith, M. 2003. What parents think about play with violent themes and what they are doing about it. Survey conducted by Leo Shapiro Associates, Chicago. Presented at the Promise of Play Conference, Yale University, March.

Turner, C. W., and D. Goldsmith. 1976. Effects of toy guns and airplanes on children's antisocial free play behavior. *Journal of Experimental Child Psychology* 21:303–315.

von Feilitzen, C., and U. Carlsson, eds. 2002. *Children, young people and media globalisation.* Yearbook 2002. Nordicom, Sweden: The UNESCO International Clearinghouse on Children, Youth, and Media.

Wang, Y., V. P. Mathews, M. J. Lowe, J. Lurito, M. Dzemidzic, and M. D. Phillips. 2002. Effects of violent media exposure by adolescents with disruptive behavior disorder as compared to control subjects: fMRI activation patterns in frontal lobe. Presented at the 88th Scientific Assembly and Annual Meeting of the Radiological Society of North America, Chicago, IL, December 2.

Watson, M. W., C. A. Caswell, K. Smith, and L. Costa. 1999. Psychological antecedents of aggression in childhood. Presented at the symposium Biological and Environmental Pathways to Aggressive Behavior in Children, at the meeting of the Society for Research in Child Development, Albuquerque, NM, April.

Watson, M. W., and Y. Peng. 1992. The relation between toy gun play and children's aggressive behavior. *Early Education Development* 3:370–389.

5. Adrift in Cyberspace: Children and Computer Play

Alborzi, H., A. Druin, J. Montemayor, L. Sherman, G. Taxen, J. Best, J. Hammer, A. Kruskal, A. Lal, T. Plaisant Schwenn, L. Sumida, R. Wagner, and J. Hendler. 2000. Designing story rooms: Interactive storytelling spaces for children. *Proceedings of Designing Interactive Systems (DIS)*.

Anderson, C. A., and B. J. Bushman, 2001. Effects of videogames on aggressive behavior, cognition, aggressive affect, physiological arousal, and prosocial behavior: A meta-analytic review of the scientific literature. *Psychological Science* 12 (5):353–359.

Ashby, N. 2003. Computer and internet use by children and adolescents in 2001. U.S. Department of Education, National Center for Educational Statistics. Report cited in N. Ashby, ed., *The Achiever*, 2(18):3.

Baars, B. 1998. *A cognitive theory of consciousness.* Cambridge, UK: Cambridge University Press.

Brown, J. A. 2001. Media literacy and critical television viewing in education. In *Handbook of children and the media*, ed. D. G. Singer and J. L. Singer, 681–698. Thousand Oaks, CA: Sage Publications, Inc.

Calvert, S. L. 1999. *Children's journey through the information age.* Washington, DC: McGraw-Hill.

Calvert, S. L., A. B. Jordan, and R. R. Cocking, eds. 2002. *Children in the digital age: Influences of electronic media on development.* Westport, CT: Praeger.

Calvert, S. L., B. A. Mahler, S. M. Zehnder, A. Jenkins, and M. Lee. 2003. Gender differences in preadolescent children's online interactions: Symbolic modes of self-presentation and self-expression. *Journal of Applied Developmental Psychology* 24:627–644.

Cole, M. 1996. *Cultural psychology: A once and future discipline.* Cambridge, MA: Harvard University Press.

Colwell, J., and J. Payne. 2000. Negative correlates of computer game play in adolescents. *British Journal of Psychology* 91 (3):295–310.

DeLisi, R., and J. L. Wolford. 2002. Improving children's mental rotation and accuracy with computer game playing. *Journal of Genetic Psychology* 163 (3):272–282.

Dietrich, A. 2003. Functional neuroanatomy of altered states of consciousness: The transient hypofrontality hypothesis. *Consciousness and Cognition* 12:231–256.

Domhoff, G. 1996. *Finding meaning in dreams.* New York: Plenum.

Druin, A. and J. Handler, eds. 2000. *Robots for kids: New technologies for learning.* San Francisco, CA: Morgan, Kaufman Publishers.

Durkin, K., and B. Barber. 2002. Not so doomed: Computer game play and positive adolescent development. *Journal of Applied Developmental Psychology* 23 (4):373–392.

Erikson, E. 1968. *Identity, youth and crisis.* New York: Norton.

Evans, R. D. 2001. Examining the informal sanctioning of deviance in a chat room culture. *Deviant Behavior* 22 (3):195–210.

Hart, D., N. Field, J. L. Singer, and J. Garfinkle. 1997. Representations of self and others: A semantic space model. *Journal of Personality* 65:77–105.

Healy, J. 1998. *Failure to connect: How computers affect our children's minds for better and worse.* New York: Simon & Schuster.

Henderson, L., J. Klemes, and Y. Eschet. 2000. Just playing a game? Educational simulation software and cognitive outcomes. *Journal of Educational Computing Research* 22 (1):105–129.

Higgins, E. T. 1987. Self-discrepancy: A theory of relating self and affect. *Psychological Review* 94:319–340.

James, W. 1890/1950. *Principles of psychology.* New York: Dover.

James, W. 1902. *Varieties of religious experience.* New York: Longmans, Green.

Ko, S. 2002. An empirical analysis of children's thinking and learning in a computer game context. *Educational Psychology* 22 (2):219–233.

Kreitler, S., and J. L. Singer. 1991. The self-relevance effect in incidental memory: Elaboration, organization, rehearsal and self-complexity. *Imagination, Cognition, and Personality* 10:167–194.

LeDoux, J. 1996. *The emotional brain.* New York: Simon & Shuster.

Lewin, K. 1935. *A dynamic theory of personality.* New York: McGraw-Hill.

Luria, A. R. 1932. *The nature of human conflicts.* New York: Liveright.

Magid, L. 1994. *Larry Magid's Guide to the New Digital Highway.* New York: Random House.

Markey, P. M., and S. M. Wells. 2002. Interpersonal perception in internet chat rooms. *Journal of Research in Personality* 36 (2):134–146.

Markus, H., and P. Nurius. 1986. Possible selves. *American Psychologist* 41:954–969.

MIT Media Lab. 2003. President's report. http://www.media.mit.edu/research/index.html. Accessed August 30, 2004.

Montgomery, K. 2001. Digital kids: The new on-line children's consumer culture. In *Handbook of children and the media*, ed. D. G. Singer and J. L. Singer, 635–650. Thousand Oaks: Sage Publications, Inc.

Morowitz, H. J., and J. L. Singer, eds. 1995. *The mind, the brain, and complex adaptive systems.* Sante Fe Institute Studies in the Sciences of Complexity,

Proceedings Volume XXII. Reading, MA: Addison-Wesley Publishing Company.

Oppenheimer, T. 2003. *The flickering mind: The false promise of technology in the classroom and how learning can be saved*. New York: Random House.

Pankoke-Babatz, U., and P. Jeffrey, 2002. Documented norms and conventions on the internet. *International Journal of Human-Computer Interaction*, 14 (2):219–235.

Provenzo, Jr., E. 2003. Virtuous war: Simulation and the militarization of play. In *Education as enforcement: The militarization and corporatization of schools*, ed. K. J. Saltman and D. A. Gabbard, 279–286. New York: Routledge.

Resnick, M. 1994. *Turtles, termites, and traffic jams: Explorations in massively parallel microworlds*. Cambridge, MA: The MIT Press.

Resnick, M. 1998. Technologies for lifelong Kindergarten. *Educational Technology Research and Development* 46 (4):43–55.

Rideout, V. J., E. A. Vanderwater, and E. A. Wartella. 2003. *Zero to six: Electronic media in the lives of infants, toddlers and preschoolers*. Menlo Park, CA: Kaiser Family Foundation.

Rogers, C. R. 1961. *On becoming a person*. Boston: Houghton Mifflin Co.

Rosenberg, M. 1979. *Conceiving the self*. New York: Basic Books.

Ruvolo, A. P., and H. R. Markus. 1992. Possible selves and performance: The power of self-relevant imagery. *Social Cognition* 10:95–124.

Sennott, S. 2003. Next in toyland. *Newsweek*. 142 (10). September 8.

Shwe, H., and A. Francetic. 1999. *Smarter play for smart toys: The benefits of technology-enhanced play*. San Mateo, CA: Zowie Intertainment, Inc.

Singer, D. G., and J. L. Singer. 1990. *The house of make-believe: Children's play and the developing imagination*. Cambridge, MA: Harvard University Press.

Singer, D. G., and J. L. Singer. 2001. *Handbook of children and the media*. Thousand Oaks: Sage Publications, Inc.

Singer, J. L. 1966. *Daydreaming*. New York: Random House.

Singer, J. L. 1975. *The child's world of make-believe: Experimental studies of imaginative play*. New York: Academic Press.

Singer, J. L. 1988. Sampling ongoing consciousness and emotional experience: Implications for health. In *Psychodynamics and cognition*, ed. M. J. Horowitz, 297–346. Chicago: University of Chicago Press.

Singer, J. L. 2003. Daydreaming, consciousness and self-representations: Empirical approaches to theories of William James and Sigmund Freud. *Journal of Applied Psychoanalystic Studies*. 5(4): 459–481.

Singer, J. L., and V. McCraven. 1961. Some characteristics of adult daydreaming. *Journal of Psychology* 51:151–164.

Singer, J. L., and R. Schonbar. 1961. Correlates of daydreaming: Dimensions of self-awareness. *Journal of Consulting Psychology* 25:1–17.

Singer, J. L., and D. G. Singer. 1981. *Television, imagination, and aggression: A study of preschoolers.* Hillsdale, NJ: Erlbaum Associates.

Strauman, T. J. 1992. Self-guides, autobiographical memory, and anxiety and dysphoria: Toward a cognitive model of vulnerability to emotional distress. *Journal of Abnormal Psychology* 101:87–95.

Strauman, T. J., and E. T. Higgins. 1988. Self-discrepancies as predictors of vulnerability to distinct syndromes of chronic emotional distress. *Journal of Personality* 56:685–707.

Strauman, T. J., A. Lemieux, and C. Coe. 1993. Self-discrepancy and natural killer cell activity: Immunological consequences of negative self-evaluation. *Journal of Personality and Social Psychology* 64:1042–1052.

Strommen, E. 2003. Using technology to create playful learning situations. Paper presented at the Jean Piaget Society Annual Meeting, Chicago, IL, June 5–7.

Subrahmanyam, K., R. E. Kraut, P. M. Greenfield, and E. F. Gross. 2000. The impact of home computer use on children's activities and development. *The Future of Children* 10:123–144.

Subrahmanyam, K., P. Greenfield, R. Kraut, E. Gross. 2001. The impact of computer use on children's and adolescents' development. *Journal of Applied Developmental Psychology* 22:7–30.

Subrahmanyam, K., P. M. Greenfield, R. Kraut, and E. Gross. 2002. The impact of computer use on children's and adolescents' development. In S. L. Calvert, A. B. Jordan, and R. Cocking, eds., *Children in the digital age.* 3–24. Westport, CT: Praeger Publishing.

Sutton-Smith, B. 1966. Piaget on play: A critique. *Psychological Review* 73:104–110.

Trotta, L. 2001. In D. G. Singer and J. L. Singer, eds., *Handbook of children and the media.* 699–720. Thousand Oaks, CA: Sage Publications, Inc.

Turkle, S. 1995. *Life on the screen: Identity in the age of the internet.* New York: Simon & Schuster.

Turkle, S. 2002. E-Futures and E-Personae. In *Designing for a digital world,* ed. N. Leach, 227–255. London: John Wiley & Sons.

Vygotsky, L. S. 1978. *Mind in Society.* Cambridge, MA: Harvard University Press.

Wilson, F. 1998. *The hand: How its use shapes the brain, language, and human culture.* New York: Pantheon.

Yi, M. 2004. Revising original Sims electronic arts creates new version of popular game. Business Section, *San Francisco Chronicle.* Sept. 7.

6. A Role for Play in Early Learning

Bergen, D. 2001. Pretend play and young child's development. *ERIC Digest*, November.

Belsky, J., and R. Most. 1981. From exploration to play: A cross-sectional study of infant free play behavior. *Developmental Psychology* 17:630–639.

Bowman, B., M. S. Donovan, and M. S. Burns, eds. 2000. *Eager to learn: Educating our preschoolers.* Washington, DC: National Academy Press.

Boyer, E. L. 1991. *Ready to learn: A mandate for the nation.* Princeton, NJ: The Carnegie Foundation for the Advancement of Teaching.

Calvert, S. 1999. *Children's journeys through the information age.* New York: McGraw-Hill College.

Christie, J. F. 1983. The effects of play tutoring on young children's cognitive performance. *Journal of Educational Research* 76:326–330.

Christie, J. F. 1985. Training of symbolic play. Special issue: Children's play, *Early Child Development & Care* 19 (1–2):43–52.

Christie, J. F., ed. 1991. *Play and early literacy development.* Albany, NY: State University of New York Press.

Christie, J. F., and B. Enz. 1992. The effects of literacy play interventions on preschooler's play patterns and literacy development. *Early Education & Development* 3:205–220.

Coolahan, K., J. Fantuzzo, J. Mendez, and P. McDermott. 2000. Preschool peer interactions and readiness to learn: Relationships between classroom peer play and learning behaviors and conduct. *Journal of Educational Psychology* 92:458–465.

Diamond, K. E., A. J. Reagan, and J. E. Bandyk. 2000. Parents' conceptions of kindergarten readiness: Relationships with race, ethnicity, and development. *Journal of Educational Research* 94 (2):93–100.

Dwyer, M. C., R. Chait, and P. McKee. 2000. *Building strong foundations for early learning: The U.S. Department of Education's guide to high-quality early childhood education programs.* Washington DC: U.S. Department of Education.

Elliot, A., and N. Hall. 1997. The impact of self-regulatory teaching strategies on "at-risk" preschoolers' mathematical learning in a computer mediated environment. *Journal of Computing in Childhood Education* 8:187–198.

Fein, G. G. 1981. Pretend play in childhood: An integrative review. *Child Development* 52:1095–1118.

Feitelson, D. S. 1972. Developing imaginative play in preschool children as a possible approach to fostering creativity. *Early Childhood Development and Care* 1:181–195.

Fletcher-Finn, C. M., and B. Gravatt. 1995. The efficacy of computer assisted instruction (CAI): A meta-analysis. *Journal of Educational Computing Research* 12:219–242.

Gilliam, W. 2004. Middletown school readiness. In a report, *The Connecticut Commission on children: Update, school readiness, early reading success* (May 3). 7–8. The Connecticut Commission on Children, 18–20 Trinity Street, Hartford, CT 06106 (860-240-0290).

Ginsburg, H. P., N. Inoue, and K. H. Seo. 1999. Young children doing mathematics: Observations of everyday activities. In *Mathematics in the early years*, ed. Juanita V. Copley, 88–99. Washington, DC: National Association for the Education of Young Children.

Goleman, D. 1990. Study of play yields clues to success. *The New York Times*, October 2.

Gottfried, A. W., and C. C. Brown, eds. 1986. *Play interaction: The contributions of play materials and parental involvement to children's development.* Lexington, MA: Lexington Books.

Greenfield, P. M. 1998. The cultural evolution of IQ. In *The rising curve: Long-term gains in IQ and related measures*, ed. U. Neisser, 81–123. Washington, DC: American Psychological Association.

Greenspan, S. 2001. Learning to read: The role of emotions and play. Interview with Stanley Greenspan and Deborah Leong. *Early Childhood Today* 16(2):43.

Haight, W., and P. J. Miller. 1992. The development of everyday pretend play: A longitudinal study of mothers' participation. *Merrill-Palmer Quarterly* 38:331–349.

Healy, J. 1999. *Failure to connect: How computers affect our children's minds—for better or worse.* New York: Simon & Schuster.

Hirsh-Pasek, K., and R. M. Golinkoff. 2003. *Einstein never used flash cards.* Emmaus, PA; Rodale Books.

Hunt, S. 2002. Back to phonics, *Child,* February.

Katz, J. R. 2001. Playing at home: the talk of pretend play. In *Beginning literacy with language; Young children learning at home and school*, ed. D. K. Dickinson and P. O. Tabors, 53–73. Baltimore: Paul H. Brookes Publishing Company.

Kulik, C., and J. A. Kulik. 1991. Effectiveness of computer-based instruction: An updated analysis. *Computers in Human Behavior* 7:75–94.

Kulik, J. A. 1994. Meta-analytic studies of findings on computer-based instruction. In *Technololgy assessment in education and training*, ed. E. L. Baker, and H. F. O'Neil Jr., 9–33. Hillsdale, NJ: Lawrence Erlbaum Associates.

Lindsey, E. W., and J. Mize. 2000. Parent-child physical and pretense play: Links to children's social competence. *Merrill-Palmer Quarterly* 46:565–591.

Manzo, K. K. 2002. North Carolina investment in teaching pays. *Education Week* 21:38–39, 42.

Marcon, R. A. 2002. Moving up the grades: relationship between preschool model and later school success. *Early Childhood Research and Practice* 4 (1):1–21.

Mayfield-Stewart, C., P. Morre, D. Sharp, 1994. Evaluation of multimedia instruction on learning and transfer. Paper presented at the annual conference of the American Education Research Association. New Orleans, LA.

Mellou, E. 1995. Review of the relationship between dramatic play and creativity of children. *Early Child Development & Care* 112:85–107.

Oppenheimer, T. 2003. *The flickering mind: The false promise of technology in the classroom and how learning can be saved.* New York: Random House.

Parker, F. L., A. Y. Boak, K. W. Griffin, C. Ripple, and L. Peay. 1999. Parent-child relationship, home learning environment and school readiness. *School Psychology Review* 28 (3):313–425.

Peth-Pierce, R. 2000. *A good beginning: Sending America's children to school with the social and emotional competence they need to succeed.* Report from The Child Mental Health Foundations and Agencies Network. Bethesda, MD: The National Institutes of Mental Health.

Raden, A. (1999). *Universal prekindergarten in Georgia. Foundation for Child Development Working Paper Series.* New York: Foundation for Child Development.

Rayner, K., B. R. Foorman, C. A. Perfetti, D. Pesetsky, and M. S. Seidenberg. 2001. How psychological science informs the teaching of reading. *Psychological Science in the Public Interest* 2:31–74.

Restrepo, S., and Z. Lucia. 1999. "Play for real": Understanding middle school children's dramatic play. *Dissertation Abstracts International* 60(2-A).

Rideout, V. J., E. A. Vanderwater, and E. A. Wartella. 2003. *Zero to six; Electronic media in the lives of infants, toddlers, and preschoolers.* Menlo Park, CA: Kaiser Family Foundation.

Riedinger, S. A. 1997. *Even start: Facilitating transitions to kindergarten.* Washington, DC: U.S. Department of Education.

Saarnie, C. 1999. *The development of emotional competence.* The Guilford series on social and emotional development. New York: Guilford Press.

Saltz, E., and J. Johnson. 1974. Training for thematic-fantasy play in culturally disadvantaged children: Preliminary results. *Journal of Educational Psychology* 66:623–630.

Sawyer, R. K. 1997. *Pretend play as improvisation: Conversation in the preschool classroom.* Mahwah, NJ: Erlbaum Associates.

Schemo, D. J. 2002. Now the pressure begins for Bush's reading expert. *The New York Times,* January 19.

Shmukler, D. 1981. Mother-child interaction and its relationship to the predisposition of imaginative play. *Genetic Psychology Monographs* 104:215–235.

Siegler, R. S., and D. D. Richards. 1982. The development of intelligence. In *Handbook of human intelligence,* ed. R. J. Sternberg, 897–971. New York: Cambridge University Press.

Singer, D. G., and J. L. Singer. 1990. *The house of make-believe: Children's play and the developing imagination.* Cambridge, MA: Harvard University Press.

Singer, D. G., and J. L. Singer. 2001. *Make-believe: Games and activities for imaginative play.* Washington, DC: Magination Press.

Singer, D. G., J. L. Singer, S. L. Plaskon, and A. E. Schweder. 2003. A role for play in the preschool curriculum. In *All work and no play: How educational reforms are harming our preschoolers,* ed. Sharna Olfman, 59–101. Westport, CT: Greenwood Publishing Group, Inc.

Singer, J. L. 1973. *The child's world of make-believe: Experimental studies in imaginative play.* New York: Academic Press.

Singer, J. L., and M. A. Lythcott. 2002. Fostering school achievement and creativity through sociodramatic play in the classroom. *Research in the Schools* 9 (2):41–50.

Singer, J. L., D. G. Singer, and H. F. Bellin. 1998. Parenting through play for school readiness: Report, year one. Prepared for United States Department of Education Early Childhood Institute. Unpublished manuscript. New Haven, CT: Yale University.

Singer, J. L., D. G. Singer, H. F. Bellin, and A. E. Schweder. 1999. Parenting through play for school readiness: Report, year two. Prepared for United States Department of Education Early Childhood Institute. Unpublished manuscript. New Haven, CT: Yale University.

Singer, J. L., D. G. Singer, and A. E. Schweder. 2004. Enhancing preschoolers' school readiness through imaginative play with parents and teachers. In R. Clements and L. Fiorentino, *The Child's right to play: A global approach.* 35–47. Westport, CT: Greenwood Publishing.

Smilansky, S. 1986. *The effects of sociodramatic play on disadvantaged preschool children.* New York: Wiley.

Spielberger, J. 1999. Head Start teachers' beliefs and representations about the role of pretend play in early childhood development and education. *Dissertation Abstracts International,* 60(2-B), 0859.

Stone, S. J., and J. F. Christie. 1996. Collaborative literacy learning during sociodramatic play in a multiage (K–2) primary classroom. *Journal of Research in Childhood Education* 10:123–133.

Strauss, V. 2003. U.S. to review Head Start program: Bush plans to assess 4-year-olds' progress stirs criticism. *Washington Post,* January 17.

Subrahmanyam, K., R. Kraut, P. Greenfield, and E. Gross. 2001. New forms of electronic media: The impact of interactive games and the internet on cognition, socialization and behavior. In *Handbook of children and the media*, ed. D. G. Singer and J. L. Singer, 73–99. Thousand Oaks: Sage Publications, Inc.

Umstead, R. T. 2003. Noggin finds new pre-k focus. *IFC Digital Media*, 2–3.

U.S. General Accounting Office. 2000. *Title I preschool education: More children served but gauging effect on school readiness difficult.* Washington, DC: GAO/HHS-00–171, September.

van Oers, B. 1999. Teaching opportunities in play. In *Learning activity and development*, ed. M. Hedegaard, J. Lompscher, et al., 268–289. Aarhus, Denmark: Aarhus University Press.

Von feilitzen, C., and U. Carlsson, eds. 2002. *Children, young people and media globalisation.* Goteborg, Sweden: Nordicon, the UNESCO International Clearinghouse on Children, Youth and Media.

West, J., K. Denton, and E. Germino-Hausken. 2000. *America's kindergartners: Findings from the early childhood longitudinal study, kindergarten class of 1998–99, fall 1998.* Washington, DC: U.S. Department of Education, National Center for Education Statistics, NCES 2000–070 (Revised).

Wheeler Clinic. 2001. *Training program in child development.* Plainville, CT: The Wheeler Clinic, Inc. for the Connecticut Department of Social Services and the Child Health and Development Institute of Connecticut.

Williamson, P. A., and S. B. Silvern. 1990. The effects of play training on the story comprehension of upper primary children. *Journal of Research in Childhood Education* 4 (2):130–134.

Wilson, F. 1998. *The hand: How its use shapes the brain, language, and human culture.* New York: Pantheon.

Yawkey, T. D., and A. D. Pelligrini. 1984. *Child's play: Developmental and applied.* Hillsdale, NJ: Erlbaum Associates.

Zill, N., and J. West. 2001. *Entering kindergarten: A portrait of American children when they begin school.* Washington, DC: U.S. Department of Education.

Epilogue

Hair, E. C., and W. G. Graziano. 2003. Self-esteem, personality and achievement in high school: A prospective longitudinal study in Texas. *Journal of Personality* 71 (5):971–994.

Harris, P. 2000. *The work of the imagination.* Malden, MA: Blackwell.

Russ, S. 2004. *Play in child development and psychotherapy: Toward empirically supported practice.* Mahwah, NJ: Lawrence Erlbaum Associates.

Russ, S. W., A. L. Robins, and B. A. Christiano. 1999. Pretend play: Longitudinal prediction of creativity and affect in fantasy in children. *Creativity Re-search Journal* 12 (2):129–139.

Shiner, R. L., A. S. Masten, and J. M. Roberts. 2003. Childhood personality foreshadows adult personality and life outcomes two decades later. *Journal of Personality* 71 (6):1145–1170.

Index

Actual Self, 122–125
adaptive thought, 167
adolescents: computer play and, 115, 118; television viewing and, 66–67, 96–97; video games and, 100–101
adult caregivers. *See also* teachers: attitudes toward play, 149; babies and, 29–30; computer play and, 129–131; concern about popular media, 93; fostering play and, 33–35; gender play and, 43–44; guided play and, 143–149; humanizing role of, 142, 145–146; imagination and, 47; intervention of, 77, 105–106, 138–139; training for, 153, 155–161; violence and, 83–84
adult play, 35
advertising to children, 69
Africa, television in, 75
aggression: adult intervention and, 105–106; global icons and, 75–76; imaginative play structures and, 87–89, 162; imitation/modeling and, 93; models of, 103–105; physical punishment and, 90; television and, 5, 70–71, 87–88, 91–97; video games and, 5, 99, 100–102, 104–106
"aggressive personality," 104–105
Ahmad, Alay, 78
AIME (Amount of Invested Mental Effort), 74
Alborzi, H., 134
American Academy of Pediatrics, 79
American Girl dolls, 46–47
Anderson, Craig, 101, 103–107
anger and television, 70–72

animism in children, 31–32
Archimedes, 20
Arieli, Dan, 133
Aristotle, 91–92
artificialism, 32
assimilation, 39
at risk children, 141, 148, 152–154; guided play and, 155–164
attention, television and, 63–64
Auerbach, Stevanne, 90
Australia: media literacy in, 80; play in, 49; television in, 79
Austria, play in, 49
autonomy, personal, 113
Azar, B., 41

babies: development of, 29–30; television viewing by, 65, 72, 78–79; toys and, 41; video and computer games and, 114
Bagley, D. M., 46
Bandura, Albert, 88, 92–95
Barber, B., 118
Barney & Friends, 67–69, 74, 88, 138
Beethoven, 22
Bellin, Harvey, 5, 156
Bender, Walter, 133
Benton, Stephen, 133
Bettelheim, Bruno, 107
Bickham, D. S., 64
Bjorklund, David, 41
Blue's Clues, 69
Blumberg, Bruce, 133
Bove, V. Michael, Jr., 133
Boyer, E. L., 150
Boyer, Ernest, 137